Daily Experience in Residential Life

LIBRARY OF SOCIAL WORK

GENERAL EDITOR: NOEL TIMMS
Professor of Applied Social Studies
University of Bradford

Daily Experience in Residential Life

A study of children and their care-givers

Juliet Berry

Department of Sociological Studies
University of Sheffield

Routledge & Kegan Paul

London and Boston

First published in 1975
by Routledge & Kegan Paul Ltd
Broadway House, 68-74 Carter Lane,
London EC4V 5EL and
9 Park Street,
Boston, Mass. 02108, USA
Printed in Great Britain by
Northumberland Press Limited, Gateshead
© Juliet Berry 1975
ISBN 0 7100 8115 4 (C)
     0 7100 8116 2 (P)

Contents

Figures

Tables

Acknowledgments

Whilst accepting full responsibility for the end product, I am thankful to many people for their help towards this book. The first group consists of those directly involved with the study who emerge anonymously in the following pages. I am most appreciative of the generous, careful help given by students in completing lengthy questionnaires during their residential placements—without the co-operation of these students and their tutors the study could not have been undertaken in this form. I also want to thank all the senior administrators and unit heads who gave permission for questionnaires to be completed in residential units for which they were responsible. It is worth emphasizing here that all units have been treated anonymously throughout the period of study; in most cases the precise identity and location of units are unknown to me —therefore no person or place should be recognizable to readers, especially as the units appear to be spread over England into Wales. There is some plain speaking—nearly always a mixed blessing, but perhaps made more tolerable when accompanied by realistic suggestions of ways in which the care-givers' lot could be alleviated. Children and adolescents in the units studied are probably less likely to see this book—but if any of them do, may I apologize now that they (not untypically) were never consulted directly about its content, so it is more appropriate for me to convey my good wishes than my thanks here.

The second group of helpers consists largely of named colleagues both inside and outside the University of Sheffield. My senior colleague, Eric Sainsbury, acted as academic supervisor for the version of the study submitted as a thesis for a Master's degree: he illustrates the truism that only the busiest people find time for extra work. I am grateful for the gentle rigour of his supervision which gave me almost complete freedom to follow my own ideas. Other immediate colleagues include Pamela Mann, who was supportive from start to finish; Mary Aveyard, who gave practical help; Michael Bayley, whose own research (into the daily care of mentally handicapped adults at home) has some bearing on mine; Deborah Page and Cissie Goldberg who contributed some sociological expertise, and Fraida Sussenwein (as well as others in the Departments of Sociology, Psychology, Psychiatry, Human Biology and Anatomy), who advised me on elusive references exploring whether the emotional climate at mealtimes has any effect on the nutritional value of food. Philip and Lily Barker, two of many local social workers whose opinion I value, have been particularly helpful in making suggestions throughout. Another local influence whose ideas I find outstandingly relevant to social work practice is Dr Colin Woodmansey in the Department of Child and Family Psychiatry at the Sheffield Children's Hospital. I have also benefited (through regular correspondence and the loan of her unpublished report) from the accrued wisdom of Miss Sybil Clement Brown, one of the few surviving members of the Curtis Committee, later Director of the Central Training Council in Child Care until her retirement several years ago. Numerous Sheffield students (quite apart from those who completed questionnaires) have contributed in recent years to my understanding of residential work—Joan Meredith is just one of these. Acknowledgment is due to the Editor of the journal *Child Adoption* for permission to reproduce a few paragraphs (mainly in chapter 1) from my paper published in 1973, and to Her Majesty's Stationery Office for permission to quote from the Curtis Report (1946). The final addition to a list which is still incomplete is my gratitude to Christine Gandy, helped by Anne Graham, Sylvia Parkin and Gillian Smith, for their persistence in typing the manuscript with proper pride in their work as well as interest in mine.

I

Ideas underlying the study

Children need from the residential worker something direct and real, and treatment surely lies in the worker's ability to provide for them real experiences of good care, comfort and control. This good care will include ... recognising that each child has individual needs, and attempting to meet the needs of each if only in a token way. The token can be used because behind it is both the recognition of the need and the will to meet it. These good experiences are not only the stuff of life, but ... have the power to become part of the child's inner psychic reality, correcting the past and creating the future.

Clare Winnicott: *Child Care and Social Work* (p. 30)

The focus of this study is on residential child care—on the patterns of everyday life as experienced by children and their 'care-givers'. Most of the ideas which emerge in subsequent discussion can also be applied to adults in residential care: to the elderly, to the mentally, physically and emotionally handicapped people who are cared for in groups either in day centres or in residential units. And virtually the same ideas can be applied to children in foster-care or even to children living in their own homes. In other words, a generic theme is the daily care of dependent people of any age, though this study limits itself explicitly to children and adolescents in residential care.

In the study, residential care is visualized as a method of social work—as a practical form of treatment for children who for some reason cannot live with their own parents. A central idea is that such 'treatment' need not rely on the immediate availability to children of highly-qualified therapists practising inside or outside residential units; effective, economical, more easily attainable treatment can be provided by comparatively ordinary members of staff in their day-to-day handling of ordinary, routine events. It will be argued that, if these daily events are to be handled constructively, the care-givers themselves require special consideration and support.

Residential work (with people of all ages) has recently been defined as: 'A method of social work in which a team of workers operates together with a group of residents to create a living environment designed to enhance the functioning of individual residents in the context of their total environment.' (CCETSW, *Discussion Document*, 1973, p. 15.)

The residents' *total environment* includes their past, present and possible future relationships and experience both inside and outside the residential centre. However, this study is concerned primarily with the *present 'living environment' inside the centre*; it rarely extends (except indirectly) to the extremely important subject of the children's continuing relationships with their own families.

Residential 'treatment' for children is an ambiguous term: it could simply mean routine methods of care or it could imply some form of therapeutic intervention. Beedell (1970, p. 79), in analysing the components of residential provision, distinguishes between holding provision, nurturing provision, and therapeutic 'integrity provision' which 'positively encourages the development of healthy individuals by adapting sensitively to them and by deliberate attempts at healing where hurt and damage have occurred'. Whilst I fully agree in principle with the above delineation, my study concentrates simply on 'deliberate attempts at healing' within the context of holding and nurturing routines, on the assumption that uprooted children in general are likely to find this helpful irrespective of their individual degrees of disturbance.

Of the thousands of children in residential care,[1] few are catered for in extra-ordinary therapeutic units headed by highly-skilled, gifted individuals whose success depends to a large extent on their rare qualities. Books have been written about the work of some of these people (for example, Dockar-Drysdale, Wills, Balbernie, Lyward); they have direct influence on a few children or adolescents, and indirectly they act as an inspiration to 'ordinary' residential child care which tends to have insufficient personal, professional and financial resources to emulate them closely. (Though of course many unpublicized community homes could in fact be helping children just as effectively.) Therefore, while I continue to recognize great value in specialized therapeutic units, it seems realistic to concentrate on the daily bread of residential treatment. In so far as any extra-ordinary units are included in this study, the emphasis will be upon their pattern of daily life rather than on any special casework or psychotherapeutic services which they may offer to the children.

Psychotherapy is an expensive method of treating disturbed children; it is unlikely ever to be available to all who might benefit from it. On the other hand, daily routines are an inevitable part of residential care, so it is expedient if these can be handled therapeutically by members of staff who may or may not be trained for their work. It can be argued (for example, Berry, 1972a, pp. 65-71) that children are helped more effectively, more meaningfully, in their daily relationships than in a regular hour set aside for psychotherapy—certainly the latter would tend to be less effective if provided within the context of inadequate daily care. I have no wish to devalue psychotherapy, especially as some therapists would prefer not to single out a child for formal treatment, but would recognize that the ongoing, total living experience is the best medium for promoting healthy social development of children (whose personalities are still in the making).

Fortunately the spirit in which a child is given and receives his daily food is not immediately dependent on highly specialized knowledge. The routine manner in which a farmer feeds his dairy cattle in winter appears simple enough; neither he nor the cows need be aware that complex calculations can be made about scientific rationing for livestock, or that the theory is derived from painstaking research. Similarly, a good deal of theory exists about child care; it is essential that some people should understand the theory and that some workers should carry out research but, when it comes to living with children, what actually happens is largely a matter of daily practice and attitudes which do not necessarily synchronize with theory even when the practitioners are theoretically trained. Recent studies (George, 1970, pp. 226-9; Triseliotis, 1970, pp. 129-31) show that a disquieting gap sometimes exists between theory and practice; that, even when social workers are fully qualified, they cannot always translate their knowledge into action.

This study, by concentrating on life as it is actually lived in residential units, attempts to close the gap a few inches and to offer some realistic rather than idealistic or theoretical solutions to problems experienced in residential life.

The first enquiry into public provision for the care of children

It is nearly thirty years now since the Curtis Committee (HMSO, 1946) reported on the care of children 'deprived of a normal home life with their own parents'. The committee worked hard and to far-reaching purpose, visiting 451 institutions of various kinds in all parts of the country as well as foster-homes and officials in numerous

3

local authorities. Here follows most of their summary of the general impressions made upon them by witnesses and by their own survey :

Para. 415 ... In the first place we are far from satisfied with the immediate provisions made for children coming ... into the care of local authorities. Some authorities indeed receive the children into establishments for temporary care where they can be studied, cleansed and cared for in an adequate and kindly way until they are placed in whatever their permanent substitute home may be but in far too many areas the child is put into a workhouse ward where there is nothing but the barest provision for his physical needs.... What is more, he may remain in such unsatisfactory conditions, temporary though they are supposed to be, not only for weeks, but for months, before something better is found for him.

Para. 416 ... The [long-term] provision for older children, in Homes or boarded out, is generally speaking on a lower level [as compared with nurseries] both of aim and achievement. Both these types of provision have recently caused public anxiety— the first because of assertions as to their out of date, harsh or repressive methods, the second because of actual disasters to children so provided for. We think the anxiety was justified, even though the general position is by no means so bad as particular incidents and statements might suggest....

Para. 417 It is right to say in the first place, as regards Homes for children, that very little evidence, written or oral, has been tendered to us that there are seriously bad conditions in existing Homes in the sense of conditions involving neglect or harsh usage. Some witnesses have come forward to describe to us their own upbringing as inmates of Homes, and in a few instances the picture drawn was a very dark one. Even allowing for some bias and exaggeration, the treatment of these particular children had clearly not been happy or successful. It must be remarked however that the evidence related to a period of ten or more years ago and that there has been much improvement since then in methods of discipline and other conditions.... We heard moreover other witnesses brought up in institutions who gave evidence of a different purport.... We ourselves have seen excellently conducted Homes run by organisations which have been attacked. We do not therefore feel justified, so far as evidence of this kind is concerned, in forming conclusions adverse

4

to the general administration of child care in any organisation or group of organisations. The witnesses in question did however bring home to us the danger, even in an organisation or under an authority with an enlightened policy, that individuals in charge of groups of children may develop harsh or repressive tendencies or false ideas of discipline, and that the children in their care may suffer without the knowledge of the central authority. A code of rules which sets a proper standard is one necessity but it is plain that no code will suffice without regular inspection and constant watchfulness that the right atmosphere of kindness and sympathy is maintained.

Para. 418 Our own survey has given us a firmer basis for conclusions about actual present day conditions.... We have seen examples of almost all levels of child care, some very good, some indubitably bad. By far the greater number of Homes were, within the limits of their staffing, accommodation and administrative arrangements, reasonably well run from the standpoint of physical care.... Where establishments fell below a satisfactory standard, the defects were not of harshness, but rather of dirt and dreariness, drabness and over-regimentation. We found no child being cruelly used in the ordinary sense, but that was perhaps not a probable discovery on a casual visit. We did find many establishments under both local authority and voluntary management in which children were being brought up by unimaginative methods, without opportunity for developing their full capabilities and with very little brightness or interest in their surroundings. We found in fact many places where the standard of child care was no better, except in respect of disciplinary methods, than that of say 30 years ago; and we found a widespread and deplorable shortage of the right kind of staff, personally qualified and trained to provide the child with a substitute for a home background. The result in many Homes was a lack of personal interest in and affection for the children which we found shocking. The child in these Homes was not recognised as an individual with his own rights and possessions, his own life to live and his own contribution to offer. He was merely one of a large crowd, eating, playing and sleeping with the rest.... Still more important, he was without the feeling that there was anyone to whom he could turn who was vitally interested in his welfare or who cared for him as a person....

Para. 419 ... The difference between the results achieved in what would appear to be precisely parallel conditions is often startling. Where a community is successful its success may be accounted

5

for in one of several ways. Enlightened central direction can do much.... Good local administration and the interest and support of a competent local committee can do perhaps even more.... But outstanding among the comments on our visits are references to the good or poor Superintendent, Matron, Housemother or other member of the staff in immediate charge of the children. On the personality and skill of these workers depends primarily the happiness of the children in their care. We have seen much admirable and devoted work by people putting their whole heart and energy into this task, sometimes in very unhelpful conditions. But such workers are too few to handle the work to be done, and some of them have had too little preparation for a very difficult task. On the whole ... this task has not been regarded as one calling for any special skill, and many of the children have suffered in consequence.

Para. 420 When we turn to boarding out, we meet a different set of inadequacies and dangers. We found in the children in the foster homes we visited almost complete freedom from the sense of deprivation which we have described among the children in Homes. Indeed the foster homes as a whole made a remarkably favourable impression. While there were some which on one ground or another we did not consider suitable places for the care of a child, there were few in which the child was not a member of the household....

Para. 422 On the whole our judgment is that there is probably a greater risk of acute unhappiness in a foster home, but that a happy foster home is happier than life as generally lived in a large community.

The above summary has been quoted quite fully not only for its relevance to the present study but because it is worth reconsidering now what the Curtis Report actually said. The committee members' efforts were rewarded in that their recommendations led to the formation of the child care service, but they may also have experienced some frustration in that their careful words have sometimes been taken out of context, distorted, oversimplified. A repercussion they may not have foreseen was the extent to which, in the next decade or so, foster-care would wax in popularity while residential care waned.[2] They reached a balanced judgment (in paragraph 422) which amounts to an obvious conclusion that the closer the relationship between child and care-giver, the greater its potentiality for good or ill. But this was often taken simply to mean that foster-care is superior to residential care.

The Curtis Report is of much the same vintage as the Beveridge Report when welfare was usually seen in terms of achieving basic minimum standards of living; when it may not have been visualized (except by educationalists such as A. Aichhorn and A. S. Neill) that group care of children could usually do more than meet their blatant needs. Since then people hope to have more than their minimum needs met; since then research (Parker 1966; George, 1970) shows that foster-care is a risky undertaking especially for older children and, with the greater emphasis on preventive work and rehabilitation since 1963, those children who do now still require care away from home tend to have greater problems and to be in care for more uncertain lengths of time (making them less suitable for fostering)—so that residential care as an alternative provision is now regarded more favourably.

Other points worth noting are that the Curtis Committee members did not absolve the current residential staff (as distinct from external administrators) from allegations of harshness; they said they hardly expected to discover maltreatment on one casual visit. They spoke with restrained compassion of the witnesses who drew a 'very dark picture' of their upbringing in homes, though perhaps one can rarely expect to get concrete evidence in these matters: children are slow to criticize their adults; deprived children can hardly afford to do so (they easily blame themselves instead). But, though it is well known that they tend to recall their upbringing either in over-rosy or in dark colours, surely their later feeling of having been maltreated does constitute a type of evidence (for example, Hitchman's autobiography, 1960). The report was perhaps over-optimistic in suggesting there had been a radical change in disciplinary methods (this was before recognition of the 'battered child syndrome'[3] when it became clear that many adults under pressure are tempted to be punitive in addition to the smaller number who actually batter) and in believing that 'a code of rules, regular inspection and constant watchfulness' would provide sufficient or appropriate safeguards against harsh treatment.

However, the members did stress the vital need for suitable staff who are prepared for and supported in a difficult task. In all, the Curtis Report does not sound altogether out of date today, even though it transformed the nature of statutory child care.

Three more recent relevant studies

Following the Curtis Report, the three approaches most relevant to my study are those of King, Raynes and Tizard, Bettelheim, and J. and E. Newson.

King, Raynes and Tizard (1971) undertook sociological studies into patterns of residential care in institutions mainly for handicapped children. They developed a Child Management Scale enabling them to show with some precision that remarkable differences can be found in different types of institution. Their major finding was that child-oriented patterns of care are more characteristic of local authority and voluntary homes than of hospital wards. For example (pp. 196-8), heads of child-oriented units organized their time differently from heads of institutionally-oriented units; they managed to interact more frequently and more warmly with children, whatever else they were doing at the time; they spoke to the children one-and-a-half times as often, were twice as likely to accept and three times less likely to reject the children than were the heads of institutionally-oriented units.

Also the work of junior staff in child-oriented units was similar to that of their unit heads; they were more accepting of the children than were their junior counterparts in hospitals. As these findings underlined the pervasive importance of the role of unit head, the authors studied factors influencing this role: they found that heads of hostels enjoyed more responsibility than heads of wards; that they were subject to less frequent inspection; that high rates of interaction with the children are associated with training in child care rather than with nursing training. The authors conclude by stating their belief that child-oriented patterns are 'better' for children and that there are likely to be long-term benefits from 'good' treatment as well as immediate rewards. At this point one wishes, unrealistically, that the Curtis Committee could have extended its concern to children in long-term hospital care, as its report in 1946 has unfortunate similarities with the hospital care analysed in 1971 but, with the reorganization of the social services and the health services (and with the multi-disciplinary research undertaken by the National Children's Bureau)[4] there is hope of 'child care' attitudes becoming less compartmentalized in future.

My study is more subjective, less statistical than that of King, Raynes and Tizard; perhaps one can afford to be somewhat impressionistic after their precision. Most of the children in the units they studied were severely handicapped; the deprived children in their two large children's homes were 'normal' in comparison. The majority of children in my sample are 'normal' in that they are not severely handicapped, physically or mentally, yet other studies indicate that deprived children in care are far from 'normal' in comparison with ordinary children living in their own family homes.[5] Only one hospital ward and one psychiatric clinic appear in my study, which is therefore not concerned primarily with hospital care, but which examines a wider range of units of the kind that King, Raynes and Tizard would expect to be 'better' in being more child-oriented. My examination of daily routines is less in organizational terms but serves rather to emphasize the fact that emotional and social caring are interwoven with the practical arrangements for physical caring.

It is necessary now to mention the work of Bettelheim (1950/71) in order to illustrate daily interactions between parent-figures and their children. Bettelheim gives a readable, detailed account of the milieu therapy practised, alongside psychotherapy, in a school for emotionally disturbed children near Chicago. Milieu therapy aims to provide an enabling environment in which the total experience of living is therapeutic by means of planned management of the residents' daily routine. Bettelheim believes children can gradually be helped to trust close relationships, and to become more self-reliant, through the positive handling of daily routines—since often it was the mishandling of these very experiences, and of the emotions surrounding them, which originally caused damage. Daily events tend to flatten into mere routine for adults, but are usually the central activities of children's lives—the medium through which they relate to, and test out, their parent-figures. In a non-threatening milieu, anxieties about cleanliness, feeding, night-time, etc. can be alleviated more directly 'on the spot' in the bathroom, lavatory, dining room, kitchen, dormitory than perhaps they can in a separate therapy room. For example, food was used to 'domesticate truants'; absconders knew that whenever they returned they would find food awaiting them by their bed-side.

Bettelheim describes how fears may be relieved in every aspect of daily life—reference will be made to some of these later on. Meanwhile, his ideas may seem impracticable in busy, short-staffed community homes here (though some therapeutic units in Britain and, for example, in Norway are following his methods)[6] but small relaxations in daily routine might make the staffs' work easier in some ways. Bettelheim suggests that 'love for children' implies the parent-figure's willingness 'to go to some trouble in answering the child's spoken or unspoken needs'. However, he adds (p. 19) that

the pressures under which most parents live often defeat the best intentioned efforts. Thus it is not even enough to do the right thing at the right moment, it must also be done with the emotions that belong to the act. Again and again in our work we have found that what counted was not so much the hard facts as the feelings and attitudes that went with them.

These ideas lead naturally to the third relevant study: J. and E. Newson (1963, 1968, 1975) gleaned their material from home interviews with over 700 Nottingham mothers of young children in order to discover what parents actually do; how they feel about their children and how they react in practice to all the situations which naturally arise in the handling of a young child. The interviewers enabled the mothers to speak candidly, but possibly any parent-figure (residential worker, foster-parent, relative of handicapped adult, teacher, etc.) could express similar sentiments if they dared.[7] Two aspects of the Newsons' research are particularly relevant to mine. First, it is clear that communication with children is not just a matter of verbal conversation; actions and attitudes speak louder (more meaningfully) than words, and the daily caring situation offers constant opportunities for the child to experience communications which are, essentially, either friendly or hostile. Second, the Newsons' studies give an almost overwhelming impression of the pressures parents experience in caring daily for young children. The fact that most mothers know how to and want to provide good-enough care does not, unfortunately, mean that they will feel able to do so at any given moment.

Looking after children is hard work, not only physically but emotionally, particularly in that children tend to arouse the most childish bits of oneself. Most parent-figures are hampered in their role by this Achilles' heel—whether they are looking after their own child or someone else's; whether it is a young child, an adolescent or a weak adult who is dependent on them. Residential staff (and foster-parents) not only have these 'normal' pressures in providing daily care but the further complication that their role cannot be defined purely in terms of parenthood. Presumably their position was far less ambiguous in earlier times when they felt responsible largely for physical care and moral training.[8] But nowadays, when the emphasis increasingly is upon close relationships between children and their care-givers, there is much debate on the nature and purpose of these relationships. Even the more lucid statements suggest that a care-giver's role is simultaneously parental and non-parental.

The paradoxical position of supplementary parent-figures

The findings of the Curtis Committee (as reported above) led to a corrective emphasis on the need for future care to be modelled on 'normal' family life in which children would be valued as individuals. Workers in the new child care service were encouraged to provide substitute parents for deprived children. But apparently, during the next decade, the very experience of trying to provide closer relationships uncovered (paradoxically) the children's yearning for their own parents. It seemed as though, in being more open to the children's painful feelings, workers inevitably became more sharply aware of the magnetic force of the natural family. Therefore, no sooner had child care staff absorbed the message about substitute parenthood than they were asked to reorientate themselves towards preventive work and rehabilitation, in which the role of natural parents was accorded greater respect than before. Presumably these conflicting pulls have existed throughout human history, but they are highlighted nowadays in proportion to the growth in social concern for children.

Here follow just a few illustrations of ways in which some exponents have tried to resolve the paradox. Clare Winnicott spoke in 1961 of her 'recent discussion' with a group of residential workers (1964/70, pp. 28-9):

> They were fully aware of the changes that have taken place in their role in relation to children.... They were no longer regarded by themselves or the children, or by anyone else, as substitute parents, although they were for the time being fulfilling parental functions.... In their new role residential staff feel at one remove from the children. They know that parents come first, and in one sense always will, even in absence, and the workers therefore have had to be more self-conscious and deliberate in exercising their own parental care.

She went on to suggest that residential workers are sometimes afraid of the satisfactions in their work, feeling guilty in knowing that these satisfactions belong properly to natural parents. She recognizes the fear as valid, but is clear that staff have to be able to enjoy acting as parents while recognizing simultaneously the child's investment in his real parents. Similarly, Tod (1968a, p. 105) appreciates that residential staff are now hesitant to risk rivalry with a child's own parents, but he sees two ways in which they may nevertheless represent parents: first, in making everyday decisions about bedtimes, food, cleanliness and clothing; second, because children unconsciously transfer to adults in positions of authority expectations formed from previous experience of their own parents.

Beedell (1970, pp. 17-18) makes further useful attempts to clarify the paradox. In order to avoid the word 'substitute', he speaks of 'parenting' in which residential care is seen as a 'stand-by' during an emergency:

But over a long period, or in the absence of a clear-cut emergency, even 'stand-by' becomes unsatisfactory and *a share in parenting* has to be acknowledged.... Biological parents can share 'parenting' with others—they can never really share except between the two of them, 'being parents'.

However, because residential care follows a major intervention in the child's life, changing his life base for a time, residential units have a positive duty to ensure that some good experience derives from the placement which is related to the general rehabilitative task (p. 21).

Beedell feels (pp. 133-6) 'we must use parental and familial words in our discussions or we shall deny some of the emotional and social realities of residential work. On the other hand, we must use them with great intellectual and emotional discrimination ....' He thinks confusions in usage of parental words are often less potent in the real situation of day-to-day life with children but that they

become more dangerous the further one gets away from that situation and the less one has a professional discipline to contain them. The result is that lay committees and bureaucratic agencies can be temptingly and saddeningly confused by them and sometimes have the power to foist confusions on residential staff.

These quotations are implying (crescendo) that an element of professionalism eliminates undue possessiveness. Righton (1972, p. 16) argues forcefully that current thinking has rendered obsolete the old, yet persistent notion of residential care as a form of total substitute care, because most children in care have their own parents, because it is psychologically difficult for children to acknowledge simultaneously two mothers or fathers, and because staff who try to perform substitute parent roles can never adequately compete with real parents. He concludes that staff (in 'planned alternative provision') have a viable and acceptable range of roles to perform as 'stand-in' parents or relatives, whilst noting their need 'to develop exceptional sensitivity to the particular style of role-performance that seems to be called for at any given moment, and to practise their ability to switch without strain from one to another'.

But what do the care-givers themselves (including foster-parents) feel about adopting an element of professionalism? And are they bewildered by the subtle complexities of the roles recommended to them by theorists? George (1970, ch. 2) demonstrates a fundamental, though often unspoken, disagreement between foster-parents and their social workers about the role-content of foster-parenthood. He says the literature is undoubtedly in conflict with the way long-term foster-parents view their role. 'Every piece of research on this matter has shown that most foster-parents view themselves as natural or adoptive parents.' He suggests (pp. 79-80) changing the title of foster-parent to 'foster care worker' because this avoids the word parent, it emphasizes the caring aspect and it allows for varying periods of care from short to long-term. However, might the title be easier to change than the attitudes?

In so far as one can distil the essence of the above debate, it seems that workers are exhorted to be parent-like without standing in the path of real parents—or, they may stand temporarily in the latter's shoes but never on their toes. And, in so far as it is recognized that this is a delicate-feat to perform, workers are advised to adopt professional caring attitudes in order to decrease the risk of possessiveness. But further complications arise through introducing concepts of professionalism and possessiveness. There will be a fuller discussion of the former in chapter 4—meanwhile it must be admitted that many qualified fieldworkers (let alone care-givers) find professionalism a controversial subject, apparently suspecting that it inhibits spontaneous relationships instead of enabling close-ness between people who were not originally motivated by mutual personal attraction. Though I share Clare Winnicott's belief (1964/70, pp. 11-14) that a social worker's professional self includes all his capacity for positive personal relationships, the problem remains that this attitude is harder for a residential worker to maintain than it is for a fieldworker who is not actually living with his clients *en masse*.

As for possessiveness, many social workers deplore this human weakness because of the obvious suffering it causes children (and their parent-figures). It seems sad that family law, in emphasizing parental rights rather than children's needs, has reinforced a traditional tendency to regard children as possessions. Yet it is clear that children need to belong, and that a kind of possessiveness is a positive aspect of parenthood—in fact it supplies the necessary drive for many care-givers to persevere. E. Newson (1972, p. 34) believes

> The crucial characteristic of the parental role is its partiality for the individual child. This is why all the other caring agencies that we can devise can never be quite as satisfactory as the 'good-enough' parent (to use Winnicott's term). The best that community care can offer is impartiality—to be fair to every child in its care. But a developing personality needs more than

13

that: it needs to know that to someone it matters more than other children; that someone will go to *un*reasonable lengths, not just reasonable ones, for its sake....

In close proximity with the above compelling words, Pringle (1972, pp. 6-7) asserts that biological parents are not always better than substitute parents. She thinks society's view of the parental role is ambivalent, contradictory and too adult-centred; she believes that willingness to undertake the responsibilities of parenthood is neither dependent, nor necessarily consequent upon, biological parenting. Although Pringle sees a main answer in the appropriate preparation and support of future biological parents, her doubts about the over-riding importance of the blood-tie are reinforced by recent studies,[9] particularly by Kadushin's evidence that even older children, removed from neglectful or abusive parents, have later responded successfully to adoptive parents. However, such questioning of the ultimate value of parenthood by right of birth carries risks in that it could either enhance or undermine the concept in public opinion. Also, there are slight indications that parent-figures are sometimes less partial to the child who attracts official interest, though not to the extent shown by birds which desert their nest on sensing human interference.

Having quoted other writers at some length, I want now to try to take the analysis of this paradoxical state of affairs a step further. Negative possessiveness towards children seems to stem from the adult's own urgent need to be loved, whereas positive 'partiality' seems to bestow on children a bloom of well-being which no amount of impartial physical grooming can achieve. In one sense, partiality is not only a desirable but a natural consequence of giving daily care. In my view, the very act of providing daily care over a period of time does inevitably arouse parental feelings in the care-giver— although such feelings may not be recognized unless they are regarded as permissible, and in any case parental feelings are ambivalent. Elsewhere (Berry, 1972a, pp. 83-4) I applied this view to adoption, where there is a clear break between the original mother who gives birth and the adoptive mother who becomes equally real through giving ongoing care. In spite of the break into two separate stages, and irrespective of their superficial differences, both women contribute something vital to the child's development; they also share a grief in common in that neither woman is able to complete the whole process.

Because adopters will be providing long-term care, it becomes their responsibility to try to hold the two stages together for the child, so that he may grow up with a sense of continuity and self-esteem from the beginning. Rowe (1971, p. 148) sees this idea of two stages as an essential element in genuine acceptance of adoption. However, it is obviously harder for foster-parents and residential workers to dovetail with 'birth parents' in this way. Residential staff are not only reaping other people's conceptions but also other people's patterns of child-rearing. This is both a strength in that they need not take the child's behaviour as a personal reflection on their ability, and a weakness in that they are tempted to project blame onto former parent-figures, or to feel fatalistic in visualizing the child's future security if he returns to his own family.

Much seems to depend on whether one conceives of parenting someone else's child as a negative form of rivalry or as a positive means of keeping the parent's place warm in the child's affections. Evidence (particularly in J. and J. Robertson's work)[10] suggests strongly that care-givers, provided they respect the child's own family relationships, have a vital role to play in *keeping alive his capacity to be parented*. In other words, no child can live in an emotional vacuum; therefore a care-giver (acting as understudy to parents who are temporarily unable to play a full, direct part) is not dividing the child's loyalties but in a sense is keeping the blood-tie flowing in his veins. And, because many children are already emotionally anaemic when they come into care, they may in addition need something akin to a blood transfusion (i.e. not a replacement but a gradual revitalizing of relationships).

If a closer identification with deprived children (reinforced by research findings) during the last thirty years has made us more aware of the pain of separation, it is also possible that we have been infected by the black-and-white outlook of childhood in our attempts to resolve the paradoxes resulting from separation. No paradox can be solved in a static moment, but it can become coherent during a period of experience. Individual workers may be tempted to seek a simple answer either in preventive work or in planned alternative provision; tempted to see 'birth parents' as more important than 'bread parents' or vice versa—instead of valuing all these facets of a comprehensive service. Without underestimating the major importance of preventive work and rehabilitation, I am increasingly convinced of the need to help the current parent-figure with whom a child is living for any appreciable length of time, irrespective of whether this figure can be termed a true parent.

No doubt there is value in previous attempts to reconcile con-flicting aspects of a care-giver's role but, in so far as these are academic exercises off-stage, it seems essential to recognize that residential workers are living with the paradox daily—they may be less interested in theoretical arguments than in an acknowledgment that their way of life is difficult. Practical support in the here-and-now situation is more relevant than continuing indefinitely to ask riddles about roles. In other words, a lengthy debate on the authenticity of various forms of parenthood tends to obscure the central fact that most adults sometimes experience difficulty in looking after a dependent person of any age, whatever the relationship between them may be called. Prolonged attempts to define legitimate roles are perhaps used as a defence in postponing the awkward moment when realistic efforts could be made *to help adults* who are struggling to care for those dependent upon them.

Finally in this section, it is appropriate to mention practical implications arising out of the ideas of Bowlby and Woodmansey, both of whom are concerned to promote the healthy development of children within their current environment. Woodmansey (1966, 1969, 1971a) cuts through ambiguity by emphasizing that any parent-figure (natural or surrogate) is likely at times to experience great emotional pressure, and that, in a battle of wills between adult and child, experiencing adult hostility is most damaging for the child (as well as being painful for the adult). Therefore it is frequently most effective to offer help with his or her negative feelings to the adult in daily charge of the child, in order to promote a more friendly relationship between them.

Bowlby (1973, pp. 359-62), discussing the growth of self-reliance, also reinforces the ideas presented in this introductory chapter. He provides weighty evidence that

> human beings of all ages are found to be at their happiest and to be able to deploy their talents to best advantage when they are confident that, standing behind them, there are one or more trusted persons who will come to their aid should difficulties arise. The person trusted provides a secure base from which his (or her) companion can operate. And the more trustworthy the base the more it is taken for granted....

Bowlby's current theoretical position clarifies earlier confusion surrounding the concepts of 'dependence' and 'protection' by stressing that it is natural (rather than infantile) for people to be fearful in unfamiliar situations. A healthily self-reliant person is able to adapt appropriately between dependence and independence; at one time he is providing a secure base for his companion(s); at another time he is glad to rely on someone else to provide him with a similar base in return. A well founded self-reliance develops alongside the capacity to rely on others.

These ideas, applied to the residential scene, suggest that children of all ages require readily available adults upon whom they can rely. In fact children who are unable to grow up consistently in their own homes have greater need of reliable alternative figures but at the same time are proportionately slow to trust them. This means that residential workers need to be exceptionally reliable in exceptionally difficult circumstances—logically then, they also require a secure emotional base from which to operate. They need not fear that ongoing support (offered either by a senior colleague inside the unit or by an external therapist) is patronizing or paternalistic because clearly the care-givers themselves require care.

Case record as illustration

The remainder of this introductory chapter develops the ideas discussed so far, through the use of case material provided by a student about a few hours of her relationship with one child during her month's residential placement in a reception centre. Her verbatim record is external to the study forming the major content of this book, but her detailed account may serve to illuminate the less individualized subsequent findings. On starting her placement (which was part of a professional social work course for mature entrants) the student felt apprehensive about her ability to communicate with children.

The child, Andy, was six years old. He had been received into care about three months previously at the request of his parents, as being beyond their control. His disruptive behaviour at home had included lighting fires, turning on gas taps and water taps, flooding the house; his school attendance was poor and he had already been expelled or excluded from three different schools. He was a premature baby who had several unexplained fractures suggestive of battering in his early months; towards the end of his first year he went into hospital for eighteen months with tuberculosis. He had returned to his family (containing one younger and three older siblings) when he was nearly two-and-a-half years old, but his parents found him unmanageable by the time he was six.

Bedtime 7.30 p.m.   Andy had been put to bed with the four other children in the nursery, and I had sat for a while reading them a story. Andy requested 'Jack and the Beanstalk', but the other children out-voted him in wanting 'Hansel and Gretel'. He was still wide awake, though quiet, when I tucked him up and kissed him goodnight. However, screams soon took me back to the nursery; he had woken the other children by jumping on their beds, and made them cry. I took him out of the nursery, settled the other children, and brought him into the kitchen with me whilst I gave the older children their supper and prepared the staff meal. After an initial burst of activity, including turning on the gas taps, the electric mixer, and feeding half the supper to the donkey through the window, he settled down to look at a book, with a very sad expression on his face, and was for the most part ignored by the other children. Eventually I carried him back to bed, talking quietly to him, and the conversation proceeds as follows, as he sits on my knee with the bedclothes wrapped round us. All the other children are asleep and only a little light comes in through a chink in the curtains:

Andy: Tell me a story—

Self: All right, if you'll be quiet, because we mustn't wake the others—

Andy: A story just for me? (with some surprise and satisfaction)

Self: Yes, just for tonight because the others are asleep, but then you must get into bed and go to sleep—

Andy: (gripping me tightly) Tell me about Jack and the Beanstalk —(I start the story and get as far as Jack leading the cow to market)

Andy: Was Jack a big boy?

Self: Well, he was big enough to take the cow to market for his mother, wasn't he—

Andy: Am I big enough to take a cow to market?

Self: Do you think you're big enough?

Andy: I'm big enough to look after the donkey—(actually he treats it cruelly. Long pause while he looks very thoughtful; silence from me while I decide nothing would be gained by reintroducing a recent incident, about which I still feel sore!)

Self: Shall I go on with the story? (he nods and I continue. As I get to where Jack's mother is cross with him for bringing home beans instead of money, he sits up straight and tense; as the beans are sown and grow right up into the clouds, and the giant's thundering voice is heard, Andy takes over, getting more tense and excited, the words come tumbling out)—

Andy: And Jack climbs up the beanstalk and kills the big giant dead (he gives a deep sigh; his body relaxes and he curls up in my arms)—Can I have the baby's bottle?

Self: I'm sorry the bottle has been put away now the baby has left us, but I'll tuck you up in your nice warm bed and you can go to sleep (he resists slightly, but then allows himself to be tucked up)

Andy: Can I have my white teddy? (pause) and my black teddy?

Self: Where did you leave them?

Andy: Over there (pointing to the shelf)

Self: (after looking to no avail) Are you sure you put them there? Wouldn't you like this bunny and this brown teddy? (he uses these to throw at the sleeping children and wakes Tommy, who cries but soon settles as I tuck him up again)—

Self: That was naughty, Andy—(great difficulty in controlling myself!) Poor Tommy, you woke him up—you must have made him jump—

Andy: (looking very defiant, standing on his bed) I want my white teddy—

Self: If you'll get into bed and be quiet, I'll look in the playroom for it—(at this point I'm not even sure he has a black or a white teddy. I do in fact find a shabby white teddy which I give him, and he puts it into bed beside him)

Andy: I want my black teddy—

Self: We'll have to look for him tomorrow—

Andy: (jumping up) I'll get him!

Self: Oh no, you won't—get back into bed, you'll wake the others—(I grab him as he jumps out)

Andy: He's in the toy box—

Self: I'm afraid he's not, I've looked there—

Andy: He's at the bottom—

Self: What's he doing there?

Andy: He's naughty—

Self: What did he do that was naughty?

Andy: He hit me—

Self: What made him do that? (no answer—long pause)

Andy: I want my black teddy (he has rearranged his white teddy on the pillow)

Self: If you'll stay in bed quietly, I'll see if I can find him again— (I do find the black teddy underneath the other toys in the box, and give it to him, but he throws it on the floor with a defiant grimace)

Andy: Give me those (pointing to the other toys he has thrown about the room; I give them to him, including the black teddy; he tucks up the other two with the white teddy and lets the black teddy fall to the floor. He is very tired by this time, and looks as if he'll settle. I talk to him quietly for just a little longer and, as I kiss him goodnight, his hands are so tight round my neck that it is very hard to get away.)

Mid-day—the next day   Andy is the first to run in from school, and jumps into my arms and kisses me with great gusto. I turn to greet the other children who all want attention and, as I help them to change their shoes, I see Andy, who must have fetched his black teddy from the bedroom, putting it in the toy box, pushing it down among the other toys. He then comes back to me and, as I help him into his shoes, he starts talking about last night, showing off in front of the other children and making them envious.

Diane:	He was naughty last night, wasn't he, miss?
Self:	Andy wasn't able to get to sleep, was he—(Andy watches me)
Tommy:	He woke me up last night—
Diane:	He made Tommy cry—he's always a nuisance—
Self:	That was a shame, but Tommy was very good and went back to sleep, didn't he—
Diane:	Did you read him another story last night, miss? Andy says you did—that's not fair for him to have two stories—
Self:	Well, you were asleep and Andy couldn't get to sleep so I just told him a little one—
Andy:	I was good then, wasn't I?
Self:	Yes, you went to sleep then—
Mark:	Will you sit on my bed tonight when you read a story?
Self:	I sat on your bed last night—I sat on everyone's bed—don't you remember?
Mark:	You didn't sit so long on mine—
Self:	Well, I'll start off on your bed tonight—(Diane, Tommy, Donna hang on my skirt and hands, saying together: No, mine, mine ...)
Self:	I know, we'll all sit on one bed for the story—then you can all hop back into your own beds—(someone calls from outside and they run out to play. During this time, Andy has been unusually quiet, standing near the toy box. I sit down whilst I untie shoelaces, and he comes and stands by me, holds both my hands together in his small ones and begins to talk about last night)
Andy:	I got up last night and came into the kitchen, didn't I?
Self:	Yes, you did—
Andy:	Was I naughty last night, miss?
Self:	Do you think you were naughty?

Andy: (long deep sigh) I wish I could be good—
Self: Do you find it hard to be good?
Andy: (cheeky laughter, ending in a thoughtful silence)
Self: Why would you like to be good?
Andy: Then I wouldn't get smacked—
Self: Who smacks you? (he gives a cheeky grin, climbs on my knee with his arms tight round my neck, and kisses me with great gusto; then he jumps down and runs out to play, shouting for me to watch his prowess on the climbing frame.)

That was a glimpse of a residential worker, faced with a typical but absurdly awkward task of trying to meet the urgent needs of one damaged child while simultaneously trying to meet the demands of a whole group of deprived children. (It is bad enough when Andy struggles against sleep in the first place just when the worker was within sight of completing that day's care of him; it is worse when he wakens his room-mates not once but twice, and it gets progressively more provoking as he disrupts the older children's supper, refuses to settle after having a story specially for him, demands an obscure toy which he then discards, and next day makes the other children jealous—so that there is danger of cumulative disturbances at bedtime in the immediate future, and residential staff naturally tend to fear that any non-conformity will be infectious.) Possibly this student is exceptionally patient; of course she is here for only a month, but one has the impression that her attitudes would endure. Certainly many residential workers respond constantly, day and night, year in year out, to similar situations;[11] others might have been provoked into loss of temper and then could have suffered further by regretting it afterwards, on remembering Andy's sad history.

It is clear that Andy was helped through his experience with the worker; it is remarkable that he manages to hold on to it as a rare, good experience. His recounting of it the following day is perhaps not so much a mischievous bragging to the other children as a desperate wish for reassurance that it really did happen and that it was tolerable for the worker. He cannot easily believe parent-figures are willing to take trouble on his behalf and he will need considerably more proof before he is convinced. Meanwhile his behaviour tests adults to the limit; though he is obviously anxious about his naughtiness, it does gain him some limelight and attention (which, even if the latter often takes a negative form, is probably preferable to indifference). Learning theorists might think Andy's undesirable behaviour is best ignored; that, even if not actively punished, it should not be reinforced by rewarding him with kindly extra attention. However, I would argue his urgent need to discover he is acceptable to parent-figures irrespective of his goodness or badness; it is only through experiencing such acceptance over a period of time that he will become more amenable.[12] There is hope for him, because he obviously has not yet given up the struggle to make friendly relationships with grown-ups.

This was not a casework interview, though Andy's reactions to Jack and the Beanstalk (and to his teddies) would have provided rich material in some child guidance settings. Probably the worker here was too pre-occupied with the practicalities of a real situation to be more than dimly aware of the underlying symbolism. Andy's responses to the story suggest not only his unsureness of his own self-image (he does not know whether he is big enough to be useful to a parent-figure) but that he doubts his ability to do anything which does not result in criticism. He has to finish the story quickly, perhaps because the giant is too powerful and frightening a figure to linger over. Although (and because) adults find Andy difficult to control, he must frequently feel vulnerable in relation to their superior strength.

It could be suggested that the white and black teddies represent the sides of himself which he sees (through other people's reactions) as good and bad; they may simultaneously stand for good (loving) and bad (punitive) parent-figures to him, or perhaps for his feelings towards his younger sibling who took his place while he was in hospital. His reactions to the black teddy could be seen as testing the worker's acceptance of his badness. He is apprehensive (as shown too by his questions in the final sequence) that his naughtiness makes him unlovable; indeed this was abundantly proved to him in past experience, yet he cannot be 'good' to order. The worker asks him some rather inappropriate and unanswerable questions—such as 'Why would you like to be good?' He can only reply, 'Then I wouldn't get smacked.' This certainly has a ring of truth, though it is impossible for him to voice his fear that the love he so badly wants is conditional upon his goodness. Children tend to be keen moralists (witness the other children's self-righteous disapproval of Andy) even when, or perhaps more so when their actions are not in keeping with their black-and-white principles of fairness and proper conduct.

However, in my view, it simply does not matter that the worker was probably not (at the time) very aware of Andy's symbolic behaviour. His actual behaviour was more than enough for her to meet, especially as she seemed to be coping almost single-handed with the entire population of the reception centre that evening.

The great thing is that she gave him *a helpful experience* of acceptance, without letting her natural exasperation and exhaustion take
over. She did not give him completely free rein; she was able to
be suitably firm when necessary, and her handling of him was
probably more immediately expedient in controlling him than any
threats or punishment would have been, as well as being far more
beneficial in the long run. Perhaps a caseworker could have made
interpretive comments, such as, 'You feel your black teddy is
naughty, like part of you, so you throw him out of bed. . . .' But, in
my view, verbal interpretation is irrelevant to the child in comparison with his experiencing acceptance through the worker's
total attitude and actions. I believe this also to be true of casework:
effective casework is less a matter of insight-giving than of giving a
helpful experience within a professional relationship. Although
casework and residential work are different methods of social work,
this attitude of acceptance is common ground between them.[13]

Another debatable point is whether the worker should have
seized the opportunity to let Andy regress to the secure babyhood
he missed, by agreeing to his request for the baby's bottle. I think
not. When one is desperate to know how best to set about helping
damaged children, it is tempting to experiment with high-flown
methods—to try anything new, ambitious, spectacular—instead of
doing the more difficult thing of just living with the child, without
pressurizing him to improve quickly against the tide of his resistance. To give an older child a feeding-bottle or to let him wear
nappies sounds impressive in textbooks—in practice the situation
would need skilled handling in a specialized unit and, more important, it might have a disconcerting effect on other children in an
assessment centre and upon the staff when they actually saw a
bigger child in the flesh sucking sensuously like a baby. If Andy's
physical regression caused angry dissent amongst the staff or hostile
teasing from the other children, it would not help him much. I
think the worker responds appropriately here: she does not say
scornfully, 'A big boy like you doesn't want a baby's bottle!' She
recognizes his need for physical comfort and gives him a comparable substitute by offering to tuck him up warmly. She makes
several token gestures towards him: part of the quotation heading
this chapter—'The token can be used because behind it is both the
recognition of the need and the will to meet it'—holds good both
in casework and in residential treatment.

The crucial question, according to the contents of this first
chapter, is how did the worker manage to respond helpfully to the
needs Andy expressed? This question will be explored in later
chapters, as it is a major *raison d'être* of the book. A short answer

meanwhile is that she responds naturally because of her own emotional maturity; it seems she has received acceptance herself, perhaps also during her training, so that she is fairly free of inner obstacles which would inhibit a professional relationship. She is acutely aware of her annoyance at some points so her anger is unlikely to take her by storm; she is unlikely to treat Andy with weak sentimentality for an hour and then to hit him the next minute. One clue to her positive attitude towards him can be found in her first paragraph, where she describes him (after some highly irritating behaviour) settling down to look at a book, '*with a very sad expression on his face*'. If she can see through to the despair underlying his devilment, she is ready to respond warmly. Critics may think she should not allow such closeness between herself and a child whom she will only know briefly, but I shall argue later that the time factor is less important for children than the availability of supportive adults during periods of crisis and upheaval. Certainly this student shows 'partiality' and a willingness 'to go to *unreasonable* lengths', but could she have persevered indefinitely without receiving ongoing support herself?

In subsequent chapters, there will be virtually no records of conversation between individual children and adults, but descriptions of daily activities will indicate both whether there are opportunities for verbal communication and whether the practical arrangements for physical caring are emotionally beneficial. In other words, the care itself is a communication, demonstrating how children are regarded by their care-givers. Residential workers are part of the child's daily environment; unlike fieldworkers they are not 'working backwards'[14] in communicating with children after a crisis has occurred. Events in residential life may be planned or unplanned, treated explicitly or implicitly, but communication (for better or worse) exists within a real situation as it happens. Words and actions are meaningful as a natural part of the complete pattern of daily care (Berry, 1972a, pp. 98-101).

The aim in further chapters is, first, to study patterns of daily care in a sample of residential units, with particular reference to staff reactions when children are unco-operative in their daily routines; second, to consider how residential workers might be supported effectively in their difficult task.

2

Outline of the study

> If, as a living creature
> I wish in all good faith to continue living,
> Where do you suggest I should lodge my application?
> Christopher Fry: *The Lady's not for Burning*

> Well-considered and sensitively contrived daily arrangements
> may provide a way of *existing*; they do not, in themselves,
> achieve a way of *living*. Adults and children have, minimally,
> to find ways to put up with one another. For some children,
> and some staff, at certain times this is perhaps all that can be
> achieved. Yet, if a residential unit is to be more than a place
> in which one marks time, children and staff have to achieve
> some sort of *relationship*.
> Christopher Beedell: *Residential Life with Children* (p. 84)

A partial answer to the first quotation will be attempted in this
chapter, in that there will be indications as to where children might
more hopefully lodge an application before entering residential
care (though of course they rarely exercise much choice in the
matter). This chapter contains a complete outline of the study,
with most of the tables and numerical findings, in order that aspects
of residential daily life for children and their care-givers can be
examined more fully and discussed more freely in subsequent
chapters.

Methods employed and the preparation of respondents

The study is based on the observations of a number of students,
mainly on professional social work training courses, during their
residential placements in a variety of institutions in various parts

of the country. The students, whether they are known to me or from courses elsewhere, were prepared by their tutors for these placements and there was some specific preparation in terms of the questionnaire. The students can be regarded as responsible observers; many of them have previous relevant experience, and—perhaps most important—they recorded their impressions not on the basis of a brief visit, as do many investigators, but whilst living in the place for at least several days and usually for one month.

In this way, the students have first-hand experience of living alongside the residents, although they retained something of the stance of outsiders as they were not (with two exceptions) actually employed; nor did they stay long enough to become identified with the régime and thereby risk becoming less aware of its impact on the inmates.[1] Inevitably, non-factual responses to the questionnaire are influenced by the judgment of individual students. However, it is argued that, since practising social workers are forced constantly to make subjective assessments of complex situations, there is considerable emphasis in social work education on ways of making such assessments as reliable as possible.

Although the study is not based on my direct observations, I shall draw on my own experience of residential work: first, six years as resident farm instructress in an approved school plus short periods in an open borstal and as a mental nurse on an admission ward; second, eight years as a fieldworker/administrator in a county children's department when I was in constant touch with a wide range of residential provision; third, five years as a social work teacher of postgraduate students who are learning the theory and practice of residential work amongst other methods. Therefore, as a student myself of residential treatment, I hope to achieve a balance between involvement and detachment comparable with the students who completed the questionnaires; in particular, by welding personal experience of residential pressures with administrative and academic perspectives, I hope to narrow the gap between theory and practice (mentioned in chapter 1).

In the construction and subsequent use of the questionnaire, great care was taken to protect the interests of the residential staff and departments concerned. Such protection of people employed in difficult work was seen as essential, though it may be at the expense of gaining an accurate picture of residential units where children are less well treated. Safeguards were provided in four ways: first, the original questionnaire was amended before use (see appendix A) in the light of discussion with senior administrators in a social services department, and several questions which might have caused embarrassment to staff (for example, about their apparent job-satisfaction) were omitted. Second, a letter (see appendix B) was sent by course tutors to each department beforehand, asking permission for the questionnaire to be completed. Third, students were asked to ensure at the beginning of their placement that unit heads saw the blank questionnaire and agreed to its being used; also, unit heads could choose whether they wished to see the completed questionnaire—although it seemed preferable for it to be regarded as confidential between me and the student at that stage, and students were asked to state whether or not the completed questionnaire had been seen by the person in charge. Fourth, all units have remained anonymous.

Initially, one or two departments expressed anxiety based on previous experience of students in residential placements being 'too idealistic' and thus unduly critical. This rarely appears to have been the case here. Even though students may be influenced beforehand by 'the literature of dysfunction',[2] it is generally agreed by tutors that a major purpose of the placement is for them to develop empathy towards residential colleagues in stressful circumstances. Also, students are preoccupied with learning to fit in to the daily routines they find practised, and perhaps there is nothing more compelling to a newcomer than to be plunged into a well established routine which is already taken for granted by the majority of residents (Berry, 1972b). And apparently students, like other people, are less ready to formulate criticism on paper than they are to express it verbally. For example, students known to me personally tended to voice stronger views about their placements in seminars than they did in the questionnaires, and it is the latter which provide material for this study.

The students

With the aim of studying a maximum number of fifty residential units, containing perhaps 1,000 children and adolescents, it was necessary to request help from other tutors in various parts of the country. Approaches were made to thirteen tutors, of whom nine proved willing to co-operate; one did not reply, one could not make suitable arrangements, and two were interested but decided with some reluctance not to take part—one of these explained frankly that questionnaires might complicate an already 'somewhat delicate' relationship with residential supervisors; the second rather similarly mentioned the difficulty of asking individual students to negotiate with unit heads at an early stage of their course 'when they cannot be expected to be as aware of the professional sensitivities of residential staff'.

Of the nine tutors who agreed to try to enlist their students' help, eight managed to do so; one (who originally hoped that a large number of students would help) passed the assignment to a colleague who later forgot to make the necessary arrangements. In all, students from ten courses took part; two of these are courses (one pre-professional) to which I am tutor, and I had some direct contact with a third local course through sharing in the teaching. All except one are professional social work courses; six are postgraduate courses.

Completed questionnaires were received within the period April 1972–February 1973, sometimes like so many drops of blood from granite. The director of one large social services department was unwilling for questionnaires to be completed (this affected placements from three courses) and at least five unit heads refused permission. However, for the most part it seemed that the students themselves had insufficient time or energy to complete lengthy questionnaires as an additional burden to their other written work. Some students who took part felt that unit heads could more appropriately have filled in practical details, and that other questions allowed too much scope (or alternatively too little space) for subjective impressions. One tutor reported 'resistance in some of the Children's Homes and I suspect the students colluded with this'. Naturally perhaps, there was a greater response from students known to me; in addition two other courses in particular made a generous contribution.

Finally, forty-four completed questionnaires were usable out of a total of fifty received. Three were excluded from the outset because these units were catering for adults rather than for children, though they may be of value in any further study of residential care for people of all ages. Two more were excluded on discovering that questionnaires had already been received from the same two units earlier in the year, and the sixth was excluded because two conscientious (or uncommunicative) students simultaneously sharing the same placement had both independently completed a questionnaire. The anonymity of the units was a disadvantage in that duplication was not immediately apparent; however, this small amount of unwitting duplication served as a slight check because there was considerable agreement between the three pairs of students who repeated each other. Apparently the placements were spread over England into Wales, but again their anonymity means that the precise geographical location is unknown.

Clearly these forty-four units do not constitute a random sample. They emerge only after a lengthy selection process, starting with the tutors' need to preserve goodwill in departments offering placements, and continuing with the tutors' routine requests for placements to external administrators who then decide which of their available units can conveniently take students. Choice may be determined partly by unit size (large enough to provide accommodation for students away from their home base) or by the ability and willingness of staff to supervise students, or by the administrators' evaluation of varying standards within their residential provision. In some cases, tutors would ask for specific units which had previously proved to be valuable placements. On the whole, it could be expected that 'better' units are offered for student placements, and that the staff concerned are more likely to agree to the completion of a questionnaire if they are fairly confident about the standard of care given to residents.

Of the forty-four students, forty were on professional social work courses, three were on a pre-professional course, one respondent was already professionally qualified but having a break from social work proper by working as assistant matron in a boys' prep-school. Eighteen of these students are known to me (eight as course tutor). There are twenty-three men and twenty-one women, ranging in age from 21-49 years old, though only four were less than 23 years, and three-quarters were aged 26 and over (details in appendix C1).

As a group, the students had considerable previous relevant experience.[3] Less than one-third had comparatively little field-work experience—that is, weeks or months before or during the current course but, of these fourteen students, one had been a magistrate and one a schoolteacher. Six students had previously been employed as social workers or trainees for at least one year but less than two years. Twenty-four students (more than half) had been employed earlier in social work for at least two years, and of these thirteen had worked for four years or longer—for example, one woman had been a child care officer for eight years; another had spent seven years in youth work plus four in social work. Five students had substantial periods of employment in residential work—one man had worked for fifteen years in a boys' approved school and intended to return after completing his advanced residential child care course.

In the future, about two-thirds of the students intended to work in local authority social services departments; others had chosen a probation, family service unit or hospital setting; a few mentioned the possibility of becoming residential workers. One foreign student was returning to her own country; in her otherwise carefully completed questionnaire she mentioned a housemother having 'previously worked in a brothel'—it seems more likely that the latter had worked in a borstal rather than as a prostitute. On the whole, the questionnaires appear to have been used with care and common sense. In a few cases it is difficult to distinguish between staff attitudes and the student's own standpoint—for instance, one respondent's insistence on the necessity for close supervision of a group of small boys suggests that she herself feared their becoming out of control.

THE PLACEMENTS

Respondents were asked, 'How many days did you stay here?' Replies would have been more definite if days off duty had been numbered alongside. However, it is clear that twenty-six students lived in the unit for one month (a traditional period, as this was formerly a Home Office minimal requirement for qualification); a further eleven students stayed for more than three weeks but possibly less than a full month; one stayed for two months. Placements of a fortnight were arranged for two students with substantial previous residential experience, and one woman spent six days (the shortest period) in a mental hospital ward. Of the remaining three respondents, one had worked for two years as assistant matron in a boys' prep-school; one was employed as social worker for a year in a school for maladjusted girls immediately before her professional course, and the third made lengthy weekly visits to a small children's home for over four months of her fieldwork placement.

An omission in the questionnaire was whether respondents were fully resident in the sense of sleeping on the premises; it can be estimated that about a quarter were not—this would be because there was no bedroom available in small units or because the student had an alternative local base. Ideally students should work day and night under the same conditions as the staff in order to have an authentic taste of residential life; but otherwise tutors normally ensure that students are present throughout the day's activities including bed-time, and it is to be hoped that students sleep peacefully (thus being absent in spirit) whether or not they are fully resident.

The forty-four residential placements fall roughly into four groups:

A *Observation and assessment centres* (14 in all) Nowadays the distinction between remand homes (once used largely by the courts for delinquent adolescents) and reception centres (for assessment of children in care of both sexes and a wide age-range) is becoming blurred. Nevertheless, the division in this study remains too clear to be ignored, even though several 'reception centres' contain adolescents on remand and some 'remand homes' are catering for older children whose foster-homes have broken down:

1 Nine 'reception centres', containing 103 boys and 67 girls.
2 Five 'remand and classifying centres', four for boys, one for girls, containing 119 boys and 26 girls.

B *Community homes* (21 in all) Again the distinction between children's homes and ex-approved schools is disappearing in theory; in practice this is still a new idea which may or may not materialize gradually in future. At present there are four clear sub-groups:

1 Five small children's homes (sometimes known euphemistically as 'family group homes')[4] containing 31 boys and 15 girls. Two of these units cater specifically for disturbed children but are included under this heading because many ordinary children's homes contain such children.[5]
2 Six larger children's homes containing 88 boys and 32 girls.
3 Six units in boys' community schools (ex-approved schools) containing 162 boys.
4 Four units in girls' community schools containing 56 girls. One of these units caters for pregnant girls, whose babies are not included in the study.

C *Special schools/units for maladjusted/handicapped children* (6 in all)

1 Four schools/units for maladjusted children: one an independent school for boys and girls; one school for boys; one run by a religious order for girls, and one mixed psychiatric clinic under the National Health Service—containing in all 90 boys and 50 girls.
2 Two units for handicapped children: one mixed nursery unit for physically handicapped run by a voluntary organization; one mixed school for 'maladjusted children with communication difficulties' (some autistic)—containing in all 23 boys and 6 girls.

D *Other places* (3 in all)
1 A small ward in a psychiatric hospital containing one adolescent girl amongst a group of adult patients of both sexes—a therapeutic experiment where patients share in the selection of members considered suitable for the group.
2 A privately owned prep-school for 72 boys of whom one is in care, with a foster-mother. The school seems to offer a service (possibly for some a social service) to middle-class families in

catering for the sons of naval officers frequently posted abroad. In any case there is room for concern about young boarders of any social class.

3 A hostel run by a voluntary organization for parents and children, containing two boys and three girls (with three mothers, and two semi-resident fathers). These five young children had spent most of their previous lives in care and were being rehabilitated with their parents whilst awaiting rehousing.

TABLE I.I *Types of unit and number of children/adolescents (see appendix C2 for a frequency distribution)*

		No. units	Total no. children	Boys	Girls
A	Reception centres	9	170	103	67
	Remand homes	5	145	119	26
B	Community homes	11	166	119	47
	Community schools	10	218	162	56
C	Special schools/units	6	169	113	56
D	Other places	3	78	74	4
	Totals	44	946	690	256

There may seem to be such diversity in the nature of these forty-four units that their daily routines hardly permit comparison. However, the basic common factor is that all the children/adolescents are in group residential care away from their own homes; adults other than their parents are responsible for meeting their daily needs. (Even the five children in the family hostel—D3—are partly dependent upon the staff, not solely in their mothers' care. Three of twenty-seven children in the Health Service psychiatric clinic—C1—are temporarily day patients, but were formerly resident and now awaiting transfer to other institutions: one for remedial education and two adolescents who will apparently require semi-permanent care in an adult mental hospital.) Otherwise all the children are fully resident. They all share common human needs; they have similar digestive systems for instance—routines must cater for their physical, mental, social and emotional needs day and night, no matter how diverse their individual problems and handicaps may be.

The total number of children in the study is 946: 690 boys and 256 girls, tended by 416 members of staff. These figures do not necessarily indicate a high average staff–child ratio,[6] because in some cases students were attached to a small coherent group of children in one unit of a large residential centre, whereas the senior staff listed are concerned with the whole place. In fact twenty-eight questionnaires provide details of *the whole place* (such as an assessment centre, school or community home); sixteen questionnaires give details of *one unit within the centre*—i.e. one house, cottage, flat, wing or ward where the whole place contains other similar units. This division into units is typical of community schools, which may for example consist of four houses, each for about twenty boys, plus other central buildings. Therefore many more than the total of 946 children will be affected by the way of life in each place as a whole.

The forty-four units include twenty-two mixed units for boys and girls together; sixteen units for boys only, and six units for girls only. (Of the forty-four respondents, ten male students and twelve female students had placements in mixed units; thirteen men and three women were placed in units for boys only; six women (no men) were in units for girls only.) Segregation of the sexes is typical of community schools and remand homes catering for adolescents (see appendix C3).

The fact that the boys in the study far outnumber the girls is partly explained in there being more units for boys only; also it has been normal practice for larger numbers of boys than girls to be housed together (in the belief perhaps that males take more easily to living *en masse*). But even in the twenty-two mixed units there are far more boys; boys outnumber girls in sixteen of these units—only three mixed units contain fewer boys than girls, and in three the numbers are equal. It is hard to escape the conclusion that boys tend to be more overtly troublesome in their behaviour and are therefore more likely to experience periods of residential care, whereas girls cause most concern in adolescence because of their sexual vulnerability. Other studies show the vulnerability of boys in their tendency to act out problems even in pre-adolescence.[7]

As mentioned above, respondents were asked to say whether or not the completed questionnaire had been seen by the unit head. Twenty-nine questionnaires were *unseen* (hopefully not through Hobson's choice—i.e. if the questionnaire were not fully completed until after the placement; in any case students could probably not be sure whether the unit head would ask to see a completed questionnaire at some stage). Seven questionnaires were *seen*: apparently these unit heads were motivated largely by constructive interest in the study rather than by suspicion; one added his own brief comments in pencil—for example, to the student's observation that most members of staff devote part of their free time to the children, he added 'over the headmaster's dead body!' Three questionnaires were *partially seen*—i.e. the unit head helped directly in supplying factual details about individual residents. One headmaster requested that no information be given about the six members of staff. Five respondents omitted to say whether the completed questionnaire had been seen. This could have been due to clumsily-worded instructions on my part, arising from my ambivalence in preferring questionnaires not to be seen but feeling it was diplomatic to give a choice.

Before presenting further factual details about the units, the children and the care-givers, it may be appropriate at this point to make brief mention of the various patterns of daily care, even though these will be explored more fully in chapter 3.

The patterns of daily care

As a main theme of the study, respondents were asked to describe the daily patterns and interactions when children rise in the morning, during washing and dressing, mealtimes, leaving for school or work, returning from school or work, in leisure activities, handling of clothes and pocket money, daily chores, bed-time, night incidents, methods of discipline and staff reactions to unco-operative behaviour in the children.

A tentative attempt has been made to grade these patterns, using as mid-point a standard where daily care sounds more than adequate though not inspired—i.e. the care is 'all right', geared towards the children's needs, analogous to Winnicott's concept (1957/64) of the ordinary, good-enough mother. My impressions have been checked independently by two other social workers, both of whom agree to a very large extent with my ratings. Accordingly, twenty-one units (nearly half) fall into the '*good-enough*' category, including three questionnaires which give somewhat limited information. Also the three slightly incongruous units in group D are best placed in this comparatively neutral category—no doubt the boys' prep-school is excellent of its kind; the parents are likely to be well satisfied with physical standards of care and to be more concerned with their sons' academic progress than is this study. These twenty-one units contain 404 children—239 boys and 165 girls, 42·5 per cent of the whole sample.

Six units seem to have patterns of daily care which are *more positive* than the above—that is, there seem to be deliberate attempts to create a therapeutic atmosphere akin to milieu therapy within the daily routines (and it can be argued that children of previously poor experience do require something more than ordinarily good care).[8] It is fair to add that three of the completed questionnaires had been seen by the unit head; two were unseen and the sixth did not specify. The six more positive units consist of an independent boarding school for emotionally disturbed children, a community school (ex-approved) for seventy boys run by a religious order on principles derived from Carl Rogers (1951), two local authority children's homes—one for adolescents, one for disturbed children; a small nursery unit run by a voluntary organization for physically handicapped children, and a school for maladjusted/autistic children with 'communication difficulties'. These last two might almost be transferred to the 'good-enough' group because the quality of care is probably elicited in response to the children's very obvious disabilities. Apart from the boys' ex-approved school (which is the second largest unit in the study and by far the largest single community school unit) these six 'more positive' units are mixed, containing in all 157 children—139 boys and 18 girls, 16·6 per cent of the total sample.

Seventeen units seem somewhat *more negative* than the mid-point standard, six quite seriously so. Obviously a large assessment centre must be structured more firmly than a small long-stay home, but this has been taken into account. The seventeen 'more negative' units include four of nine reception centres, four of five remand homes, one of five small children's homes, three of six larger children's homes, four of six community school units for boys (none of the four parallel ex-approved school units for girls—by a narrow margin in one case) and one special school for maladjusted boys. In all, the seventeen 'more negative' units contain 385 children—312 boys and 73 girls, 40·8 per cent of the total sample.

TABLE I.2 *Unit type related to three patterns of care (further details in appendix C4)*

		More positive	Good-enough	More negative	Total no. units
A	Reception centres	0	5	4	9
	Remand homes	0	1	4	5
B	Small children's homes	1	3	1	5
	Larger children's homes	1	2	3	6
	Boys' community schools	1	1	4	6
	Girls' community schools	0	4	0	4
C	Special schools	3	2	1	6
D	Other places	0	3	0	3
	Total units	6	21	17	44

Fuller descriptions of daily patterns will be given in chapter 3—for example, mealtimes are often strained occasions in 'more negative' units, while other routines may be highly regimented and impersonal. The quality of separate routine activities does of course vary within most units; few units are consistently or completely negative in all respects. Table 1.3 shows twelve aspects of daily life, and the number of cases where each aspect separately was rated 'good-enough' (//), 'more positive' (+) or 'more negative' (−) in each of the three overall patterns. Where there is any doubt, sometimes because of limited information, aspects are rated 'good-enough'.

TABLE 1.3   *Twelve aspects of daily life in three patterns of care*

		+ 6 more positive + // −			// 21 good- enough + // −			− 17 more negative + // −			Total of 44 units + // −		
1	Getting up	3	3	0	0	20	1	0	7	10	3	30	11
2	Washing/ dressing	2	4	0	1	19	1	0	4	13	3	27	14
3	Mealtimes	6	0	0	0	16	5	0	4	13	6	20	18
4	Off to school/ work	1	5	0	0	21	0	0	9	8	1	35	8
5	Back from school/work	1	5	0	0	21	0	0	11	6	1	37	6
6	Leisure activities	3	3	0	3	18	0	0	9	8	6	30	8
7	Pocket money/ clothing	2	4	0	1	19	1	0	8	9	3	31	10
8	Household chores	2	4	0	2	17	2	0	7	10	4	28	12
9	Bed-time	3	3	0	2	18	1	0	5	12	5	26	13
10	Night incidents	3	3	0	1	20	0	0	8	9	4	31	9
11	General interaction	6	0	0	0	21	0	0	0	17	6	21	17
12	Discipline	6	0	0	0	21	0	0	0	17	6	21	17

This suggests the possibility of there being more tension inherent in getting up in the morning, mealtimes and household chores than in returning from school, and leisure activities. A most important factor is staff attitudes towards children who are unco-operative in their daily routines. Apparently it is 'normal' in residential child care to keep discipline by a system of rewards and punishments. Therefore units are assessed as 'good-enough' when mild punishment is a regular feature, though in my view the problem is not that children require punishment 'for their own good' but that adults are tempted to administer it in order to ease their own pressures and uncertainties. Rewards as well as punishments seem almost irrelevant in the more positive units, whereas there is great reliance on both in the more negative units. Tables 1.4 and 1.5 show

TABLE 1.4 *Number of times (and nature of) rewards mentioned in three patterns of care*

Rewards	Total times mentioned	More positive	Good-enough	More negative
1 Praise	11	0	5	6
2 Extra sweets/food	4	0	1	3
3 Extra home leave	6	0	3	3
4 Delayed bed-time/ similar privileges	8	0	3	5
5 Extra pocket money	4	0	2	2
6 More latitude/more staff attention	6	0	3	3
7 Extra outings	7	0	4	3
8 Bonus cigarettes	3	0	1	2
9 Higher marks	4	0	3	1
10 Prizes/cups for achievements	1	0	1	0
11 Wear best shirt/own shirt evenings	2	0	0	2
Totals	56	0	26	30

the relative incidence of sanctions, according to the number of times each item was mentioned by respondents. Outsiders may feel the nature of some of these rewards indicates an odd state of affairs; two odder still (not included in Table 1.4) are that one remand home's special privilege is permission to take Matron's dog for a walk, and that one unit head defines a reward as 'not losing pocket money'. We seem more ingenious in devising punishments than rewards.[9] The subject of control and discipline will be discussed further in later chapters; however, it is clear that rewards and punishments are inter-woven. Lack of reward can imply punishment and vice versa, which may be why the more positive units rarely resort to either (except that workers in one unit for extremely difficult children are occasionally exasperated to the point of slapping their legs). Rewards are a mixed blessing in many ways (beyond the fact that some of those listed above are concerned with basic needs rather than luxuries): for example, in one unit prefects were said to receive extra money for reporting misbehaviour in other children. Items such as having 'tuck' restricted or winning silver cups are naturally found mainly in the boys' prep-school. What the tables do not show is the intensity and frequency of sanctions and the accompanying attitudes—some of this will emerge in chapter 3.

Respondents were asked to describe the prevailing attitudes of the staff towards discipline: whether these attitudes were strict,

TABLE 1.5 _Number of times (and nature of) punishments mentioned in three patterns of care_

Punishments	Total times mentioned	More positive	Good-enough	More negative
1 Loss/postpone home leave	15	0	6	9
2 Official caning/corporal punishment	8	0	0	8
3 Unofficial slaps/cuffs/clips on ear, etc.	11	1	2	8
4 Threats/scolding/shouting	19	0	8	11
5 Child not spoken to by staff	3	0	1	2
6 Threat to whole group aimed at unknown culprit	4	0	3	1
7 Lock in detention room	6	0	3	3
8 Delay food/send from mealtable	8	0	4	4
9 Extra household chores	13	1	4	8
10 Withdraw privileges (unspecified)	15	0	8	7
11 Loss pocket money/fines	13	0	6	7
12 Stand on landing/sleep in corridor	2	0	0	2
13 Cigarette ration docked	7	0	3	4
14 Sweets docked	1	0	1	0
15 Stop from playing games	4	0	1	3
16 Stop from watching TV	7	1	2	4
17 Stop/curtail outings	16	1	10	5
18 Send to bed early/during day	16	1	7	8
19 Loss of marks or points	3	0	2	1
20 Physical exercises	2	0	0	2
21 'Therapeutic' use of group disfavour on individual	1	0	1	0
Totals	174	5	72	97

quite firm, or relaxed. Replies suggest that attitudes tend to vary according to circumstance: for example, control may be tightened according to the time of day, and when conformity is regarded as essential for particular daily routines; or control may be firmer for an influx of newcomers and relaxed again when children know the routine. The category 'quite firm' varies in the amount of friendliness it contains. In other words, there is some flexibility in units other than those where discipline is consistently strict. On the other hand, nearly half the respondents mentioned spontaneously

TABLE 1.6 *Prevailing attitudes among unit staff towards discipline*

	More positive	Good-enough	More negative	Total units
Strict discipline	0	0	4	4
Strict/quite firm	0	0	8	8
Varying from strict/ firm/relaxed	0	3	2	5
Quite firm	0	3	2	5
Quite firm/relaxed	3	13	1	17
Relaxed	3	2	0	5
Totals	6	21	17	44
Inconsistent attitudes in unit	1	10	10	21

an atmosphere of inconsistency within the unit, often quite seriously dividing the staff into two camps. This was nearly always caused by conflicting attitudes about methods of controlling children : in some cases younger care-givers were seen as more tolerant; in other cases older, experienced workers are described as more confident and therefore more relaxed in handling groups of children.

An encouraging aspect is that no fewer than twenty-five respondents mention spontaneously the uncritical attitudes of staff towards enuretic children, and twelve of these comments relate to the more negative units—being implicit in positive units. 'Wet beds create no concern' is a typical comment elsewhere. The prevailing attitude seems to be matter-of-fact provision of clean sheets without fuss. This clear evidence of non-punitive reactions is hopeful in suggesting that residential workers could gradually learn similar tolerance towards other provocative symptoms—such as attention-seeking behaviour. Also, four units (though three of them still sound somewhat negative) have in recent years undergone a radical change for the better through the influence of a new unit head who is less strict, or through the same head changing former policy— for example, one headmaster caned twenty-six boys two years ago, two last year and has now stopped altogether because (the respondent says) of his awareness that Labour councillors are now in control locally.

This grading of units according to their apparent quality of care in daily life patterns is not a particularly constructive activity; therefore it should not be emphasized except in relation to the urgent need of residential workers for training and ongoing support which enables them to give positive care. The next two sections indicate the extent to which workers derive support both within the neighbourhood and from the children's own families.

Integration of units into the neighbourhood

Respondents were asked to state the number and nature of community contacts, and to say whether the unit was well integrated into the neighbourhood, or fairly well, or isolated with few contacts. The responses require four categories rather than three. Only four units in the sample are said to be well integrated locally (two children's homes—one small for disturbed children, one larger; the school treating communication difficulties and the ex-approved school for pregnant girls). Nine units are described as fairly well integrated; eleven as fairly isolated, and twenty as isolated with few contacts. Possibly these figures also reflect the students' own sense of isolation during their placements.

TABLE 1.7 *Integration of units into the neighbourhood*

	Well integrated	Fairly well	Fairly isolated	Isolated	Total
Reception centres	0	1	4	4	9
Remand homes	0	0	0	5	5
Small children's homes	1	2	0	2	5
Larger children's homes	1	2	1	2	6
Boys' community schools	0	2	1	3	6
Girls' community schools	1	0	1	2	4
Special schools/units	1	1	2	2	6
Three other places	0	1	2	0	3
Totals	4	9	11	20	44

In all, approximately seventy per cent (actually 70·9 per cent) of children in the study are living in units which are isolated or fairly isolated. In addition, a similar proportion of resident (as opposed to non-resident) members of staff are in the same plight—i.e. 70 per cent (actually 71·1 per cent) are at least fairly isolated from the neighbourhood. If the incongruous prep-school is omitted, then these figures are even higher: nearly 77 per cent of children and 75 per cent of the resident staff.

Two-thirds of the 'good-enough' units are isolated or fairly so.

One-third of the 'more positive' units are similarly isolated: this proportion would have been much lower had not the large community school for seventy boys been isolated; also the school for thirty-five emotionally disturbed children has a well reasoned policy of *not* cultivating neighbourhood contacts in the belief that the children need primarily to learn to relate to their care-givers. Nearly 90 per cent of the 'more negative' units are at least fairly isolated.

These figures, although they show a correlation between isolation and less positive units, should not be taken as a clear implication that workers in more negative units are poor at making social relationships both inside and outside the unit. Several other factors are involved. Twenty-two units (half the sample) are *geographically isolated* in the first place, in many cases situated on or beyond the town or city outskirts; only five of these are said to be relatively well integrated. At least ten units are situated in rural surroundings, but half of these appear to be quite well integrated. Apparently we still place too much faith in the benefits of fresh air as opposed to the fug of the child's former environment.

This leads to the factor of *social isolation*. First, at least six units could be seen as potentially socially isolated in 'a select residential area' or 'in the stockbroker belt'. Second, social stigma may affect some units more than others. For example, nineteen units (remand homes, community schools, 'maladjusted schools') might be seen by local people as catering for 'naughty children', and in fact fifteen of these places are at least fairly isolated, whereas units catering for obvious physical and mental handicap are more likely to attract public sympathy. Even the pregnant girls, whose community school is well integrated into the neighbourhood, are there for an obvious purpose, and are thus more acceptable perhaps. But many respondents mention local suspicion or ignorance in relation to reception centres and children's homes.

Another possible related factor might be termed *architectural isolation*. Of eight large old converted houses, usually standing in their own grounds, seven tend to be isolated, even though some are within the town or village; all seven large old houses with modern extensions are rather isolated, whereas only fourteen of twenty-two modern purpose-built units are isolated or fairly isolated (Hall, 1965). (Another sub-group here is six units purpose-built in the nineteenth century which risk *historical isolation*.) Then there is the question of whether a whole, coherent home is likely to be more integrated locally than a small unit which is part of a bigger establishment and which may tend therefore to relate mainly between units in the centre. This seems to be borne out by the finding that ten of the twenty-eight *whole* units are at least fairly well integrated, whereas thirteen of the sixteen units forming *part* of a bigger centre are at least fairly isolated. One place at an obvious architectural and social disadvantage is described (perhaps in exaggerated terms) as 'a very old rambling monstrosity—a mansion on the outskirts of the city in a very expensive suburb. Some of the building is unsafe.'

The nature of this limited number of neighbourhood contacts varies considerably. In some fairly well integrated units, contacts are mainly of an official nature—for example with the Women's Institute, Rotary Club, Toc H, amongst other organizations—so it is not clear how far these are personal, individual relationships. (One respondent wondered whether local warmth for the unit extended as far as individual boys.) The Church seems quite active generally, and may be extremely helpful or possibly merely discharging an impersonal, moral duty towards unfortunate children. The local cinema manager and shopkeepers may well enjoy a reciprocal relationship (unless they are tempted to advertise their patronage). Natural contacts are formed spontaneously in playing with neighbours' children or in being invited to neighbours' homes, so better integrated units are those where inmates are able to offer informal hospitality themselves. One unit, although fairly isolated, contains children indigenous to the neighbourhood who thus identify strongly with it. In many cases, the units' closest contact with the wider community comes through their own non-resident and domestic staff—potentially an excellent bridging device.

Unfortunately, the fairly few existing contacts are not always friendly. Several respondents mention local hostility or complaints, perhaps exacerbated by incidents arising when children abscond. One respondent (in a children's home) recorded five complaints from neighbours during his placement; another said that the local authority spent £300 on erecting a higher fence after a well heeled neighbour complained about the football continually going over into his garden. The primary school whose catchment area includes the family hostel will not accept its children, ostensibly because they might be short-term pupils, but the parents perceive this as discrimination, claiming moreover that they are regarded locally as living in 'a nut-house'.

Positive neighbourliness, while not of primary importance in comparison with internal relationships between residents, does no doubt give pleasure to the children and proves supportive to the care-givers in easing their daily pressures. But, by the end of this chapter, three more kinds of isolation will be discovered, in addition to the frequent lack of integration within the neighbourhood.

Visits from parents and relatives

Respondents were asked both about the general pattern of such visits, and : How frequently do parents visit? How many children have no visits from parent(s)?

The amount of contact between parents and their children in residential care (irrespective of whether this is sometimes unsettling for all parties including the staff) is of course vitally important to the children and can also be a comfort to the staff in sharing their responsibilities. Most units (at least thirty-seven) sound open to receiving regular visits from parents, though about eight of these keep restricted visiting hours, and one children's home finds visiting days rather stressful. The picture in general is of the staff being very welcoming to parents in theory, very willing to offer hospitality and to discuss matters of mutual interest, but in fact the pattern of parental visiting is fairly infrequent.

One obvious reason for this (apart from other factors such as geographical isolation and the practical and emotional obstacles which prevent regular contact) is that many of the children are themselves going home regularly for weekends—sometimes every week, sometimes monthly or perhaps three weekends a term—as well as for longer holidays. This is not only true of special boarding schools but it is becoming normal practice for adolescents in community schools to have frequent short home leaves. Therefore the forty-four units fall roughly into two groups : in at least sixteen units some or all of the children are going home regularly, so there is less need for their parents to visit them. Even so, some parents do visit periodically—perhaps for open days and special events—for instance, parents of the children with communication difficulties come to the school for birthday parties.

However, in about thirty-one units (merging slightly with those above) children are more reliant upon their parents visiting them. At a very rough estimate, it seems that up to 36 per cent of these receive virtually no parental visits. If the proportion without parental contact is related to the *whole sample*, then the number is 25 per cent—a figure which tallies exactly with another recent study (Rowe and Lambert, 1973, pp. 42-5, 155). In general there seems to be far less visiting from other relatives and friends— indeed the latter are discouraged in some remand homes and community schools, perhaps being feared as a contaminating influence.

Where parents do visit, units vary in whether arrangements are casual or formal; whether visits are spontaneous or made by appointment (so that the child is readily available) and whether the staff use these opportunities for discussion. One small home is on friendly,

Christian-name-terms with parents, who seek advice and reassurance from the housemother. Many units allow parents to take their child(ren) out for the day; others enable frequent telephone conversations between parents and children. Less constructively perhaps, one unit 'compelled the boys to write home weekly', and it is still customary for letters in and out of some adolescent units to be censored by the staff in case plots are hatched. In contrast, the prep-school boys whose parents are abroad nearly all have relatives nearby, or other boys' families take them out. These service families know each other and can keep an eye on each other's children as appropriate. 'Without exception the boys go to their parents every holiday, going by plane to every corner of the world.'

Having now set the scene, in which children and staff are thrown together all the more because of their limited contact with the outside world, it is time to give further details about the residents.

THE CHILDREN

These 946 children and adolescents are very much alive as individuals to the forty-four respondents who met them in the flesh; they are fairly real to me, having been given the Christian name (not surname) of each one, but they may be less easy to visualize here. It is tempting, although impracticable, to name and describe each one separately now. (As a gesture, there are, amongst many others: 47 Davids, 39 Michaels, 38 Stephens, 31 Pauls, 29 Peters, 27 Johns, 15 Kevins, 13 Susans, 10 Christines, 9 Patricias, 6 Jennifers, 4 Alberts and an Aaron. The girls, though fewer in number, have a wider range of names.)

Number of children in care

At least 657 (nearly 70 per cent) of the children are in care or subject to care orders;[10] a very few more than is apparent may be in care in three of the special schools. The 30 per cent not in care include most children in special schools, adolescents on remand as distinct from those awaiting assessment after Court appearance, and (with one exception) the prep-school boys, the girl in a psychiatric hospital ward, and the five young children with their parents in the family hostel.

Age of children

The youngest child is a baby girl of four months old, with her mother in the family hostel. The nineteen children under the age of five are in this family hostel (having been in care previously), a few are in small homes and a few tagging on to older siblings in reception centres. The small number of young children bears out the expectation that foster-placements are generally considered

TABLE 2.1   *Age of children and adolescents*

Age in years	under 1	1	2	3	4	5	6	7	8	9
Boys	—	1	3	4	2	6	8	10	33	38
Girls	1	1	1	5	1	—	16	5	8	7
Totals	1	2	4	9	3	6	24	15	41	45

Age in years	10	11	12	13	14	15	16	17	18
Boys	40	69	82	82	129	120	57	6	—
Girls	13	15	13	35	34	41	44	14	2
Totals	53	84	95	117	163	161	101	20	2

more appropriate for them.[11] One toddler in a children's home has already experienced a foster-home breakdown; he may be more fortunate in a future attempt now being planned. Many of the eight- to twelve-year-olds are in special schools. Adolescents are in most places, especially in observation and assessment centres and community schools. Table 2.1 shows a peak of fourteen- to fifteen-year-old boys; also comparatively more adolescent than pre-adolescent girls. The sharp drop in young people aged over sixteen illustrates the usual attempts to establish them elsewhere well before they are discharged from care at the age of eighteen. It also illustrates the rather sad fact that places in residential care are scarce and costly, so young people cannot usually regard this as a home base (unlike foster-homes which have stood the test of time) while they find their feet in the adult world.[12] But a few of those over seventeen years in the study are staying on by choice for a little longer, having no other plans.

Brothers and sisters living together

Fifty pairs of siblings had been placed together, including three sets of twins; also eleven sets of three siblings (including girl triplets); two sets of four siblings and three sets of five siblings. Even more than these might have been expected, in view of the risks attached to placing siblings together in foster-homes.[13] There is a saying amongst farmers that 'the worst enemy of a sheep is another sheep' (disease-wise) and this has a grain of truth when applied to siblings in care: they are a mixed blessing to each other, in that a failed placement for one jeopardizes the other's security. Brothers and sisters were mainly together in reception centres and children's homes, though there were a few brothers in remand homes and community schools. The prep-school contained thirteen pairs of brothers; many of these older brothers are described as being actively concerned to support their younger brothers (especially during initial home-sickness), whereas older siblings in other places were often too needy themselves to have much to give to younger siblings—though no doubt there is some comfort in being together.

Length of stay

The findings apply simply to the duration of the present placement, not to previous lengths of time spent in care elsewhere. Many of the children, especially those in assessment centres and special schools, will have come straight from home; many others have spent long periods of their lives in previous placements—a few are described as institutionalized. The length of stay here is also limited by the fact that two units had only been opened quite recently (less than a year before the students' placement). A third factor is that several units (community schools, for example, and some catering for disturbed children) have a prescribed maximum length of stay —perhaps of up to two years.

Detailed figures in appendix C5 show that 69 per cent of the total had been living in their present unit for over three months, 39 per cent for over one year, and nearly 13 per cent for over three years. These periods may feel even longer to those directly concerned.

With regard to the shorter periods, some children had only recently arrived in long-term placements; others (for example in assessment centres) were obviously there short-term and many of them would be moving on to other forms of residential care. Where children have only come into residence briefly and expect soon to return home, the quality of care is still equally important because such children are in a crisis-situation (Parad, 1965). Also, in a few cases, children and adolescents were having a very prolonged stay in an assessment centre, waiting for plans to materialize.

Of the seventeen children who had stayed in their current unit (mostly children's homes) for seven years or more, seven boys and four girls had been there for over seven years, one girl for over eight years, one boy for nine years, one boy and two girls for ten years, and one boy for twelve years. Surprisingly perhaps, there were vague plans to place several of these children in foster-homes in future.[14]

Future plans for the children

These are plans made by the staff and departments concerned, hopefully involving discussion with parents.[15] Possibly the children's own plans would be vastly different, partly because their hopes and fears arouse fantasies, and they do not always participate in the planning.

Future plans are so many and various that they will not fit into a neat table. Fifty-six per cent of the children could expect to stay where they were for the time being: of these there were no definite plans for 12·8 per cent (often because of intractable home circumstances); 5·5 per cent expect to return home eventually depending on a change in family circumstances (for example, when the father remarries or comes out of prison).

There is a flavour of waiting for plans or people to mature:[16] 11·3 per cent are awaiting the age of about thirteen (that is, to leave the prep-school and a unit for disturbed children); 7·9 per cent are awaiting school-leaving age, and 2·8 per cent the age of eighteen years; 9·8 per cent were still being assessed and 2·5 per cent were awaiting Court appearances.

Of the total, 6·8 per cent expected to return home in the near future. There were plans (sometimes vague) for 3·4 per cent to move to foster-homes; 3·1 per cent were to move to children's homes; 5·2 per cent were going to community (ex-approved) schools; 3·1 per cent were awaiting vacancies in special schools or psychiatric units. A small group of 0·7 per cent were so difficult that they were to be transferred to places considered more able to contain them (such as a different remand home, a detention centre, or a 'closed approved school'). In fact, more than this small group would be in the same boat, steered towards deeper or more strictly controlled waters.

Some 2·3 per cent of the total were becoming more independent but were still unable to return home: of these 1·2 per cent were going into a hostel; 0·8 per cent into lodgings or a flat; 0·2 per cent into the Army and 0·1 per cent (one girl, with her baby) planned to marry. No answer was given to this question for 7·4 per cent of children: these were mainly seventy boys in one community school, where the general tenor is such that it seems likely to make appropriate individual plans, except that it seems to lack co-operation from fieldworkers.

The degree of settledness in the children

Respondents were asked to say whether each child seemed settled, or fairly settled, or unsettled or very unsettled. In the written instructions, no attempt was made to define these terms, largely because degrees of settledness are familiar to most people with any experience of meeting children who are living away from home. The students seem quite clear in their responses. They are not only aware of children violently acting out distress and uncertainty but also of those who are quietly withdrawn or depressed, attracting less attention. The responses were not intended to be taken as an indication of the quality of current care (particularly as good care does not straitjacket symptoms of grief, resentment, envy and anxiety)[17] but simply to show how far children appear resigned or reconciled to their circumstances, and therefore as an indication of the pressures on residential staff when children are unsettled.

Table 2.2 shows the overall pattern of settledness. Children described as settled include seven who were said to be 'too settled' in the sense that they would be reluctant or unprepared to leave when

TABLE 2.2 *Degree of settledness in the children*

	Settled	Fairly settled	Unsettled	Very unsettled	Not known	Total
Number	418	349	132	38	9	946
%	44	37	14	4	1	100

the time came. (It is not only foster-children who are expected to keep their roots in a suitcase.) More than seven may well be in this predicament, since 'too settled' was not a recognized category in the questionnaire. The *settled children* also include thirty-five comprising the whole population of an independent school for emotionally disturbed children described *en bloc* as follows:

> None of the children wish to leave. All children are consulted as to whether they wish to come to the school after spending a day here. The family and, if relevant, the caseworker are also consulted. An extremely thorough assessment is made in order that those children who are most likely to be able to make use of the treatment are selected. There are very few runaways— the school offers a primary experience of containment.

The *fairly settled* children include twenty-one comprising the whole school for maladjusted children with communication difficulties (some autistic) described thus: '... [their] main difficulty is in forming relationships. Apparently they do settle ... many of them

48

as far as I can see live in a world of their own.' *Unsettled children* include current absconders, a few of whom respondents had little opportunity to meet. '*Not known*' includes some very recent arrivals.

So it could be said either that 56 per cent of the children are less than settled, or that 81 per cent are at least fairly settled. In any case, almost one-fifth are unsettled or very unsettled. If these findings are related to unit type, the picture is as shown in Figure 2.1. Perhaps the main aspects of interest here are the clear indica-

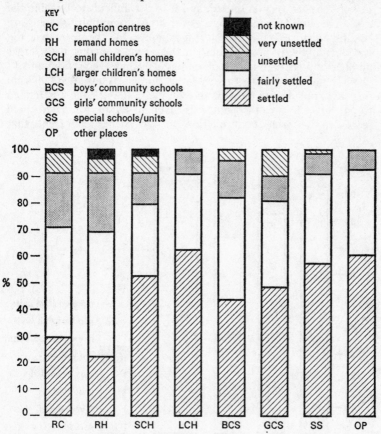

FIGURE 2.1 *Settledness in children related to unit type*

tions of the proportionately greater number of settled children in children's homes and special schools as opposed to a small number in assessment centres, though of course the degree of settledness in one child may be given to some extent in relation to his immediate fellows, and therefore it is of fairly limited use to compare unit type in this way. The children's homes of smaller size contain only forty-six children, but the lower proportion of settled children as compared with those in larger children's homes may partly be explained by the fact that two small homes cater specifically for disturbed children. Again, the number of girls in four community school units is quite small but it is interesting that, while 48 per cent are said to be settled, a relatively high proportion of almost 11 per cent are very unsettled, and it is not difficult to imagine the explosive form this takes. Figures for boys' community schools are possibly distorted throughout the chapter by the fact that the one outstandingly positive unit in this group contains a far larger number of boys than in any other single ex-approved school unit.

No single unit contains a very large number of unsettled children; they are spread over most of the sample.[18] If settledness is related to patterns of care, the picture is given in Figure 2.2. Here there seems to be some contradiction to the earlier statement that

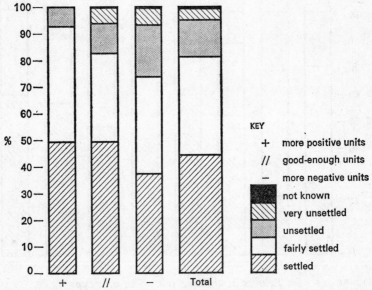

FIGURE 2.2   *Settledness in children related to three patterns of care*

settledness was not intended to be taken as any indication of the quality of current care, but rather to highlight pressures on the staff. It is clear that the more negative units contain nearly 25 per cent of unsettled or very unsettled children (as compared with 16 per cent in good-enough, and 7 per cent in more positive units). It could be that workers in more negative units are less able to tolerate uneasiness in the children and therefore influenced the respondents by drawing attention to restless behaviour; or perhaps the children are to some extent reacting to a somewhat unsympathetic environment, which in turn may tend to convince the staff that such children will get seriously out of hand unless tight control is maintained. Whatever the explanations, it is hard on these workers in the more negative units to be living with the higher proportion of one unsettled child in every four.

Relationships between children and residential workers

Respondents were asked to say whether each child seemed to be on good terms with the staff in general, or on fairly good or on poor terms. (They were also asked to say with whom on the staff each child seemed closest. This proved too difficult a question for many of them to attempt or for me to analyse, although several respondents made valiant efforts to identify the main support-figure chosen by individual children. The limited number of responses suggest that this person can be anyone on the staff including a domestic helper, gardener or night supervisor, but that it is more likely to be either the worker most closely involved in giving daily practical care, or the unit head (or deputy), perhaps because the child senses he or she has greatest power in furthering the child's well-being. Unit heads tend to be larger than life-size in the inmates' eyes.)

The first part of this section alone was a tough assignment, and the findings should be taken with a pinch of salt. Again no attempt was made in the written instructions to define the nature of good and less good relationships, partly in the hope that social work students are usually tuned in to the quality of personal interactions. But it is easy to understand why comparatively few research workers[19] have the temerity (or arrogance) to try to pin down relationships into clear categories—ambivalence is only one of the problems to be taken into account. In some cases, respondents simply wrote 'good', 'fairly good' or 'poor' according to their perception; very often they added a fuller description of the relationship, or gave details, leaving me to form an opinion, or occasionally I have made an estimate based on other evidence in the questionnaires as a whole. There seemed to be a tacit agreement between us that the care-givers, being grown-up, bear the lion's share in determining the quality of these relationships; the children are not lambs in any case but cannot usually in their circumstances respond on purely reciprocal terms.

The children said to be on *good terms* with the staff include the entire population of two schools (thirty-five emotionally disturbed children and seventy boys in a community school) where the question was really irrelevant as applied to individual children because all are 'accepted' in the casework sense of the word— that is, care-givers are usually able to look beyond unattractive behaviour through to the child's underlying needs. It does not seem as though the two respondents in these placements were carried away by their admiration for staff attitudes—acceptance on this scale is rare but unmistakable when seen in action. Children on good terms also include all twenty-one with communication difficulties, as the workers' main preoccupation lies in trying to reach abnormally inaccessible children: '[The children] are generally on good terms with the staff but as they have such individual attention they naturally or apparently get closer to their own housemother....' Those *'not known'* are mainly newcomers.

With all these qualifications, Table 2.3 shows the picture with as much care as possible. The figure of 46 per cent for children on

TABLE 2.3   *Children's relationships with residential workers*

	Good terms	Fairly good	Poor	Not known	Total
Number	437	361	123	25	946
%	46·2	38·2	13·0	2·6	100

good terms with care-givers would be reduced to 33 per cent had it not included the 126 mentioned above as being accepted in casework terms rather than in worldly terms of their likeability and what they themselves could contribute positively to a relationship with an adult.

Indeed, a striking aspect of this whole section was the extent to which many respondents did link the quality of the relationship directly to the likeability or otherwise of individual children: out of 648 detailed comments on individual children, 271 (42 per cent) demonstrated that it was the child's personality and behaviour which largely determined his popularity with the staff, rather than the child's basic and special needs determining the workers' attitudes. Whether this was really how the staff reacted or whether it should partly be ascribed to the students' own standpoint is blurred, but the former appears largely true and of course respondents could afford to be more accepting during their comparatively short placements. It is fair to add that the questionnaire possibly slanted responses in the direction now being criticized; it was a mistake that it offered as *an example* of part of the response 'staff regard him as likeable though cheeky'.

These 271 responses, where care-givers seemed to relate according to the child's personality and behaviour, fall roughly into two equal groups. In the first half, children said to be on good terms with the staff were seen by them as pleasant, helpful, open or perhaps as attractively naughty. The other half on poorer terms were almost always said to be perceived by the staff as sly, or deceitful, manipulative, attention-seeking, conceited, superficial, disruptive or troublesome in some way. Apparently a most serious obstacle in these relationships is for a child to seem sly. Again, it seems cheekiness can be tolerated, but 'insolence' is extremely provocative—though of course the word insolence only features in the vocabulary of adults who regard children as their inferiors. My argument throughout this section is that staff-child relationships are in danger of being poor, or of only being 'good' because the child is cowed into likeable conformity, unless care-givers can offer a professional relationship based on acceptance (C. Winnicott, 1964/70, pp. 29-30).

When the tentative findings are related first to unit type and second to patterns of care, the picture is as shown in Figures 2.3 and 2.4. In so far as Figures 2.3 and 2.4 are significant in such a complex realm as relationships, they speak for themselves. (But no figures are self-fulfilling prophesies as related to the three patterns of care, because columns were first added separately without cross-reference between sections of the questionnaire; it is hard to see trends until composite numbers are translated into tables.) It is advisable not to place too much weight on the figure of 90 per cent good relationships in the six more positive units because, while it is genuine enough in one way, probably only the two largest of these positive units are outstandingly so (thus swaying the results because they contain 105 children); the third is still finding its feet as a therapeutic home or hostel for difficult adolescents, whilst the remainder contain such very handicapped children that the staff are constrained to treat them in a very special way. (And yet, in theory at least, should this not be true in virtually all forty-four units?)

Subsequent chapters will be devoted both implicitly and more explicitly to the whole question of relationships in practical terms of daily residential life.

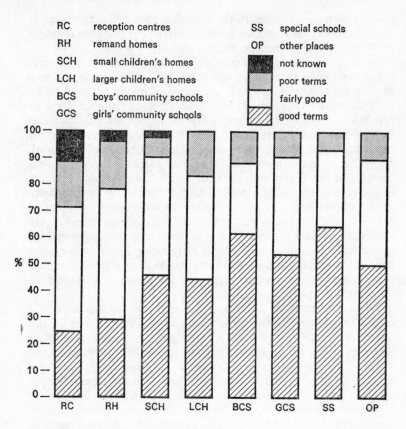

RC	reception centres		SS	special schools
RH	remand homes		OP	other places
SCH	small children's homes			not known
LCH	larger children's homes			poor terms
BCS	boys' community schools			fairly good
GCS	girls' community schools			good terms

FIGURE 2.3 *Relations between staff and children according to unit type*

Relationships with other children

The provisos made in the previous two sections apply even more here. Although respondents were clearly alive to the importance of relationships between children, and apparently quite sensitive in their perceptions, it was a tall order to expect them to give these details, especially in the largest units containing up to seventy-two boys and in assessment centres with a floating population. Three respondents did not tackle this section, so that sixty-six boys in two community school units and one remand home are omitted from the tables. The category *not known* therefore consists largely of newcomers (see Table 2.4).

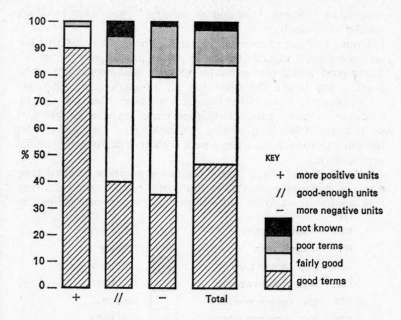

FIGURE 2.4 *Relations between staff and children in three patterns of care*

TABLE 2.4 *Relationships with other children*

	Good terms	Fairly good	Poor terms	Not known	Totals
Number	294	405	155	26	880*
%	33·4	46·0	17·6	3·0	100

* 66 boys omitted

The thirty-five emotionally disturbed children in one school are regarded *en bloc* as being on *good terms* with each other: 'Children are noticeably concerned for and tolerant of each other.' The twenty-one children with serious communication difficulties inevitably have poor relationships within the group, but they are included amongst those on *fairly good terms* on these slender grounds: 'They do not on the whole form relationships with each other. They play on their own a lot and they fear some children more than others because of their aggressiveness. Many of them as far as I can see live in a world of their own.' Those of us who live in the ordinary world may choose whether fairly good or poor is the more appropriate category—and add or subtract 2·2 per cent to either column accordingly.

Serious bullying (mentioned frequently in the units catering for adolescent boys) suggests that both parties are on *poor terms*, but 'fairly good' seems reasonable for one boy who 'would like to be a bully but hasn't the heart for it', although this ambiguous description may imply either that he is too nice at heart or that he lacks the necessary guts. 'Fairly good terms' includes a great deal of bickering, tale-telling, rivalry and picking on each other.[20] So the usual three pictures emerge here with even more qualifications than hitherto.

It is hoped that initial juggling with the numbers involved here does not risk making the tables too contrived to warrant drawing conclusions—apart from the adjustments explained above, the

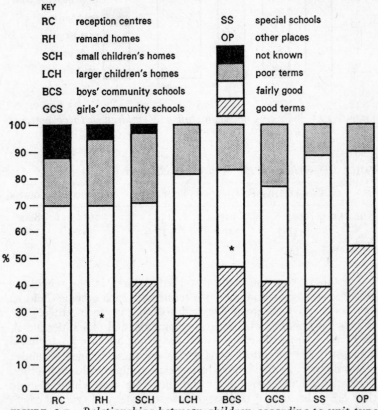

KEY

RC	reception centres	SS	special schools
RH	remand homes	OP	other places
SCH	small children's homes		not known
LCH	larger children's homes		poor terms
BCS	boys' community schools		fairly good
GCS	girls' community schools		good terms

FIGURE 2.5   *Relationships between children according to unit type*

* 66 boys omitted, in 1 remand home and 2 community school units

numbers are not shop-soiled. The children's relationships with each other appear to mirror, more darkly, their relationships with the staff. This is what might be expected, even though the principle of do-as-you-are-done-by is proved more in experience than in research as yet.[21]

Often in this study a child on poor terms with the staff is also on poor terms with his fellows—a universal scapegoat (in 81 cases out

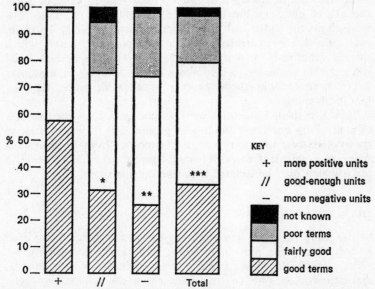

FIGURE 2.6   *Relationships between children in three patterns of care*

* 49 boys omitted from 1 remand home and 1 community school unit
** 17 boys omitted from 1 community school unit

of a possible 123)—and these children cannot accurately be termed scapegoats because eighteen units contained more than one such child, and two units each contained as many as nine. In other cases a child on poor terms with the staff (who suspect him of being a bad influence perhaps) is a hero amongst his peers, or vice versa if his mates resent his toadying to the staff, who like him. There is some correlation between unsettled children and those with poor relationships generally: of 170 children described as unsettled or very unsettled, seventy-four (43·5 per cent) were on poor terms with the staff, sixty-two (36·5 per cent) on fairly good terms, thirty (17·6 per cent) on good terms, and four (2·4 per cent) not specified.

An exception to the above pattern of mirrored or parallel relationships (with those between children on a lower plane) is found in

the boys' prep-school, where the boys seem marginally to enjoy
even better relationships between themselves than with the staff.
Possibly this is because they have sufficient confidence in their own
family ties to be free to mix with each other, or perhaps the staff
do not recognize much need to provide emotional support, except
to new boys. In contrast, children in care are typically more
dependent on residential staff for their security; no doubt many
form friendships amongst themselves and find support in sheer
strength of numbers, but other children tend to be seen as rivals
who dilute the individual adult attention each desires. To them,
adult affection is expendable, like a set amount of butter which
spreads generously on very few slices of bread. Also each child
is a constant reminder to his fellows of the adverse circumstances
which have brought them together by accident rather than by
family planning.

Typically then, residential workers not only have the problem
of controlling unrelated children in groups, but they also have to
try to share their affection amongst a clamorous group of youngsters
who are ambivalent towards parent-figures and each other, in a
place which may be isolated from the outside world.

THE RESIDENTIAL WORKERS

In the study there are 416 workers—i.e. all the direct caring staff
in forty-four units plus some senior staff with responsibility for
other units besides these: in all 178 men (eight places have no men)
and 236 women, plus two workers whose sex is unknown here.
This is because their headmaster requested that no information be
given about the six relevant members in the unit concerned; little
is known beyond their consisting of two housemasters, two housemothers and two teachers, so subsequent tables will often contain
two or six cyphers.

Teachers are included when they are at least partially integrated
with the care staff, but not (in five cases) when the division is
architecturally sharp. Social workers attached to the units (only
eight-and-a-half, mainly concerned with difficult adolescent girls)
are not included but may emerge from time to time. Neither
are domestic staff included individually though they often hold
importance far beyond their basic function, but night supervisors
and relief staff are included where relevant. In addition, some
places have a range of visiting experts: psychiatrists, psycho-,
physio- and speech-therapists, GPs, clerical staff—these are valued
but not included, being external to the daily care.

Table 2.5 shows, in three separate sections, the proportion of men and women; of married women and single women; of resident and non-resident staff. Traditionally, single women have been the

TABLE 2.5 *Proportions of men and women, resident and non-resident workers*

	Men	Women	Single women	Married women	Resident staff	Non-resident staff
Number	178	236	114	120	290	126
%	43	57	49	51	70	30

N = 414 (2 unknown + 2 women's marital status unknown)
In 3rd section N = 416

mainstay of residential child care, but fewer will be available in the foreseeable future;[22] fortunately men and married women are increasingly ready to hold the fort—which may become less fortified through having both sexes involved, as well as refreshed by married women who are perhaps less likely to be totally immersed in their work. Seventy-eight of the married women are working apart (though not necessarily living apart) from their husbands; forty-two married women are working in the units with their husbands —i.e. there are forty-two married couples working together in twenty-eight units. They are welcome, unless any one partner is less comfortable in residential work than the other. An omission in the questionnaire was reference to *their own children*, if any: respondents mentioned none, but their presence tends to cause even more divided loyalty in residential staff-parents than amongst foster-parents (Lambert, 1968). The remaining 136 men not working jointly with wives may or may not be married—in any case their wives are off-stage. All the men are full-time workers; at least twenty-four of the married women working apart from husbands are part-time, but may nevertheless be working long hours on a shift system.

Seventy per cent of the workers are fully resident, including 8 per cent who have separate staff accommodation in the grounds and who may not be regarded as fully resident by their colleagues (or by external administrators). Thirty per cent of workers (spread over thirty-four units) are non-resident in the sense that they are not sleeping on the premises.

A note on working conditions

Respondents were asked about the number of hours worked during a typical day; time off each week; the amount of time spent on routine chores, and the availability of domestic help. It would be tedious to quote information in minute detail, but certain patterns

59

emerge. In approximately thirty-four units, the staff work an 8-9 hour day; in two units slightly less; in six anything from 10-15 hours a day. Of course many work far longer than their stated hours; it is a problem that unforeseen situations arise frequently out of normal working hours.

Some units use a shift system, with night supervisors, which stabilizes working hours, but it is noticeable that smaller units (typically small children's homes) involve much longer hours as well as more domestic chores. In one such home, the staff were 'disgustedly working to rule', having been forced into a 45-hour week after a customary 60-hour week, which now allows them little opportunity to give the children individual care. Another problem, mentioned in several cases, is lack of domestic help at weekends, so that workers not only have the children home from school but are busier with cooking and washing up.

With regard to time off, about two-thirds of the units allow two clear days (usually consecutive) each week; others give one day plus a few hours here and there (for example, two or three evenings a week), but about half the total give regular additional weekends off at intervals of anything from two weeks to twice a term.[23] At least one unit enforces regular time off, lest workers save up lost days and later go off on a prolonged holiday; others are rather irregular. Only one unit was seriously short-staffed, but another unsettled place soon would be, as seven out of eleven members were leaving (two for training). One large children's home is also a training unit, with a small permanent staff of four members, supplemented by changing groups of four to eight students.

Domestic help seems adequate or even plentiful in thirty-two units; two units are served by a cleaning firm on contract which seems less satisfactory; remand homes and some community schools tend only to have cooks, using the boys to do most of the cleaning themselves as part of their daily routine; one school is helped by CSVs; all adults in the family hostel share the tasks democratically. In three units, young children may feel the fairies are responsible as housework happens when they are asleep. One respondent included mention of the window-cleaner's visits; others were equally meticulous in listing details.

The availability of domestic help obviously affects the amount of time care-givers can devote directly to the children. In one-third of the units, workers are largely free of household chores so have plenty of time to play and talk with children; in over another third, chores are fairly time-consuming, almost totally so in a few cases (perhaps when domestic busyness is used as a defence against involvement with inmates). Elsewhere, typically in remand homes and to a lesser extent in community schools, there is the tiresome, friction-provoking chore of supervising the adolescents moodily tackling most of the housework. 'The staff are told to work *with* new boys instead of just supervising them.' Housefathers seem more prone to supervising domestic work than housemothers.

Nowadays there is probably less emphasis on spit and polish; a few places let dust settle but, until residential workers are valued for less tangible aspects of their work, the temptation remains for them to seek external approval by maintaining unnecessarily high standards of cleanliness, while relationships risk being festooned with emotional cobwebs.

Age of residential workers

These ages are more approximate than those of the children. Table 2·6 shows a wide age range, somewhat concentrated in middle-age, when more married women appear. Eight people over middle-age are night supervisors, including five night nurses in the psychiatric clinic run under the health service. In many cases, units contain a good mixture of people of all ages; some are clearly divisible into older experienced members and very junior staff, perhaps in their late teens. The girls' remand home stands out in having no less than fourteen middle-aged or older women plus one married couple in their late thirties. Age has not been linked to length of service, except that younger members are usually newer to the work.

TABLE 2.6 *Age of residential workers*

	All care-givers		Men		Women		Single women		Married women	
	No.	%	No.	%	No.	%	No.	%	No.	%
Under 21	20	4·8	3	1·7	17	7·2	17	14·9	0	—
Early 20s	66	15·9	29	16·3	37	15·7	32	28·1	5	4·2
Mid-20s/ early 30s	90	21·8	45	25·3	45	19·1	25	21·9	20	16·7
Early middle-age	93	22·5	47	26·4	46	19·5	18	15·8	28	23·3
Middle age	89	21·5	29	16·3	60	25·4	11	9·6	49	40·8
Late middle age	47	11·3	22	12·3	25	10·6	7	6·1	18	15·0
Not known	9	2·2	3	1·7	6	2·5	4	3·5	0	—
Totals	414	100	178	100	236	100	114	100	120	100

Length of service in present unit

The workers' length of service is not only of great importance to long-stay children but to the workers themselves: if they survive the first few months or years, then time passes until it may become difficult for them to visualize returning to the outside world. At one extreme care-givers may gradually be drained by overwork; at the opposite pole they may settle into a rut which is not easily vacated —paradoxically, residential life for the staff is tougher than many outsiders could endure and yet it also protects people from some of the 'normal' pressures of the outside world.

Figure 2.7 does not take into account individuals' total length of service in residential work, which in some cases would be very much longer—for example, possibly in the cases of some fairly recently promoted unit heads, or of one woman who has worked in her present children's home for seventeen years but whose total length of service is thirty years. Also, as with the children, length of stay is limited by the length of time the unit has been in existence —only a few months in two cases. Figure 2.7 is a simplified version of appendix C6.

The numbers show quite a sharp drop after four years. The record is held by a man who has worked for thirty-five years on the farm of the outstandingly positive ex-approved school for boys. He belongs to an exceptionally long-serving staff: together twenty of them (omitting a few newer members) have served a total of 195 years—an average of nearly ten years each.

On the assumption that residential workers are unlikely to remain indefinitely in an acutely uncomfortable situation, it might be interesting to relate length of service over two years, and over four years, to the three patterns of care. Table 2.7 and Figure 2.8 are based on the 396 workers whose length of service is known. (This omits eighteen workers, 4·3 per cent of the sample, consisting of six men and twelve women, eleven working in good-enough units and

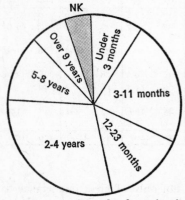

Approximately 33 per cent of workers have stayed in their present post for less than one year; 40 per cent have stayed from one up to four years; 18 per cent from four up to nine years, and 6 per cent for over nine years. Total sample 414.

FIGURE 2.7   *Length of service in present unit*

nine in more negative units.) Full numerical details are given in appendix C7, but the table and bar-charts given here show more positive units combined with good-enough units because numbers in the former are comparatively small.

TABLE 2.7 *Length of service over two years and over four years linked to patterns of care* (see appendix C7)

	More positive and good-enough		More negative		Totals	
	No.	%	No.	%	No.	%
All known staff	242	100	154	100	396	100
No. staying over 2 years	108	44.6	86	55.8	194	49.0
No. staying over 4 years	54	22.3	45	29.2	99	25.0

The bar-charts give a fuller picture of the sub-divisions (within patterns of care) of men and women workers, single and married women, and a further sub-division of married women according to whether they are working with or without their husbands. The main finding here is that workers not only do stay in the 'more negative' units but they stay proportionately longer than those in the 'better' units. (This would be more surprising were it not for Monsky's earlier findings.)[24] Perhaps the general concern about turnover of residential staff has tended to obscure another problem that authoritarian workers show an unfortunate propensity to gather moss, when it might be in the children's interests for them to be rolling stones. The only exceptions to the prevailing trend here of lengthier service in more negative units are amongst single women (who are not apparently persistent stayers anywhere and whose numbers are in any case relatively small in the negative units) and amongst men in more positive units whose numbers are swollen by long-serving men in the one outstanding ex-approved school.

Numerous speculations arise now. Do certain types of worker gravitate to certain types of unit or are they influenced for better or worse once there? Both are possible in my experience. If the questionnaire had asked: 'How many years has this unit been in existence; in what year was it opened?', responses would have indicated whether there was more scope for workers to remain long-term in negative units simply because such units had a longer history. In fact the questionnaire does provide clues if the number of old purpose-built units are compared with modern purpose-built units: of the six units dating from the late or mid-nineteenth century, five are good-enough, one is positive and none is negative; of twenty-two modern purpose-built units (excluding converted old houses) ten are good-enough, four are positive and eight negative,

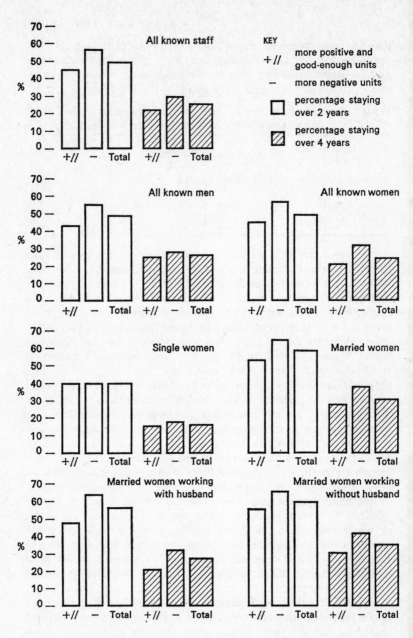

FIGURE 2.8 *Staff service over two years and over four years linked to patterns of care* (numerical details in appendix C7)

so this factor does not appear to be of much significance.

Further speculations: perhaps negative units are only uncomfortable for the children? Evidence in the questionnaires suggests otherwise. Do workers in negative units tend to be sadists, masochists or martyrs? Answer: probably not more so than most of us. Are pressures greater in negative units because they are dealing with more difficult children? Possibly there are more actors-out in negative units, but the whole sample (apart from the prep-school boys) contains a large number of disturbed children. Perhaps workers in good-enough units exhaust themselves by trying to be nice, and therefore leave? This is tragic, if so. There is a higher proportion of women in good-enough units and a higher ratio of men in negative units: does this imply that women in general are kinder than men? No—in any case married men with family responsibilities are usually less mobile than single women; this also applies to married women who feature particularly in negative units but who are less likely to go elsewhere if their family home is situated nearby. Many of the total number of long-serving staff (including several married couples working together) are in senior posts: is it then difficult for them to relinquish better paid jobs, or have these workers shaped the units' patterns to their own satisfaction? Are negative units so isolated socially and so unlike ordinary life outside that workers lose touch with their former values? Are workers in negative units less sensitive to start with or do they become hardened during long periods of stress? Factors of training and subsequent support are becoming increasingly relevant in trying to answer these questions.

A relevant factor in this debate is the difficulty for established workers of trying to withdraw or move on from the residential scene, irrespective of their degree of harmony in the present post (and this is borne out in my experience) partly because the unit represents both home-base and work-base. Also hitherto, their specialized training has not qualified them professionally for other forms of social work; nor do they always have opportunities to discuss the development of their career with external administrators.[25]

Several of these speculations will be discussed further in chapter 4; the two remaining aspects to explore now are the qualifications of workers in the sample and their opportunities for in-service development and consultation.

The workers' training and qualifications

First, a note about the forty-two married couples in the sample, as in five cases both partners are qualified in residential child care, whereas some others complement each other in having an alternative or additional teaching or nursing qualification. More than half the married couples are in early middle-age or older (including three in their late middle-age); about a third are young couples, and in four cases one spouse is considerably older than his (or her) partner.

In nineteen out of the forty-four places, the unit is headed by a married couple (only in small children's homes is the wife likely to be the senior partner, with her husband in outside employment); in eleven places the head is a single woman, and in fourteen places the head is a man who might have a wife off-stage. In twenty-two cases, the unit head has a relevant qualification in child care, including three who have completed advanced courses in residential child care. The general picture for all workers in the sample is as follows:

20·2 per cent have a relevant qualification in child care (this figure is comparable with but higher than a recent national estimate).[26] These eighty-four workers are thirty-seven men, five of whom have a Senior Certificate; another five are also teacher-trained; one has additional in-service training, and in five cases the respondent thinks but is not certain that the worker is child care trained. Of the forty-seven women, similarly in six cases the qualification is probable rather than certain; three young women have a Preliminary Certificate; one has the Senior Certificate; two have an additional teaching qualification, and two have extra in-service training.

14.2 per cent are primarily trained as teachers. These fifty-nine workers are thirty-four men (seventeen of whom are employed here mainly to teach); three have an additional qualification for teaching in special schools; two have extra in-service training; one also has training in youth leadership. Of the twenty-five women in the group (again seventeen are employed mainly to teach), three have a further qualification for working in special schools; one is also a trained nurse, and one did not complete her teachers' training course.

7·2 per cent are primarily trained as nurses. These thirty workers consist of twenty-four women (nineteen employed specifically as matrons, or as nurses in units for handicapped children); seven have NNEB training; the remainder are SRN/SENs. In addition four have in-service training; two are registered mental nurses (RMN) and two have special training for work with handicapped children. Of the six men, five are employed as male nurses in two psychiatric units; two are SRNs, and five are RMNs in addition to basic training.

7·5 per cent have none of the above qualifications, but have had *further/higher education* which may be more or less relevant to the present post. These thirty-one workers include twenty-five men, twelve of whom are graduates (one school chaplain also with theological training); two are trained youth workers; eleven have appropriate training for instructional posts—for example, in farming, industry and various trades, and a PE teacher trained in the Army. Of the six women in this group, three are graduates (one in psychology); one has a diploma in librarianship, one in occupational therapy and one in business management.

14·9 per cent (who should appear higher on the list) consist of sixty-two workers with *in-service training in residential child care*. These are twenty-three men and thirty-nine women. (In addition to these with in-service training alone, the whole sample contains six women and three men who have other training followed by in-service study.)

29·8 per cent have no training at all, though of course they may have valuable previous experience (it is not specified whether one man with 'a lifetime's experience as a prison officer' finds this relevant in his present remand home). These 124 workers consist of thirty-seven men, and eighty-seven women—many of whom are experienced housewives.

6·3 per cent where no details are known, apply to twenty-six workers, mainly in two units.

Inevitably, but with some trepidation, these findings must now be related to the three patterns of care. Figures here are based on each worker's main qualification; to include the details given above of secondary qualifications would make the tables too complex. Because numbers in more positive units are comparatively small, the two Figures 2.9 and 2.10 show more positive combined with good-enough units. Figure 2.9 includes unit heads with the rest of the staff; Figure 2.10 relates only to unit heads. (Full numerical details are given in appendices C8 and 9.) Advanced training in child care is shown separately in Figure 2.10 but not in Figure 2.9. At least two heads of positive units are skilled therapists (influenced by Carl Rogers, Bettleheim, Donald Winnicott and others) but presumably without formal qualification. The 'not known' category in these two diagrams applies only to negative units, suggesting that they may possess even more qualified staff than is apparent.

These findings, comparing the patterns of care, give cause for concern. It looks at first sight as though child care training is not as effective as we have hoped. This is particularly depressing in

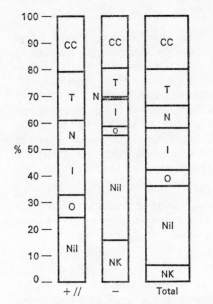

KEY to Figures 2.9 and 2.10
+ //   sum of more positive **and** good-enough units
−   more negative units
CC   Child care qualification
(A   Advanced child care)
T   Teaching qualification
N   Nursing qualification
I   In-service
O   Other training
Nil   No training
NK   Not known

FIGURE 2.9   *Staff training in relation to patterns of care* (numerical details in appendix C8)

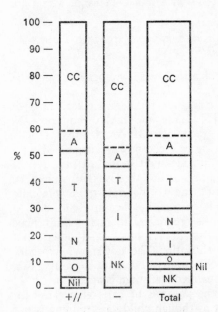

FIGURE 2.10   *Training of unit head in relation to patterns of care* (numerical details in appendix C9)

68

view of the tremendous efforts made in postwar years to develop residential child care courses.[27] It can of course be argued that proportions of around 20 per cent are still very low in any case, so that qualified staff are sometimes isolated in any setting. A single staff member (except possibly the unit head) cannot be expected to take responsibility for the tone of the whole unit; one professionally qualified worker will have only limited influence if all his colleagues are untrained. Therefore it is worthwhile to look at clusters of variously trained colleagues within units.

In Table 2.8, R stands for a worker with a relevant qualification in child care, T for a teacher-trained worker, N for a trained nurse, and I for a worker with in-service training. It seems that well qualified workers in negative units are no more isolated amongst their colleagues than are qualified workers in good-enough units —indeed, if anything, slightly less so. This raises the rather sinister implication that, although professionally qualified colleagues normally boost morale by confirming each others' positive attitudes, it is also possible for them to collude with each other in dropping former values and standards. If one imagines a young, recently qualified newcomer to the staff, then presumably he would tend to be more easily demoralized in subsequent practice through finding that his experienced, qualified senior colleagues imply by their daily attitudes that their former training is divorced from the reality

TABLE 2.8 *Relative isolation/colleague support for professionally qualified workers in three patterns of care*

	More positive	Good-enough	More negative	Total units
One R alone in unit	o	1	1	2
One I alone in unit	o	1	o	1
Two to three Is only	o	o	2	2
One R + colleagues with I	o	1	3	4
One R + several T/N or Is	2	2	1	5
Two Rs + other T/N or Is	o	4	1	5
Three Rs + other T/N or Is	1	2	2	5
Four Rs + other T/N or Is	2	1	2	5
Six Rs + other T/N or Is	o	3	o	3
Five Rs with no other trained colleagues	o	o	2	2
No Rs but at least 2 Ts and/or Ns	1	6	1	8
Not known	o	o	2	2
Totals	6	21	17	44

situation. To argue that these findings suggest personality is more important than training is an over-simplification, because attitudes and values are carefully evaluated both in selection of candidates[28] and during training itself, which is intended to be a thought-provoking and strengthening process.

To me, the discouraging findings in this section do not imply that training is almost irrelevant, but they do highlight the gulf between theory and practice referred to in chapter 1. We have tended to assume that residential workers, once qualified, will continue to put their knowledge and skills into practice for indefinite lengths of time. But no amount of initial training, however good, can prepare workers for all the subsequent pressures they will meet sooner or later. Care-givers have to react spontaneously to a wide range of planned and unplanned situations in the context of their everyday life; in the heat of the moment theoretical understanding and good intentions can easily melt down the drain, leaving only an uneasy sense of failure to maintain former standards. Therefore some kind of ongoing support and consultation is essential.[29]

Opportunities for ongoing support and consultation

Several sections of the questionnaire attempted to gauge what types of support workers receive internally and externally. Respondents were asked about the general pattern of visits from parents, relatives, friends and fieldworkers; about the number and type of staff discussions/meetings; about the number of visits from fieldworkers and external senior workers; about opportunities for consultation (with regard to children, the workers' pressures and their own development) and, lastly: 'Are any of the children receiving casework help or psychiatric treatment of any kind? Do the staff consider this effective?'

All these aspects will be explored more fully in chapter 4, but brief mention is made here in order to complete the outline of the study as a whole. Taking the last questions first, there was a mixed response to the section about casework/psychiatric treatment directly for the children. Where *good/effective help* is given, it is largely built into the units' basic pattern because of their special function in treating disturbed children. For example, the family hostel has frequent visits from a psychotherapist who is freely available to parents, children, and individual workers as well as meeting the latter for general discussion. '*A little help*' means that a psychiatrist, psychologist or social worker visits occasionally or that a few children attend child guidance clinics—in some cases the staff see little point in these arrangements, or it seems outside

TABLE 2.9 *Availability of casework help/psychiatric treatment for children*

	More positive	Good- enough	More negative	Total units
Good/effective help	4	7	0	11
A little help	1	4	6	11
Inadequate help	0	5	4	9
No external help	1	2	4	7
Not applicable	0	2	3	5
Not known	0	1	0	1
Totals	6	21	17	44

their province, invested with an element of mystery or mistrust. *'Inadequate help'* is a shade less welcome. It may mean that care-givers find the treated child just as difficult as before, or difficult in a different way (and in practice this can be a problem, in that a child who has actually been helped by treatment may well prove more assertive, less amenable than before). *'No external help'* means either literally none, or that the staff feel nobody other than themselves is available. *Not applicable* includes the boys' prep-school (although the one boy in care there presumably has a social worker discreetly in the background) and four assessment centres where respondents and/or the staff perceive psychiatrists and social workers visiting 'for assessment not treatment'.

The question of direct casework treatment for children is relevant to the study largely in terms of whether care-givers feel their own daily pressures are shared or eased by means of such external support: apparently more than half the sample feels to derive little comfort. This question is linked with the sections about visits from fieldworkers,[30] which evoked some strong responses. Here the

TABLE 2.10 *Frequency of visits from fieldworkers*

	More positive	Good- enough	More negative	Total units
Frequent visits	0	2	1	3
Fairly frequent	4	4	1	9
Variable/erratic	0	8	6	14
Infrequent/rare	1	4	9	14
Not applicable	1	2	0	3
Not known	0	1	0	1
Totals	6	21	17	44

respondents conveyed messages of isolation, frustration, hostility, self-sufficiency, resentment, wistfulness, bewilderment.... As potential fieldworkers themselves, it was an awkward question for them to answer. For one headmistress of a girls' community school who 'feels she is fortunate' in the co-operation she receives, there are numerous others where the majority of staff feel seriously neglected by fieldworkers or that they are merely used as a dumping ground. '*Variable/erratic*' visiting was sometimes related to resentment that a few children were visited regularly by their particular fieldworker, whereas other children in the same unit had infrequent visits. 'Most of them don't know who their social workers are anyway.' Another source of resentment is when fieldworkers discuss plans only with the unit head, without meeting less senior caregivers who are closely involved on a daily basis. Again, a general impression emerges of busy fieldworkers visiting when constrained to do so by statutory reviews, case conferences and assessment reports for Court, but otherwise (from the care-givers' viewpoint, especially when they are not included in discussing these plans) not making sustained efforts to visit.

In addition to a good deal of solid evidence about a definite lack of visits, there is a fairly pervasive sense of residential workers feeling cut off, left to their own devices, and—even though actual visiting may be somewhat more frequent than the staff feel it is—this too is evidence of a kind. However, several responses indicate that there is no simple answer, such as a strong recommendation for regular visiting: residential workers are ambivalent, partly preferring to be 'free of interference' or quite naturally wanting 'better liaison rather than support' from less senior fieldworkers. Unfortunately, there is a lack of recognition (even amongst respondents) that the fieldworkers' concern for children and for their immediate care-givers is interwoven, although there is an obvious negative link in that a fieldworker's real or perceived neglect of the child arouses the care-giver's resentment both for the child's sake and her own.

With regard to staff discussions/meetings, the general picture is of a great deal of informal discussion over tea and coffee breaks (sometimes too much shop at mealtimes for the taste of some members). Meetings happen less easily if there is a shift system, or if there is a sharp division into teaching and care-staff. The majority of units have formal staff meetings at widely varying intervals; some are seen as valuable, others as merely going through the motions. A very few have virtually no formal discussion or have got beyond it: 'The care staff feel they have no-one to whom they can turn to discuss their problems'; 'Any opportunity to discuss any of the above subjects (children/pressures of job/own development) had to be fought for, and most of the staff have given up trying.' Respondents were not asked about the degree of uniformity amongst the staff, but almost half mentioned spontaneously an atmosphere of inconsistency or a division into two camps—nearly always arising from conflicting attitudes about methods of controlling the children.

The question about opportunities for consultation was deliberately left open to allow for flexibility of response and to see what the concept implied to individual respondents. My conception of consultation is in terms of direct concern for the care-givers by giving them (individually or in groups) regular opportunities to discuss whatever pressures are uppermost at the time—either with an external senior caseworker/therapist or with a senior member internally, especially if the latter is receiving external support himself. Most respondents had a similar conception; others were confused; a few replied in terms of the support they themselves received as students (which presumably gives some indication of how supportive the unit is to members of staff). On the whole, consultation seems to emanate from within the unit rather than from an external person—i.e. it is the unit head or deputy who is often described as being freely available to anyone at any time. It is a gift in both senses of the word when a busy person is able to create that impression. In addition to daily availability, a few unit heads arrange regular individual weekly sessions with each worker.

TABLE 2.11 *Residential workers' opportunities for consultation*

| | Internal consultation | | | | External consultation | | | |
	More pos.	Good-enough	More neg.	Total	More pos.	Good-enough	More neg.	Total
Very good/ excellent	4	4	0	8	3	3	0	6
Good opportunities	2	8	4	14	0	4	0	4
Fairly good	0	9	3	12	2	5	1	8
Poor opportunities	0	0	10	10	0	6	14	20
Ambiguous response	0	0	0	0	1	1	2	4
Not applicable	0	0	0	0	0	1	0	1
Not known	0	0	0	0	0	1	0	1
Totals	6	21	17	44	6	21	17	44

A clear link is shown between the availability of support for care-givers and the quality of care they give in turn. The single instance of *'not applicable'* relates to the boys' prep-school, which has internal support but naturally no external social work help, though there will be some broad educational oversight of a privately owned school. The two more positive units said to receive only *fairly good* external support are first, the nursery unit for physically handi-capped children where 'the senior staff do have a high level of consultation and are satisfied with it. The child care staff are less satisfied, some feeling there should be more consultation, especially about the children—personal problems are generally felt to be adequately dealt with....' (Again, the fact that care-givers' prob-lems are often directly linked with the children is not recognized here.) Second, the exceptional community school for boys, while having an excellent internal support system, lacks external help from social workers. However, presumably other external sources are available—possibly from Rogerians in the USA, and within the wider religious order to which the Brothers belong, not to mention God (who may be conveyed as accepting or punitive, according to the individual life experiences of believers).

These last, most important aspects have been treated sketchily here, but will reappear as central issues further on. This long chapter is concerned with numerical details of interactions in the daily life together of 1,406 people (946 children and adolescents plus 416 workers and 44 students); the bare bones will be given more flesh later. Far more emphasis has been placed on the three different patterns of daily care than was originally intended: this is destruc-tive if it is used as evidence against some residential workers; my aim is exactly opposite—to demonstrate as constructively as pos-sible that the care-givers themselves require care if they are to give helpful daily experiences to the children. Chapter 4 will consider the needs of residential workers in greater depth.

3

Daily life for the children

All creatures have to live and, to do that, they have to make
a living. That means they have to get food somehow and
a shelter somewhere.... Of course, the thing we call Living
(which includes the other oddity, dying) is a very easy thing to
do. So many creatures do it.... There are camels and Chaucers;
snails and Shakespeares; Wordsworths and winkles.... They
have all managed to do exactly the same thing that I did....
James Stephens: *James, Seumas and Jacques*

An ugly fat snail slithered into a garden
He sat upon a stone and cried
Becau he did not like to be alone
He had no friends
He did not go intoo a hole
  because he was afraid of worms
by Andrew (aged 6½) in *Early Years at School* (BBC Publications)

Andrew seems to have considerable fellow-feeling with the snail
in his poem, or to be projecting his own misery on to this unhappy
invertebrate. And James Stephens is emphasizing similarity of experience in all living creatures, yet his paired examples illustrate
large differences too. It is not only reasonable to assume that an
insect and a poet enjoy rather dissimilar lives, but acceptable that
they should do so. However, it is less acceptable that a homogeneous
group like human children should have very different life experiences, especially when they are being cared for away from their
own homes in a comprehensive system of planned alternative
provision. There is some comfort in the idea that children, in
common with other creatures, show resilience in maintaining a

75

spark of vitality even in adverse circumstances, but they cannot hold on entirely by the efforts of their own green fingers.

In this chapter, aspects of daily life in the forty-four residential units are described and discussed in greater detail, with particular reference to the problems of communicating with children individually and in groups, and to methods of handling unco-operative members who rock the communal boat when they fail to conform with the daily patterns established by their care-givers. (Table 1.3 showed twelve aspects of daily life in the three patterns of care.)

The signs in brackets after each of the numerous examples given below refer to the three grades of 'good-enough' (//), 'more positive' (+), and 'more negative' (−). In every case, the first sign given relates to a specific part of the daily routine and the second sign shows the estimated quality of care in the unit as a whole: for example, the sign (//−) indicates that a particular aspect of daily routine is rated 'good-enough', while the unit as a whole seems somewhat negative. Where respondents give limited information, aspects are taken to be good-enough. Only a limited attempt will be made here to link the type of unit with each example; this is a deliberate omission in order to highlight the common human needs of inmates in all units. If we had evidence, for instance that young delinquents' stomachs tend to atrophy or that cold baths are beneficial to cerebral palsied children, there would be more relevance in linking unit type with differing patterns of daily care.

The 946 children and adolescents are in the foreground of this chapter as it discusses how their everyday needs are met, but the fact that care-givers have similar basic needs must be remembered silently alongside.[1] Residential workers, unlike fieldworkers, live with those whom they are trying to help, which naturally at times causes conflict between their concern for others and self-interest. Care-givers, being human, may also be hungry or queasy at communal mealtimes, tired at the end of the day, and perhaps no more eager to rise from bed in the morning than are some of their dependants....

Getting up in the morning

Seven o'clock seems to be the earliest rising time in the study; a more usual time is 7.45 or 8.00 a.m., often at least half-an-hour later at weekends. The main difference between units lies in whether inmates rise like clockwork automatons and almost sleepwalk themselves down to breakfast, or whether there is some resistance so that this is a fairly tense time of day easily leading to arguments with callers or between inmates, or whether children are given some leeway to rise at their own pace. Much depends on whether only one worker is waking a large number of children; on the age of children and whether they have to travel some distance to school or work, and whether they are expected to perform household chores before breakfast, not to mention the relative incidence of enuresis and encopresis. (Evidence of non-punitive attitudes towards enuretic children in nearly all units was stressed in chapter 2. The problem of soiling is harder to tolerate.)

Bettelheim (1950/71 pp. 82, 92) suggests that disturbed children often find it difficult to face a new day with much confidence: 'They lack the emotional strength needed to overcome their lethargy and their desire to retain the security and comfort of a nice, warm bed.' If children are to forfeit the physical comfort as well as the pleasure of wish-fulfilling fantasies, the care-giver must 'try to arrange the world the child meets on awakening—in such a way that it becomes obvious to the child that by changing from the world of his bed to a more active way of life he stands to gain greater pleasures, without running graver risks.' This sounds idealistic in comparison with most places in my study, with a few exceptions:

'Getting up seems unhurried ... each child may spend one morning in bed per week if he wishes. If a child wishes to stay in bed for another reason which is acceptable (e.g. depression), permission is related to the particular child's development.... Teaching staff also help in bathing and dressing' (+ +). Similarly, in a therapeutic unit for adolescents of both sexes, they 'are woken at a time personally suitable for school/work on weekdays. They can get up when they like at weekends and holidays, but there is a time limit (10.30 a.m.) on the possibility of breakfast' (+ +). Again, in a third unit for disturbed children, 'they are allowed to waken at their own pace and are not dragged out of bed ... [sometimes, in the holidays] they can stay in bed if they wish and breakfast is reserved for them' (+ +).

Such permissiveness may cause former advocates of disciplined, clean living (such as Baden-Powell) to protest in their graves but of course, when practicable, it encourages a more harmonious start to the day. (In fact the above examples show a flexible framework of warm control; to let sleeping dogs lie indefinitely can amount to a subtle form of rejection.) In my experience, it is clearly written on adolescent girls' morning faces from which side of bed they have arisen; everybody's interests are served when they can be helped to emerge on the right side. 'The general mood for the day is often determined at this point and on more than one occasion I have seen staff create unpleasant situations which could have been avoided with a little more tact ...' (– –). 'The older girls especially need a lot of encouragement to be in time for breakfast' (// //). 'Children have to stay in bed until told to get up ... at 7.15 a.m. on schooldays and 9 a.m. on other days. Staff shout from the door of each bedroom that it is time to get up' (– –). That was a children's home; in a more homely one, the two schoolboys get themselves up early and have breakfast with the housemother in her dressing-gown; then two other housemothers arrive to help dress the younger children (// //).

The prep-school boys 'more or less get themselves up—the head boy ringing the rising bell—with supervision by two matrons; they each make their own bed—bigger boys often help younger ones, matrons lend a hand ...' (// //). Another fairly neutral though slightly dreary example: 'The housemaster just opens curtains—not much chasing out. Boys wash ... and get on with routine small jobs.... It works automatically. NB relief housemaster has far more difficulty' (//–). One respondent perceives workers exercising 'a normal parental role i.e. drawing curtains, talking, pulling back bedclothes if necessary, then occasionally tipping out of bed etc.' (// //). Some units experience greater difficulty: 'Most of the staff had to coax the children out of bed but when Mr B or Mr E were on duty children got up immediately (they are less tolerant than other staff)' (// //). 'The Sisters take it in turn to call the girls ... the staff member calls each girl individually. Some are easier to call than others.... An assistant housemother usually follows the Sister round to make sure that no girl has gone back to bed again' (// //).

Here is a rather grim routine in a school for maladjusted boys: 'Youngest boys [aged under 10 years]—housemother wakes at 7.30. Enuretic boys strip beds, shower and dress, apart from shirt. Others wash, dress (apart from shirt), half-make bed. All boys go to boot room to clean school shoes, bring shoes to dorm, placing by bed. Wash hands, put on shirt, tie and jumper. Tidy drawers. Breakfast at 8 a.m. Routine is very important. Some of these younger boys must be very closely supervised otherwise they would not be ready until lunch-time. They are very unpredictable and any number of fights can occur within the first ten minutes of the day' (– –). That respondent seems to have absorbed the routine and the attitudes rather too easily. Several other units start the day with tight control and tension: '... supervision usually consists of hurrying along and stopping arguments and fights' (– –). 'The main job seemed to be to ensure that everything was done effectively and also to maintain discipline. There was little time to hold conversations ... punctuality was regarded as being of considerable importance ...' (− −). 'On being called, the children are expected to put their feet on the floor right away and then make their beds ...' (−//).

This section merges with the next. In one-quarter of the forty-four units, children are given household tasks before breakfast, typically in remand homes and ex-approved schools, and less often in units for girls than for boys (offset in one place by allowing some informal football between breakfast and continued work at 9 a.m.). Most children, in virtually all units, make their own beds, which (in addition to washing and dressing) would seem enough at this point without starting to clean and polish the building.

Washing, dressing, bathing, toilet

Most children in the study are physically able to wash and dress themselves; occasionally older children (but usually care-givers) help younger children. Extra time is allowed in the nursery unit with physically handicapped children, and in the school containing some autistic children, for helping them to learn to manage as independently as possible. Elsewhere, in the more relaxed units children either receive friendly supervision or tactful reminders if they are noticeably neglecting to wash; in the stricter units there seems to be greater emphasis on hygiene, perhaps partly as a hangover from the days when it was assumed to be the outward sign of moral standards. 'Washing is not an obsession as in some cottages' (in a girls' community school). In another such unit, the girls' hair is checked weekly for fear of head-lice. Newcomers and returned absconders are often bathed on arrival; sometimes they will certainly need a bath but otherwise their contamination from the outside world may exist largely in the workers' imagination.

A typical problem after children leave residential care is their apparent carelessness over personal hygiene: this may be related to poor self-image and depression, or to the possibility that they were drilled in a manner which subsequently feels incongruous in the ordinary world. Therefore, it seems sensible for residential workers to give children some experience in deciding when they want to bath and in choosing which clothes to wear today. This does happen in the more flexible units, where it is also normal practice for adolescent girls to look after their own underclothes rather than have a few inmates laundering for all. When related to individuals, the overall pattern is inevitably less tidy. Here follow some contrasting examples:

'Speed and efficiency are regarded as of paramount importance during this [early morning] operation. Children are constantly supervised during all these activities. Even 14 year-olds are escorted to the lavatory' (− −). 'Staff supervise all washing and bathing ... no allowance is made for privacy of any kind. Staff are asked to note cuts and bruises (which may be signs of bullying) and also the boys' attitudes to washing etc. The boys are always encouraged to keep themselves clean and tidy in appearance' (− −). 'As there is one member of staff supervising, the majority of children do not clean their teeth or wash properly in the morning. The staff member spends most time travelling between the two bedrooms and bathroom ensuring none of the children have got back into bed ...' (? // //). 'Because of the number involved, this is done in a fairly regimented fashion—the boys sit on lockers ... and go to wash/toilet etc. in groups of 5-10' (− −). '... The emotional state of the child very much dictates the extent to which these routines are adhered to' (+ //).

Few respondents recorded much about the use of lavatories, though two mentioned that there were no set times, which suggests that some idiosyncratic bowel and bladder habits are allowed. In two remand homes, the staff themselves put a set amount of toothpaste on each brush. In comparison with washing, bathing seems to offer much more scope for play and conversation, especially with younger children. Bettelheim (1950/71, ch. 11) recognizes that, while some children prefer bathing alone, for others it is a natural opportunity to learn the pleasure of being touched by a safe adult (some having had earlier experience of painful scrubbings, scolding for being dirty, or sexual assault). In one unit, children had a temporary craze for bubble baths, and were encouraged to start early if they were to be ready by supper-time. In smaller units, bathing can continue throughout some evenings, with children returning downstairs in their dressing-gowns, or it might even be the main entertainment sometimes when caregivers 'lack inspiration for evening activities' (// //).

Mealtimes

Eating together offers an excellent thrice-daily opportunity for care-givers to communicate affection through the symbolism of food. The emotional truth of the Proverb—'Better a dinner of herbs where love is, than a fatted ox and hatred therewith'—is widely recognized; possibly there is more actual nutritional value also in food eaten comfortably.[2] Bettelheim (1950/71, pp. 156, 163-4) says food and eating are symbols of security, demonstrating that satisfaction is available:

It is remarkable how even children who have always had ample food will unconsciously equate a parent's disapproval with the unspoken threat of being deprived of food.... Eating with others has been so unpleasant for some children that they have first to relearn with only one other person that eating does not need to be a misery.... Children who have always fought with their parents at mealtimes, for example, are particularly slow about learning to enjoy meals at the School.... Since there is no emphasis on eating or table manners, and since the child may eat or not eat as he pleases, he can neither control nor provoke us through not eating or through his complaints. Moreover, other children set a vivid example by their enjoyment of food, although it is equally important to convince the child that he cannot control or deprive others of eating by his own misbehaviour.

At one extreme children may be greedy for satisfaction through food; at the other extreme they may show hostile dallying, messiness or plain refusal, with numerous variations in between, including a range of cultural habits.

In about three-quarters of the sample, children eat with their care-givers sitting at the same table, having the same food; in seventeen of the larger units, several small tables are provided for one adult (occasionally two) each with a group of children. In seven of the larger units, mealtimes cannot promote friendly relationships through eating together because only one worker is present—purely in a supervisory capacity; in one such unit, workers regard this duty as a most distasteful part of their daily routine. In six places, where the unit forms part of a large centre, it is customary for some lighter meals to be prepared and eaten in separate cottages, houses, flats, etc. but the mid-day meal is served centrally for everybody together: 'Lunch is in the canteen, treated as a bit of an occasion, often with visitors present. Girls are expected to collect staff dinners from the hatch but there is no formal "waiting" as such' (// //). In two of the more positive units, several workers devote their attention to individual children's needs but tend to have their own meal separately afterwards: this arrangement is surprising at first sight, though evidently planned for the well-being of all parties concerned. In a third positive unit, workers and adolescents discuss at their 'community meetings' how best to organize mealtimes. A few units operate self-service systems; more often workers serve children or the latter help themselves to food on their own table.

Mealtimes appear to be pleasant events in at least ten units; unpleasant in thirteen, with the remainder more or less lukewarm. Two are particularly regimented: 'The boys are allowed to walk freely up to the dining room from the House, but have to line up and wait before being allowed in to sit. Each table is directed up to the hatch in turn to receive their meal. Again only one member of staff is on duty ...' (− //). 'When the bell rings, girls proceed immediately to the dining room, where they have specific places. They must say in turn whether they want the meal.... One girl has the job of pouring tea and being given one spoonful of sugar per cup by staff. Girls queue up at the staff table for one spoonful of jam.... Rations of sugar etc. [like toothpaste here] seems to be purely for economical reasons' (− −). Meals are rushed in at least two units: 'Speed and efficiency in feeding seems to be very important. Little social intercourse takes place at mealtimes' (− −). 'Exactly 20 minutes for breakfast, and all other meals. They commence by standing behind their chairs until silence prevails and prayers. The meal is a little more relaxed—however, the boys must behave and use good table manners. This is carefully controlled ...' (− −).

Next follow two particularly unpleasant and one outstandingly pleasant example. 'The boys eat together around one large table. The meals are supervised by one member of staff, who does not have the same food as the boys. I found this quite embarrassing at times. Boys would often say, "First digs on your meat, Sir" or "How I'd love some of that". I thought their food poor—too much [carbohydrates].... Table manners are enforced very rigidly. Grace said before every meal ... I did not always enjoy the mealtimes. Always a great deal of tension present amongst the boys' (− −). 'Painful experience. [The housemother-in-charge] sits at the head of the table shouting "10p. off your pocket money for holding your fork incorrectly ... the next person I see eating with their mouth open will go straight to bed" ...'; apparently she has extra food and sometimes, if she is overfaced, either a child or the dog finishes her leavings directly from her plate (− −). 'A very relaxed and happy time. The children only eat what they like and if they do not wish to eat, pressure is not brought to bear to make them. There are no set places and children are allowed to sit where they like' (+ +).

Saying grace is mentioned by few respondents, but seems a mockery in some circumstances—less meaningful in any case than affectionate attitudes. There is considerable emphasis on good table manners (in the children) in fifteen units, and on noise level in at least seven units. Children are adept at chattering freely with their

mouths full, whereas of course most adults prefer to eat peacefully, so mealtimes in residential life do tend to be feared by some
workers as a situation which may escalate towards loss of control.
'Mealtimes are rather chaotic. Children find it hard to stay on
their chairs for many minutes at a time' (// //). There is some
variation in whether children are free to leave the table before
everyone has finished.

Only two respondents recorded food of poor quality; in general
it sounds good, with plenty of scope for second helpings. A few
mentioned excellent menus, which may occasionally offset the
emotional flavour: 'Strict routine ... although there is no choice
of menu, standard of food is very high and diet well controlled.
Helpings are generous and "seconds" always available. The boys
clear up as directed by master present. Excessive noise discouraged'
(// −). Four respondents mentioned the staff having different food,
or the same with extras, or different equipment. Rarely (perhaps
naturally enough in small units) is there a choice within the menu:
'Food does not cater for individual likes and dislikes; if a boy
dislikes something, he just does without, but the meals do vary and
a lot of thought does go into the menu' (// −). One respondent
said the larder is kept locked; another said 'Children have free
access to the kitchen where they do some cookery themselves.
Food is left out at night—bread is always available ...' (+ +).

The way in which food is given and received has strong emotional
undertones for both parties in terms of personal acceptance and
rejection. Therefore it can be hurtful to care-givers when children
refuse or criticize food prepared for them.[3] Several respondents say
that criticism is not tolerated, or that the boys only criticize
privately between themselves, or that workers ignore criticism but
resent it as ingratitude. '... Mark [aged 9] criticized every meal put
in front of him. He was made to eat all his meals even if it meant
sitting at the table for two hours' [in a school catering specifically
for maladjusted boys]. Some workers are able to handle complaints
more constructively: 'A girl may talk about "food in this dump"
... this is usually ignored. If there is a serious complaint the housemother may support the child, e.g. if the milk is sour, and find an
alternative' (// //). In at least six units, children must eat what
is put before them; in about twelve units, they are free to eat as
much or as little as they like, with contradictions in some places—
such as having to consume the amount they estimated they would
want beforehand, especially a second helping for some illogical
reason. Apparently a child's eyes should not be bigger than his
stomach. Some capricious feeders are treated inappropriately:
'Apart from two faddy children no-one is forced to take any food

they don't like.'

It is doubtful (in my view) whether food eaten at pistol-point contains much nutritional value. Occasionally a child's refusal leads to ugly incidents: for example, the remains of a five-year-old boy's dinner was kept aside for him to finish at teatime, or: 'One boy [in a unit for "extremely disturbed" older boys] didn't like swedes which were served with the dinner one day. He was forced by the member of staff to eat them and was consequently sick. He ran out of the dining room in an extremely upset state. The member of staff brought him back into the room and made him eat his sweet. Another boy remarked that the staff member had left something on *his* plate and this resulted in him being thrown from the dining table and made to scrub the playroom floor throughout his lunch hour.'

Punctuality and preliminary hand-washing are important in some places; in at least two units any child late for a meal must wait until everybody else has finished before he may begin. Several respondents mention inconsistent expectations or that workers in charge of separate tables show varying degrees of strictness. 'Expected eating behaviour varied according to staff members, Mrs C and Mr E withheld food until children were silent' (− //). 'Rituals vary from table to table.... Rituals tend to be complicated and confusing to a new child.... There is also a tendency for new rulings to develop on the spur of the moment. At the beginning of my placement I was told children should not serve themselves but later staff were told off for not letting them do this' (− −). In contrast, physically handicapped children in the nursery unit 'follow the small rituals of mealtimes quite happily, and even make up their own, which the staff fall in with ...' (+ +).[4] In the family hostel, mothers organize their own and their children's breakfasts and teas, but the mid-day meal is shared by the whole community; in the ex-approved school for pregnant girls 'older babies eat with their mothers at table'; in both places there is a good balance between enhancing and supplementing all aspects of care given by inexperienced mothers.

In this section (as in others) examples are drawn from virtually the whole sample, without constant repetition from a few negative units. Unfortunately it seems that earlier battles or deprivation experienced by children in their own families are sometimes re-enacted and reinforced when they come into residential care.

Going to (and returning from) school or work

Here, as in a Shakespearian play, is a comparatively relaxed interlude after tension—which of course is literally the way in which many care-givers will experience the children's hours of school or work, although they may well be extremely busy with a range of unit activities on their own.

In just over half the forty-four units, school or work classes take place on the premises, seeming more within the centre's control than when children go out to neighbourhood schools, but which may entail a formal handing-over of tidy bodies (standing to attention in one place or in crocodile formation sometimes) from care-staff to teachers, often after a community assembly for morning prayers. In a few units, some children are occupied on the premises while others go out; in the remainder there is a general exodus into the neighbourhood.

The second major characteristic in this section is that the children's return in the afternoon is markedly warmer, more casual and relaxed than their departure in the morning. There is an obvious practical reason for this in that care-givers (as in ordinary families) have to plan in the early morning towards a time deadline of which they are often more aware than are their charges, and perhaps there is also a more subtle psychological reason in that care-givers frequently seem anxious that 'their children' shall make a good impression either in the outside world or with their own teaching staff (with whom some care-staffs are uneasy). This phenomenon—where parent-figures dread their child 'showing them up/letting them down in public', and enter into a tacit bargain with him that standards can be relaxed at home on condition that he conforms outside—is well described in the Newson studies.[5]

A few examples: 'Children have to do their job, clean their teeth and get ready for school, inspected by Mrs A before being allowed to go. Most children have something that does not please her and have to get changed or re-clean trousers, shoes, etc.' On returning from school, the children change their clothes 'and are told to play "up the garden", away from the staff who are preparing tea' (— —). Children 'sometimes need gentle reminders to get ready for school with staff helping ... talking to them about school activities.... Never any particular problems about them going. Often kissed goodbye and waved to from the window.... Children are greeted warmly on return from school, asked how they have fared, but sent immediately upstairs to change into playclothes ...' (// —). The return is 'much more informal than leaving for school. Girls usually bring some product of their labours to show the housemother, and talk freely about incidents in school. ... Most housestaff praise the girls for their achievements and show concern if anyone has behaved badly in school' (// //). 'All children tend to drift into the kitchen on returning from school for a little chat ...' (// //). In the family hostel, the mothers are expected to rise in time to see their own children off to school; they also collect their offspring from school, helping each other when necessary and rarely asking the staff to understudy for them.

In general, little difficulty is experienced with children who are reluctant to attend school,[6] though some workers go to considerable trouble in smoothing frightened pupils' paths. The pattern on return varies: a few units introduce more household chores at this point or mass shoe-cleaning or 'showers, strictly supervised', but most children are given time to relax and enjoy leisure activities before and after tea.

Leisure activities during weekdays and weekends

Possibly this is the aspect which has changed most since the first survey undertaken by the Curtis Committee (1946, for example paras 247-9). Only exceptionally nowadays would a residential unit have nothing to offer, or regard free time as time wasted. The present climate of opinion sets great value on creative use of leisure,[7] so perhaps the main danger today is of children being given too little opportunity to choose what they wish to do, or to refuse to participate. Apparently some tension remains between the concept of free expression and the fear that Satan tempts idle fingers into mischief. Some uneasiness also arises through lack of appreciation that uprooted children, whose inspiration may have withered, are sometimes unable to play constructively on their own.

The majority of units in the study (thirty) cater adequately for leisure activities; six show rather more positive attitudes and eight somewhat more negative. To avoid repetitive lists of typical activities, here follow a few examples:

'If the weather is fine all the children are outside playing football, cricket, etc. For the smaller children there is a sandpit and swings.... There was a big contrast in the extent to which staff joined in the children's activities.... Indoor games—table tennis, chess, Monopoly, table football, colouring books.... After school, the children have about five hours of play only interrupted by tea ... [sometimes] they are taken for walks, visits to the local park, swimming baths. Other available activities are basket-making, painting, and of course watching TV (about 50 per cent stay in the TV room from 7.30 onwards, some being persistent watchers).... At weekends efforts are made for the children to go out somewhere special on Saturday, usually in staff cars. On Sunday there is semi-compulsory church attendance in the morning' (// −). In another reception centre, 'There are no formal leisure activities but the staff create certain interests such as painting, woodwork, model-making, sewing, etc. or assist the children in following their own interests and sports. Within the unit there is a hobbies room, table tennis, billiards, TV, record player and numerous indoor games. The grounds while not extensive have a tennis court where football, cricket, rounders, etc. are also played, there is a climbing frame for younger children, and tree-climbing and hut-building is not restricted. Unfortunately the unit has no transport but walks, swimming, visits to museums ... are made available and staff with cars take small groups to the sea. One group spent five days Youth Hostelling during the holidays with a member of staff' (+ //). 'The only unorganized or unsupervised leisure activity is TV both on weekdays and at weekends. The boys have to earn this by not having any points marked against them during school, work or in the house. Approximately a third of the boys gain this privilege' (− −). 'The majority play in the large grounds—not allowed in the house during the morning unless it is raining. Staff seldom play with children ...' (− −).

Having read many lists of fairly formal activities, it is entertaining to learn of a few others chosen by children when left to their own devices: 'Boys create their own interests—e.g. illicit smoking, also catching rabbits and bird-nesting.' 'Each child has a little garden of his own and some derive enormous satisfaction from tending their plot.' 'The wooded area includes a fallen tree—"the log"—where depressed individuals or twos go to talk or smoke surreptitiously.' 'Much time is spent on caring for pet mice—feeding, cleaning, building new cages....' 'Some go out to interested families in the neighbourhood or to visit the cemetery and read grave-stones—a popular pastime!' Many of the children with 'communication difficulties' (some autistic) enjoy listening to music. Some boys in an ex-approved school help with gardening at an Old People's Home. These examples suggest that children can derive vicarious satisfaction in caring for other people, animals and plants; also that some special pleasures are introspective, highly individual or verging towards the forbidden.[8]

One unit (for disturbed children) seems almost to encourage a split between 'good' and 'bad' activities—it is debatable whether such extremes can be integrated constructively, especially in the absence of any safe adult: 'Only games of a quiet nature can be played in the playroom, noisy games are played in the basement playroom. Almost anything "goes" in the basement playroom— there are no windows and the lights are covered with a metal grille. A piano, table-tennis table and a number of wooden chairs were smashed during my stay. Most of the younger children play unsupervised in the basement whilst older children watch TV or do their homework [upstairs].'[9] However, the whole sample contains only one example bizarre to the point of sickness where (if we are to believe the respondent) senior staff frequently initiated water-fights which they perceived as a healthy outlet for their hostility whilst many of the children were soaked, shivering or trying to hide further afield. (The student said that on his last evening there he was saturated with water, then coated in flour and garnished with a raw egg.)

The main contrast lies in whether or not leisure activities allow some individual freedom. A few units seem intent on a grim pursuit of character-building: 'Physical activity is felt to be good.' In others there is time to do anything or nothing: 'Patients [in the psychiatric ward, with regular opportunities to join in psycho-drama, music and painting sessions] may just chat, wash, go to bed or visit the pub, go to town, dances ... as they wish—very free atmosphere.' Again, in a community school unit, 'The house-mother is available in the evenings and would often talk to boys singly or in groups—sometimes while they came to help her with small jobs in the kitchen, e.g. ironing!' Similarly, in some units adolescents are permitted to be bored or lethargic: 'Like all adolescents, they complain of boredom. However [here follows a long list of spontaneous activities] the philosophy behind this community is that it should operate as a community, and adults and children should intermingle as individual personalities. There-fore leisure is no more structured than in any home with a small "h".' But in a very few places boredom goes unrelieved: 'Girls spend their afternoons and evenings reading old comics and books or playing one of the two games available—i.e. draughts and Frustration!'

Another contrast centres on whether or not workers appear to enjoy playing with children. In some small homes, housemothers sound preoccupied with chores while children play rather dis-contentedly alone. In larger homes supervision of play is virtually a duty, and the outcome depends very much on how far care-givers can throw off their cares: 'Staff supervise several activities or join in games, taking care not to play too skilfully and dis-courage the girls.... There is rather a lack of stimulating creative activity for those not interested in sports, and boredom occasionally sets in. On the other hand, if staff offer encouragement or a display of enthusiasm (e.g. for toffee-making) the whole cottage can be busily occupied till bedtime.' Several respondents observed that younger workers participate keenly whereas older workers merely supervise. Apparently one or two students brought new life to the place but received a mixed response: 'For the period I was there, I organized a table tennis room with excellent equipment and this was met with enthusiasm by the girls. As I was leaving however, I noticed that the equipment had been dismantled.' Again, workers vary in whether they can tolerate risky amusements; some are relaxed about tree-climbing for instance, but elsewhere 'whilst we were told that there were no restrictions, tree branches were sawn off up to twelve feet from the ground...'.

On the whole, weekday activities happen within the precincts (apart from regular outside commitments, for instance to youth clubs) whereas weekends can be dreary for those children who are not going home or having visits from parents; alternatively some units plan special events and outings at the weekend, often with a mass exodus to spend pocket money.

Management of clothing and pocket money

Because this section will be quite brief, it is worth bearing in mind that both clothing and pocket money carry emotional significance in terms of self-image, individuality and personal worth (Bettelheim, 1950/71, pp. 46-7, 265-74). With both aspects it is difficult in residential life to avoid an element of dull uniformity; care of clothing for a large group involves complex overall planning even when shorn of frills and fancies. Inevitably perhaps, larger units and those containing a higher proportion of potential absconders (for example, remand homes, community schools) are more likely both to have uniform clothing (so that runaways are easily recognizable) and to control pocket money carefully (so that runaways cannot conveniently speed their passage). Pocket money is also closely controlled when inmates are thought to be light-fingered, and of course some children in several units have already forfeited a proportion of the money due to them, through misbehaviour. These factors explain some of the discrepancies in examples given below.

In nearly three-quarters of the sample, arrangements sound at least reasonably adequate; care-givers in a few units take extra trouble in helping children to choose and look after their own clothes and in preparing them for handling their own money in future, whereas about ten units sound somewhat more negative—quite apart from using these material things as a medium for punishment. Looking first at some examples: 'The children [in a reception centre] wear their own clothes and have a free choice—although advice is given—in the purchase of any new clothing. House-mothers appear to keep a fairly close check on the condition of clothing although the children are responsible for it. Pocket money is issued at the weekend and the child has complete freedom in what he does with it—staff do of course offer advice. The children generally pay for their pleasures such as swimming, speedway, etc.' (// //). 'Clothes for school are issued to girls [in a community school unit] but there is no uniform as such. They produce some very creditable efforts in sewing classes, go on shopping expedi-tions to choose their own materials and can also shop on Saturdays for their own clothes which they wear in leisure time. Sharing of clothes goes on on a large scale. Each girl is given a set amount of pocket money according to age, most of which goes on cigarettes' (// //).

'When a boy comes in [to a remand home] his own clothes are stored away and he is issued with a set of clothes from the home (he does keep his own shoes though). There is of course a set routine of wearing best shirts for dinner and the change of cloth-ing is laid down for each week. There is little use for pocket money and boys' money is kept by the staff' (— —). 'Mrs A [in a children's home] buys clothing and complains that the girls do not say thank you. They do not choose their own dresses and shoes, and appear to have insufficient clothing for their needs. Pocket money is paid out by Mr A on Saturday mornings. They are not allowed to have it at other times' (— —). 'Housemothers strictly control all clothing [community school unit], in fact all her time is spent either in repairing clothing or cooking. The boys are allocated 40p. per week spending money but spend most of this in replacing worn out clothing, e.g. jeans, shirts, socks and replacing lost ties, hankies ...' (— —). 'Clothing [in a remand home] is either provided by the family or by the centre.... The girls may not change clothes at any other time than that specified. Any money allowed to girls is held by the superintendent who will buy as they request within reason. Girls are not allowed to handle money' (— —).

In some units where children are not in care, parents are responsible for providing clothes. Presumably parents of the prep-school boys can afford to comply with the characteristically long list of requirements, but a problem arises in the psychiatric unit run by the health service: 'All clothing and pocket money have to be provided by parents, unless the children are in care. There-fore there is some inequality. If the parent does not contribute, children can earn some money for carrying out some minor domestic task ...' (— //). In several places, children's clothes are put out for them by the staff, sometimes in a fairly impersonal way; an extreme instance is where children are not allowed to open their own clothes drawer except under supervision. Only one respondent says that each boy's clothes are marked with his *number*; in another community school unit boys do their own simple mending. The outstandingly positive ex-approved school run by an order of Brothers tends 'to lack a woman's care' in the aspect of clothing.

Another variable is whether or not pocket money is supplied on request; most units seem to have a fairly formal weekly hand-out. One respondent describes 'a tortuous and complicated ritual after Saturday lunch, which seems highly disorganized with complex financial transactions being carried out with individual children (savings, debts) whilst everyone else waits'. Payment is usually followed quite quickly by an opportunity to go out shopping; here again conflict sometimes arises when children want to spend all they have immediately (commonly on sweets or cigarettes) whereas workers hope to encourage habits of thrift and saving. Some children willingly put aside a small proportion of their money towards a future goal (assuming it has not been decimated by fines beforehand); a few save under compulsion.

Children's responsibility for household chores

Here the three main variables are whether tasks are orientated towards the whole building so that a boy can be cleaning far more lavatories or corridors than would be found in any ordinary home, or whether these jobs are geared to real outside life; second, whether extra chores are given as punishment on top of a fairly heavy routine daily commitment (which tends to devalue all tasks in practice); third, whether care-givers work pleasantly alongside children or supervise them in an atmosphere of mutual resentment.

Many larger units organize routine duties so comprehensively that there is little scope for inmates to offer help in a spirit of spontaneous goodwill. Twenty-eight units appear to have 'good-enough' attitudes towards sharing domestic tasks, with four markedly positive and twelve more negative. Because this section was introduced in chapter 2 in the discussion about availability of domestic staff, limited further detail is given here. The fact that virtually all children make their own beds was noted earlier; also that in about a quarter of the sample, children (typically adolescent boys) start other chores before breakfast. Apparently the enforcement of high standards is sometimes perceived as conducive to character-building—for example, making beds to 'super neatness', though there is no logic in the punishment of forcing restless boys to strip and re-make their beds during the night. Unnaturally high standards are perhaps merely building future husbands who are reluctant to lift a finger in their own homes, and wives who either sit apathetically amidst domestic chaos or strive incessantly for sterile cleanliness.

Some examples: 'Older children [reception centre] are responsible for making their own bed and keeping their rooms moderately tidy. There is little involvement in other household chores' (// //). 'Children [in a small home] are asked to do little except setting tables, washing up and making beds. If they offer, they are usually allowed to help with other things' (// //). 'A high standard is not expected but they are all made to feel that they each have a part to play in the running of the unit' (// //). 'Girls [community school] have to clean their own bedrooms, help prepare breakfast and tea and also do some routine cleaning of the cottage.... Unfortunately scrubbing is sometimes used as a punishment. Some housemothers manage to make domestic chores quite a family affair, others allow them to become dull routine if they insist on them being carried out with monotonous regularity' (// //). 'Kitchen work [boys' remand home] is most sought after—possibility of bonus food and cigs from Kitchen staff ...' (// —).

'Chores are discussed at the weekly meetings [between staff and adolescents of both sexes]. There are no set chores, however it was decided at one meeting that they would tidy their rooms and change their sheets on Sundays' (+ +). 'Having jobs is seen as a sign of "bigness" and welcomed' in a school for disturbed children (+ +). 'The boys [remand home] are responsible for most household chores under staff supervision.... The staff don't like the domestic duties (which last all morning) and neither do the boys ... after a few weeks the monotony of it all can cause friction.... The boys know they are being assessed constantly but, although many make a conscious effort to aim for a good report, few are able to be unnatural for very long ...' (— —).

Dreary as some of these examples may sound, the Curtis Committee reported a markedly grimmer picture—they actually saw some dirty homes, as well as instances of child labour which would seem intolerably harsh today (1946, for example paras 190, 234).

Bed-time

Respondents were less forthcoming than might have been expected of this evening hour, when care-givers often feel quite tender towards their charges, not least because the day is nearly over, and children are sometimes less defended. Twenty-six units sound 'good-enough' at bed-time, with five more positive and thirteen where the sun is liable to sink on the workers' wrath. Bettelheim (1950/71, p. 304) suggests that, if we can cultivate the ability of disturbed children to enjoy unbroken sleep, 'we have gone a long way towards settling them down, making them less anxious, less tense, and in general more comfortable. This service, once achieved, then makes our work during the day very much simpler.' He goes on to compare children's needs at both ends of the day; whereas a child on waking in the morning needs to be convinced that it is safe to meet the day's activities, at bed-time he must feel he is safe even when his (and his adults') watchfulness is relaxed.

In both cases (when rising, and when settling for sleep, as well as during the remainder of the day) care-givers' attitudes in mediating these routines largely determine the degree of safety experienced by individual children. There seems to be a fairly general implicit recognition in the forty-four residential units that a calm atmosphere is soporific, but the main difference lies in whether care-givers are obviously concerned to provide quietly reassuring, comforting interaction or whether excitement is avoided merely by using a somewhat regimented, impersonal routine. Naturally perhaps, younger children receive more consideration, while many adolescents are virtually putting themselves (and their childish feelings) to bed. Larger units tend to have definite bed-times either *en masse* or according to age, while children in smaller homes may be coaxed more casually or equally are able to retire early if they wish, so there is a great contrast between homely and more institutional places. Several respondents mention some flexibility in bed-times, with extensions granted at weekends, holiday periods or to fit in with TV programmes.

Stories are part of the ritual in at least seven units, usually for younger children, apparently with the idea of giving them pleasurable attention as well as for expedience in lowering the emotional temperature. Children in one special school ask for individual stories, but in addition records (music and stories according to choice) are played over a loud-speaker for about an hour afterwards. A similar technique is mentioned in only one community school, though adolescents in the therapeutic community probably have transistors in their own bedrooms. Apparently it is mainly younger children who are tucked in and kissed goodnight; individual prayers are said with workers in perhaps two units, one containing physically handicapped children. Workers make a point of saying goodnight to all children individually in at least seven units, with the headmaster himself making a final round in the boys' prep-school. A few units are characterized by a changeover from day care-staff to night supervisors; in some cases children have special relationships with the latter. In other cases night-staff are less personal or bring an element of rivalry: 'The children [in the psychiatric unit] were taken upstairs to bed by the night staff, who jealously guarded this duty and wouldn't tolerate any interference from the day-staff.... I felt that not enough individual attention was given at bed-time—this could have been given had the day-staff helped to put the children to bed' (— //).

More examples: 'The girls [aged up to sixteen plus in a "maladjusted school"] go to bed at 9.30 unless they wish to go at 7.30 because of illness or tiredness. Two or three staff members are on duty but often all the housestaff are present. Some girls want to talk ... most of them like to be kissed goodnight and tucked into bed with dolls and teddies. This time of day is usually quite intimate ... with anxieties being discussed. The staff leave when every girl has settled down for the night' (+ //). In a large children's home, they 'are allowed to read at the discretion of the staff on duty. Younger ones will have a story read to them, and a night-light to help them settle down. The staff ... reassure the children at this time, and check that bedspreads are folded back, clothing is ready for morning and other clothing put away' (? + //). 'Depending on staff on duty [in a reception centre] ... children talk and interact freely. Other staff prohibit this and one finds that when they're on duty there generally isn't time for the younger ones to have a story either. Some staff allow wakeful children to look at books, others don't' (— —). 'The regimented pattern again comes into operation at bed-time. Washing and then putting on pyjamas is done so many at a time and then the boys are filed off to dormitories where they normally read comics for a short while before lights out at 9.30-ish. The staff member would check periodically—incidentally the dorms are locked' (— —).

Although in many units this is a comparatively relaxed, friendly time of day, there is also a sense of care-givers being torn between a wish to settle children down contentedly and feeling their patience wearing thin. Some wait for calm to prevail; others withdraw hopefully (ignoring a low buzz of conversation) or 'a member of staff remains on duty outside bedrooms until the older children go to bed, to listen for any disturbance'. The day is not over yet.

Night incidents

Most sections interlock, and this one follows closely on bed-time, partly because care-givers who are willing to give extra attention then are apparently less likely to be disturbed later on. (A local fieldwork teacher said recently, when discussing how to handle demanding and dependent clients, that our generosity is the best form of self-protection.) About thirty-one units sound to cater adequately for night incidents (which can rarely be ignored because of the sheer number of sleepers liable to wake), with four more positive and nine markedly more negative. A clear distinction is found between seven units served by night supervisors *awake* on duty, and the majority where day care-staff are *asleep* whilst remaining on call, either at random or on a rota system. In this majority, the degree of availability varies; positive units tend to have workers sleeping in adjoining bedrooms or using an intercom system, so that they seem more responsive both day and night.

Indeed, an interesting feature of the questionnaires is the varying perception of what is meant by night incidents. Three-quarters of the respondents were aware of minor or major disturbances, but these fall into two groups: first, of units which react in terms of controlling disruptive behaviour (stopping fights, homosexual activity, absconders); second, of units which react in terms of distressed children's need of adult support. Briefly, the former are concerned with nuisance-value and the latter with needs—apparently staff attitudes prevailing during the day are carried over into the night, or even magnified then. For example, some respondents mention individuals who suffer from nightmares, restlessness or who rock and moan in their sleep; others mention disturbances caused by loud talking, quarrelling, whistling, prowling, bullying, pillow-fights ... and include a note of punishments considered appropriate.

A small children's home is 'generally quiet but some nights children seem easily excited and will not settle down ... usually a firm tone is all that is required but at other times some children are smacked ...' (− −). 'If there was trouble at any time [in a remand home] the usual punishment was to remake bed(s) or threats of scrubbing for next morning ...' (− −). 'Individual girls [community school] occasionally demand attention by walking about or shouting in the night. A member of staff will talk to her and try to find out what is troubling her. If she persists with the disturbance she will be asked to take a sleeping tablet. Occasionally a girl may have to be moved to a separation room, in which case a psychiatrist is often called in the following day' (? // //). 'Few incidents at night were noted [remand home]. Raiding of one dormitory by another happened occasionally ... a boy was found wandering ... no evidence of homosexual activities at night. Staff had their suspicions during the day, however ...' (// //). In a reception centre, '... one 6-year-old girl was reprimanded for crying in her room. Two 10-year-old boys were caned for going into a girls' dormitory at 6.45 a.m.' (− −). 'As they are emotionally disturbed [some autistic] there are often incidents during the night. One child gets up and may strip his bed four or five times, makes it up again and bangs his head a few times before getting into it.... Aggression towards other children on waking. Nightmares.... Housemother sleeps in adjoining room' (// +).

Apart from three-quarters of respondents who were directly aware of incidents, the remaining quarter said these were either very infrequent or non-existent. In a few cases this was associated with the student being non-resident; in a few units it seems unlikely that children would dare to provoke any further criticism at night in addition to their daily dose, whilst other places seem genuinely peaceful. One respondent said there were merely odd scares from the natural creaks and bumps of an old house; another answered 'only crying incidents'. In at least two units, children are sufficiently confident in the staff, and concerned for each other, to seek help for their fellows: 'Should a girl be ill, upset, or want to run away during the night it is usual for one of the older girls ... to find a staff member for help.' And in the boys' prep-school 'I have known a prefect cope himself in cases of bad dreams or similar upsets—they are exceptionally nice to each other.'

A changeover from day care-staff to night supervisors may or may not bring a bonus: 'Many children [in the mixed adolescent unit] are restless at night either because of "settling in" or some disturbing incident in their recent experience of work, school, family. They get up and usually make their way to the dining room to the night supervisor who will give them a warm drink and a sympathetic ear. Even the most grown up adolescent is often tucked in after this.' But in a remand home, 'it seemed that where day staff might talk to boys involved in an incident the night staff would not. Their immediate recourse was usually solitary confinement for the boy or boys concerned.' Where there are no night supervisors, some units for older boys (including boys aged over twelve in one place) have locked dormitories, associated with bells, or an alarm system, fire practice and the locking away of day clothes. The girls' remand home had about two new admissions after midnight each week, when the procedure was to bath the newcomer, wash her hair, lock her clothes in the bathroom and take her to sleep in a detention room so as not to disturb the other girls (though in fact this manner of reception must be fairly disturbing for everybody, including the staff and especially the newcomer).

In all, there are remarkable differences in the handling of night (and day) incidents, when the degree of disruption seems to be linked more to the workers' varying responses than to the children's actual behaviour problems.[10]

At this point, a new day is about to dawn (when some children will wake inconveniently early, and a few may be isolated to stand silently in the corridor) so readers may choose now whether to read on, or whether to turn back to the beginning of the chapter, and re-read it several times in order to gain a cumulative impression of residential life.

Interaction and control

These two remaining aspects of interaction and control are not only mutually interdependent but pervade all fore-going sections. The rest of this chapter first considers these two aspects in detail and then discusses some relevant concepts. The overall grading of units depends largely on the total picture in each unit of communication, care, comfort and control: thus an overall impression is gained of twenty-one 'good-enough', six 'more positive' and seventeen 'more negative' units. The gist of further discussion concluding the chapter, arising from evidence in the questionnaires, is that the daily care itself is a continuous communication, for better or worse, particularly in relation to children who are uncooperative with their care-givers.

Twenty-seven places (including six 'more positive') sound at least adequate in their general interaction between staff and children. In a few of these, the prevailing atmosphere is remarkably friendly, with a flavour of a firm hand not within an impotent kid-glove but within a warm aura of acceptance. In the majority, care-givers are interacting fairly freely with children throughout most daily routines, using opportunities for play and conversation to some purpose. Even so, several respondents recognize that workers often find themselves prevented in various ways from communicating as fully as they would wish. The most typical limitation is caused simply by numbers: examples are given of ten children all demanding attention simultaneously; of interaction being 'constant and close' but usually in groups without 'very much opportunity for close individual relationships to develop', or of its depending on individual workers whether plentiful opportunities are actually taken.

In fact, children themselves are adept in seizing opportunities, provided the régime allows openings and children are confident enough that their overtures will not be rebuffed. (Naturally, people in urgent need of attention are inclined to choose awkward moments for putting themselves forward, partly through blindness to other people's pressures and busyness; also to seek attention from a preoccupied person is a surer test of its availability.) But again variations occur : in a school for maladjusted girls there is constant opportunity for conversation of all degrees of formality and informality, including the house-staff 'just being around'; in a small, basically friendly children's home, housemothers 'did not mind' being interrupted from their domestic chores to attend to children, but there is little chance of 'private conversations'. The prep-school respondent (who has considerable previous experience of residential work with children in care) describes how one boy, worried by his parents recently having been posted abroad, and conveying this worry in terms of fearing his plane-journey to join them in the holidays, has talked of his journey 'for weeks ... every single morning while making his bed [but now, at last] even shows signs of looking forward to it'. Again, in a special home for disturbed children, 'so long as there was only a couple, there is no objection to children chatting to staff cooking the meal. One or two children would stand by the sewing machine while a housemother mends clothes.'

It is characteristic of ordinary home-life that parents have limited time free to devote themselves entirely to their offspring, and therefore much communication happens not only within children's daily routines but also within the parents' parallel routines of cooking, washing, shopping, gardening.... For example, some students at the beginning of their social studies course were given an observation exercise when they were asked to record the interaction between a mother shopping in a supermarket and her young child(ren); several students said there could only be minimal interaction because the mother was intent on shopping. However, they agreed later that this is a plain fact of life, and moreover a fact which frequently affects communication adversely; indeed their observations reflected considerable conflict between toddlers, who regarded shopping as anything from a bore to an adventure, and their mothers who had the double task of shopping and child-minding. The added difficulty in residential life is that larger numbers of older, unrelated children are often wanting more than ordinary attention just because of their personal circumstances.

Workers and units vary in how far they seem able to lay themselves open to children's demands. Apart from the attitudes already mentioned in about three-fifths of the units, seventeen places are markedly more negative. Apparently interaction is often severely limited : either it is restricted by over-emphasis on discipline (including as many as eight places where interaction may consist largely of 'telling the child off', giving orders, 'talking *to* boys rather than *with* them'); or 'individual attention is almost non-existent', or an atmosphere of dumb resentment reigns when certain workers are on duty. Interaction in remand homes seems to be affected by their assessment and holding functions: 'Since staff and boys do virtually everything together, the opportunities exist though some members of staff find it easier to "come down" from their position of authority to talk with the boys.' 'The daily routines provide an opportunity for staff to observe the behaviour of boys in different situations ... if a boy does not do what is required of him then any interaction takes the form of coercion to enable him to conform—the boy is thus observed under pressure.' 'In the afternoons and evenings the girls stayed in the common room and there was a barrier between staff and girls.'

Even more serious perhaps, in at least one remand home, is a deliberate policy of avoiding relationships on the grounds that these would be short-lived anyway—such a policy ignores the fact that adolescents on remand are in a crisis-situation when they are (at least in theory) more susceptible to short-term influences.[11] The questionnaires show a sharp contrast between the hardened bravado of boys in restrictive units and the obvious distress of similar boys in units allowing more expression. In one reception centre, spontaneity may be reduced by the edict: 'It is hoped that Residential Staff be concerned solely with the assessment and needs of the children'; some workers there 'are available if a child requires help or talking, others organize games in which everyone must participate and there is restricted interaction with individuals'. In a second reception centre, 'both children and staff are expected to be occupied at all times and cannot just sit and talk'. In a third such unit, there is 'very little interaction between domestic and clerical staff and children [who] are considered by most to be bad and in need of close control'. And in a fourth reception centre, the respondent says 'All my conversations etc. took place off duty.'

In a large, short-staffed children's home, the respondent observed little interaction 'except at mealtimes and obvious points of contact.... Children mostly seem to interact with each other, with occasional displays of excessive behaviour (shouting or violence) to cause a reaction from staff....' Such displays are not uncommon in the seventeen negative units, suggesting either that they contain a higher proportion of actors-out[12] or the corollary that a lack of satisfying communication with their adults is one factor in provoking children to extreme behaviour. This leads directly to the question of discipline.

Control and discipline

Evidence will be cited to suggest that in residential life it is typical for a care-giver to perceive an individual inmate as maddening, whereas the whole group appears plain frightening—thus it is not uncommon that the care-givers' fear of the group becoming beyond their control causes them to jump heavily on individual inmates (like swatting one of a cloud of mosquitoes). Individual children must not step out of line lest the whole line is unlinked and liable to run amok. Equally, the maxim 'divide and rule' suggests staff mistrust of group solidarity—the very word crocodile-formation is a reminder that real crocodiles bite. If the residential situation is visualized as potentially leading to mass confrontation between staff and inmates, then a small number of adults would inevitably lose any overt tug-of-war with a large group of adolescents (or elderly residents, or prisoners, or psychiatric inpatients; even one crying baby, one child refusing to eat or to sleep or to go to school, can make his adults feel powerless). What is remarkable to outside observers, as Stevenson (1972) points out, is the rare occurrence of mass confrontation—but the underlying fear of being outnumbered in a major clash between 'them' and 'us' is real enough for the care-givers directly concerned. Often the battle simmers underground, with a series of minor eruptions between representatives of the two opposing sides.

Chapter 4 considers these fears and pressures from the care-givers' viewpoint; meanwhile this chapter continues to examine repercussions on the children themselves. In the section about patterns of daily care in chapter 2, tables showed the relative incidence of rewards and punishments, and prevailing attitudes to discipline, in the forty-four units. The tables did not show the intensity and frequency of sanctions and the accompanying attitudes; some of these aspects may emerge more clearly now. To take an obvious example, there are times when it seems to be in the interests of all concerned that a disruptive or depressed child should be separated temporarily from the group, and Table 1.5 shows that it is common practice in at least six units for adolescents to be locked in a detention room, and in at least sixteen units for younger children to be sent to bed early or confined to their bedroom during the day.

Leaving aside the question whether solitary confinement in a detention room can ever be enforced in a positive way, there are tnree distinct ways in which a child can be sent to bed. First, he can be sent in a hostile, rejecting way, when he is more likely to brood resentfully than to recover his equanimity. Second, he can be sent in a comparatively neutral manner on the understanding that he shall reappear the moment he is ready to mix again in company, in which case the onus is on him to regain his social poise—and it is difficult even for adults to emerge from 'a bad mood' when they are left to make the first move of their own volition. Or third, his bed can be provided as a temporary 'place of safety', as an undemanding place of comfort to which he is helped to withdraw and from which he will be helped to rejoin the group in due course when refreshed—in which case no battleground exists at any stage; neither child nor adult risks losing face. Critics might argue that a highly disruptive child would refuse the offer of his bed, but he is less likely to resist if the unit has an established pattern of making such offers, and if children have seen the method work in practice.

Clearly the third is the most effective method of treatment, the easiest, least painful for both parties, but it requires considerable maturity and freedom from hostility in the care-giver. The crux of the matter is whether care-givers are willing and able to respond positively to children's immediate needs for care, comfort and control. The forty-four questionnaires are replete with contrasting examples, and it is largely on this basis that the units divide themselves into three groups of twenty-one 'good-enough', six 'more positive' and seventeen 'more negative' units. (For instance, though it is encouraging that twenty-five respondents, including twelve from negative units, mention spontaneously the non-punitive reactions to enuretic children, it is possible to take a further positive step beyond the typical attitude of 'wet beds create no concern' by recognizing that the child himself may well feel concerned or distressed about his enuresis.)

With regard to prevailing attitudes to discipline, it may be sufficient to take one example from each of the three patterns of care. In a *good-enough* community school unit, disciplinary methods depend 'largely on the personality of the member of staff concerned, depending on a relationship which he may have formed with a boy. Most difficult situations are dealt with by firmness of tone or a quiet talk just away from the group—the boys usually respond to one or other of these. There is the occasion when, because of an irate temper, a situation is not as quickly controlled as it could have been. Discipline is quite firm ... the boys are fairly co-operative according to how they are handled....' In a *more positive* community school unit, discipline is 'relaxed ... the aim of the school is to establish a safe situation in which the boys can admit and acknowledge their feelings without fear. There is a healthy absence of rewards and punishments as such. Boys are continually "rewarded" with kindness, understanding and care—this applies to all boys, particularly those whose behaviour is "more difficult". There is a grading system but very much in the background and geared to each boy's response' and apparent readiness to cope in the outside world. And in a *more negative* (reception centre) unit, 'Discipline is very strict. The children are in general co-operative. The staff consider it vital that they should conform.... In general, a child who cried or criticized (e.g. food) would be regarded as misbehaving. Treatment might vary considerably depending on which member of staff was on hand but since the staff themselves are uneasy if children are not acting in a predictable fashion it is more likely that the child would be reprimanded than given sympathy.'

These examples give a rough indication of the range of prevailing attitudes to discipline, but the most striking feature overall is the haphazard nature of control within units. 'Depending on staff on duty—some require strict discipline and appear (to me and therefore presumably to the children) to make up rules on the spur of the moment.... Other staff allow potentially dangerous activities (throwing stones) to continue with only mild warnings.... Some bluster and make threats that they can't possibly carry out. Others set out clearly the limits and what will happen if they are exceeded....' Overall, the vast majority of units have care-givers who attempt to reason with unruly children but, in more than half the sample, reasoning easily turns to threats. There is of course a narrow margin between reasoning and nagging; between pointing out cause and effect, and making threats—nor is it easy to reason with children who are unaccustomed to thoughtful explanations from parent-figures. Insecure children seem irresistibly tempted to test the validity of a threat, so the use of threats tends only to inflame situations with resultant dangers of harsh punishment, ineffectual blustering or weak permissiveness.

Comparatively few units sound confident in their ability to maintain a relaxed but safe environment, and it seems clear that such confidence depends partly on open communication, both between workers, and between them and the children. For example, 'Discussion is seen as essential in dealing with incidents. After the visit of a parent, one girl and two others were upset and the disturbance showed signs of spreading: prompt communication between members of staff enabled them to contain this situation which is a typical one.' 'Staff may at any time ask to discuss rules which are not felt to be helpful—e.g. in a staff meeting, the wisdom of expecting girls to attend church on Sundays was questioned.' In other places, lack of discussion seems to lead to aggressive outbursts:

'The boys generally acted out their dislike of the school or their fear of other boys by verbal aggressive outbursts directed towards the masters, and at times towards the housemothers as they were almost certain to make an emotional response. I witnessed two incidents when boys were emotionally upset and they chopped down the flowers in the gardens of the unit ... were punished by loss of privileges.' 'The boys do not seem to discuss their problems in an open way but rather appear to act them out in some form of unacceptable behaviour. One lad helping to demolish a brick wall started acting a bit dangerously by throwing bricks about in a careless manner. When told, he reacted very stubbornly and cheekily. Moments later after quietly being taken aside, he was in tears and expressing his [unrealistic] fears about a brother whom he thought might be sent to Ireland.'

Sometimes children turned to the students for discussion. Mark, aged nine, saw his placement in a 'maladjusted school' as a punishment: 'He told me how it was his fault that one of his pet mice had been killed by his cat.... He felt very guilty about this and seemed to connect it with being sent to the school.' 'Several times I was approached by boys with worries about the future.... At these times they obviously lost their "hardness" and came across as insecure little boys. The older boys wanted verbal reassurance, the younger ones wanted some physical contact—an arm round the shoulders....' Occasionally the student's efforts were undermined by other workers: for instance, Peter aged ten, newly admitted to the psychiatric clinic, was upset when his parents failed to visit him—'he refused to go into the dining room for tea ... I remained with him and he eventually started talking about his feelings. Miss L came in and listened for a few minutes and tried to interrupt but soon left. After ... about 10 minutes, Peter started crying, but at this point Mr B came in. He jokingly threw Peter in the air, saying that all children must be in the dining room.... Having worked in another unit where one person usually worked through a difficult situation from beginning to end, I found this rather offputting. However, it happened quite often between the permanent staff....'

There is great variation in how far care-givers are aware of, and able to handle, distress underlying non-conformity. 'Staff have an unhappy tendency to label *any* untoward activity as attention-seeking. A small child who was retching but not actually vomiting was told to stop making a fuss because she was just attention-seeking—she later developed a minor attack of gastric 'flu.... A disproportionate amount of time is spent with the activists thus reinforcing their needs to claim attention and the feelings of the quiet, depressed ones that they are not worth anyone's interest.... Keith [aged eight] went to his mother's funeral during my placement and on his return hardly mentioned the event but became very aggressive towards other children and members of staff.' In a remand home, '... less obvious examples of upset in the boys e.g. separation anxieties, fears and worries are less likely to be picked up by staff and the behaviour concurrents more likely to be treated firmly.' Small mishaps can snowball rather than be taken as a chance for children to see, with help, how things can be put right again; an extreme example is given of a child in a reception centre who spilt paint on his shirt cuff: 'One member of staff called him careless and left it at that. Another member upon seeing the cuff scolded him and dragged him to the washroom. Finally he was fined by a third member.'

Certainly trivialities tend to escalate in residential life. 'Small incidents, such as forgetting to put a cup on the table, would often result in there being an almighty row.' In a children's home, one boy was sent to bed for a whole Sunday after failing to say hello to the housemother-in-charge; because this unit dealt so severely with minor incidents, the staff were at a loss to 'know what to do with a boy who ran away for two days'. Some respondents did their utmost to excuse insensitive reactions from care-givers: 'In only one case was a child scolded for [enuresis/encopresis]. At the time that person was about to be taken ill with an infection and was probably not in full control of his temper.' The same respondent said little punishment was used in his reception centre, but he noted that a fourteen-year-old coloured girl unwilling to attend school one day was not spoken to until 7 p.m. He felt staff attitudes to discipline were normally relaxed, but 'strict rules are enforced where safety is concerned—e.g. when the eldest boy encouraged the rest to disobey requests to come out of the sea, he was forbidden to go on further outings for a fortnight'.

Fears in the care-givers, either for the children's safety, or of loss of group control, are vividly illustrated. After watching a morning TV programme during school hours, one large group refused to return to the school building; 'about five of the younger staff were present, and seemed fearful of exerting any authority. A "messenger" was sent for the headteacher. He talked over the matter with the children, pointing out that it was unreasonable to expect to watch TV all day ... everyone returned to school. No more was heard of the subject.' And in the adolescent hostel, 'David, usually co-operative, was entertaining his girl-friend in his room when his elder brother, recently out of prison, suddenly arrived. Within the short space of two hours the brother disappeared down the drive with David's "bird". David was very upset—not verbally—but he led one or two other boys into all sorts of crazy mischief, which gradually became more violent and destructive. [Three workers were unable to control the situation, then] the deputy warden was called and the mischief calmed. She did not wave a magic wand—she reacted similarly to the other staff—told the boys not to be fools, to come down from the roof and that they did not need to break the windows, etc.—but because she was "Jill" whom they liked and respected—they growled their way down. The minor crisis was over.'

A similarly threatening situation in a remand home was resolved less competently. 'On one occasion when the football game became a shambles, all the boys were sent running round the pitch. One boy in particular was most unco-operative and a member of staff took it upon himself to cut him down to size in front of his peer group. The rest stood around while he was given a thorough verbal dressing-down and then set to scrub for the afternoon. A few days later a similar situation arose involving about four boys.... In the end they were beaten' [the first official caning for about two years]. There are many examples of units where a few workers exert natural, quiet, effective authority whilst others resort to bullying tactics. In at least two community schools, the cane is used particularly to punish bullies, without apparent realization that caning is a form of bullying in itself which encourages brutality.[13] One community school has changed ostensibly from its former strict authoritarian régime, but the housemaster believes that the resultant uncertainty in some of the staff has led to even greater use of unofficial physical punishment—'the boys are hit regularly ... hair pulled and heads banged. Boys accept all this as natural.'

Another respondent describes the staff tensions which may follow relaxation of disciplinary methods. 'There has been a great change since the appointment of the headmistress [eighteen months ago] and this has formed a split in staff opinion. The school had very strict discipline, which the headmistress has relaxed. Because there is now less conformity, some staff feel that all discipline has disappeared. The school once had repressed "good" children. Of late it has developed into a school which has wilder, more outgoing but happier children. With a small percentage of children being disruptive, in general the majority are reasonably co-operative for most of the time. Some staff feel the children should conform

—mainly staff here for a long time. The housestaff *do not* wish the children to conform for conformity's sake.'

On a much smaller scale, several respondents recount graphic examples where children themselves have been uncertain of their own feelings while care-givers try to adapt with more or less sensitivity. 'After tea one day, the 5-year-old [in a large children's home] fell off his chair when fooling about. He immediately began to laugh but, when told it was his own fault that he fell, he began to cry. The same member of staff who had chastised him then had a look at his arm upon which he had fallen and offered sympathy and joked with the boy to comfort him until he had stopped crying.' In the nursery unit for physically handicapped children, 'Mandy twisted over in the bath, accidentally on purpose, got under the water, was fished out by Miss F and cried very hard. She seemed to have frightened herself, and was angry with Miss F, who hadn't helped her quickly or been sympathetic because she had done this before. Miss F reacted to her screams by whispering to her and tickling her, and when this comfort was refused, Miss F took Mandy's fear seriously, and waited for her to quieten before reassuring her.' Other respondents indicate how teasing from care-givers is perceived realistically by children either as a sign of affection or of hostility (Berry, 1969). 'Moodiness and sulking, which are common [in a girls' community school] are usually treated by gentle teasing and joking, but it was sometimes overdone and led to more trouble.'

The handling of temper-tantrums also varies. Temper-outbursts from adolescents are likely to be seen as violent behaviour, perhaps requiring seclusion in a locked room. Smaller bodies expressing similar violence are easier for care-givers to hold in their arms until the tempest subsides, in the knowledge that the experience of losing self-control is frightening to the child himself (Dockar-Drysdale, 1973, ch. 11). In at least three units, such holding is common practice—'If a child is in a panic or is being particularly aggressive, he is generally held tightly until he feels calmer.' An impressive example arose in the family hostel, where two-year-old Paul had a temper-tantrum and two other *mothers* (taught by the staff?) encouraged his own mother, Kathy, to hold him firmly until it had subsided. Kathy then commented that in the past she had only been able to hit Paul, which exacerbated his tantrum.[14] Another positive example in a reception centre occurred when a young boy had a tantrum because he could not go on a swimming trip in case his mother visited—his uncertainty of the latter's plans was enough to cause panic. He hid briefly in a cupboard, while a worker telephoned unsuccessfully to try to see whether his mother would come; then a compromise was reached by deciding with him that he should join the others at the swimming baths later on if his mother did not turn up.

Elsewhere, examples are given of children being expected to emerge unaided from their emotional upheavals. 'One child has regular outbursts of temper and nearly always directs her attack upon her sister. Afterwards she is always terribly upset, but is not forced to continue with normal routine—she is allowed to get over it in her own time and gradually she will return to the main group, anxious to please and do well. It is left to her however. No effort is made to go to her.' It often seems that disturbed children are expected to reach standards of self-discipline which the care-givers, though adult, are quite unable to match in their own self-control. Again numerous examples are given of younger children and adolescents who, when frustrated by the staff, vent their aggression on each other. 'If Maria [aged six] was reprimanded ... she would go away afterwards and often hit a smaller child.'

So, an impression is gained of a pecking order of aggression in some units, where weaker members may find themselves at the mercy both of workers and their fellows. (Rivalry between children is of course very difficult for parent-figures to handle, but a policy of sympathizing with the victim without attacking the aggressor seems to be the most immediately constructive way of handling fast-moving interaction.) Workers in some units appear to attempt to control bullying amongst the inmates; occasionally there is a hint of tacit collusion between staff and group to allow intimidation of unpopular children. For instance, in a community school, 'Pat feared she was going to be beaten up by the other girls one evening and she locked herself in the toilet for protection. The staff felt she should sort this problem out for herself. She is a manipulative, unpopular girl, and the staff often discussed her in a derogatory way in front of the other girls. . . .' In at least four units, group pressures are deliberately exploited by the staff's method of punishing the whole group for the misdeeds of an unidentified culprit. Typically, a whole unit for adolescents is threatened with forfeiting its tobacco ration, and the foreign student describes something similar in a large children's home: 'There has been a fairly large amount of underpants missing. The Home felt that it was done deliberately by the boys. Therefore the children were asked to produce the missing pants. Failing to redeem the missing pants, the children would have to share the cost for replacement.'

More subtly, a very few units which aim to create therapeutic communities, deliberately or unwittingly pressurize individual non-conformists by means of group disfavour. The psychiatric ward (containing one adolescent girl with adult patients) conducts group meetings daily with compulsory attendance, and uses 'formal censure in meetings of behaviour regarded as counter-productive to the group's efforts to help fellow members'. In such confrontations, there is a difference between helpful discussion of each other's problems, and destructive tactics (either from leader to group, or between group members) which exploit the particular need of adolescents for peer group solidarity. 'Following a group meeting at which the warden expressed his anger with the group [of adolescents] about their broken agreements, Michael was seen outside in a very aggressive mood. This kind of reaction is not unusual. The deputy went outside to see Michael who hurled both sticks and abuse at her. However, she eventually persuaded him to calm down and come in and then to see the warden. He welcomed him and the boy immediately saw that the warden was no longer angry, which is what had originally concerned him. After a very understanding and warm talk ... Michael went very happily to bed about 11.15 p.m.'

All these examples (drawn from the whole range of question-naires) illustrate the pressures of residential life upon children and upon their care-givers, who may be extremely patient and painstaking in very difficult situations or who may equally react in ways which cause unnecessary pain and trouble to all concerned. The haphazard nature of care-givers' responses, the discrepancies between their own theory and practice, and the prevalence of inconsistent attitudes within units, amply demonstrate the prob-lems of living together—and the temptation of care-givers to rationalize their methods of treatment in terms of the children's needs when they are in fact often reacting to their own pressures. Workers may have a deliberate policy of confronting naughtiness or equally of ignoring attention-seeking behaviour but, in the heat of the moment, their beliefs are influenced to a considerable extent by their own fears and hostility.

One last example, in a 'good-enough' reception centre: two nine-year-old coloured boys were half-an-hour late for mid-day dinner having gone to play in the local park; therefore they were made to wait in silence for half-an-hour while everybody else finished their meal, and then they were given their dinner. Presumably it was thought necessary to teach them punctuality, especially as the domestic staff went off duty after dinner but, to an outsider, this punishment was neither appropriate (considering the natural un-punctuality of small boys out at play) nor logical (since in effect the boys were made to be an extra half-hour later than they were in the first place). It would have been quite enough to ask them to hurry up once they arrived, and then their jaunt would not have ended unpleasantly.

Punishment is frequently thought necessary in order to 'teach a lesson' to the offender. A point in favour of skilled behaviour therapists,[15] even if one is not an advocate of their methods, is that they do give careful thought to the exact nature of the lesson they wish the child to learn—i.e. treatment depends on the demonstration of a clear cause and effect whose logic can hardly escape the child. In contrast, amateur dispensers of rewards and punishments may unwittingly teach confusing, irrational lessons, being motivated largely by their own exasperation. But in either case (of amateur or of skilled behaviour modification) there is a danger that the main lesson learnt by the child is that powerful adults are less concerned about him personally than about his nuisance-value to themselves (Woodmansey 1966, 1969, 1971a). Ultimately, the personal concern he receives will determine whether he is able to behave in a considerate way to other people.

The most valuable lesson, in my view, is for children to learn by daily experience (in their own homes, or in foster-care or residential care of any kind) that their parent-figures can care for them and control them without becoming worn out, hurt or hostile in the process but whilst remaining on friendly terms. This idea (easier said than done) is compatible with behaviour modification theory—very briefly, that people learn from their own direct experience—though the two types of treatment look and feel different in practice, stemming from dissimilar philosophical bases.

The depressing picture throughout most of this section is not wholly accurate but arises partly because more negative than positive examples have been given. It is less easy to select positive examples because helpful control tends to blend into the landscape with fewer glaring features: in fact, there is less to say about peace than war (as newspapers demonstrate) and part of the effective control in positive units happens simply because care-givers have cultivated the landscape so that it is not riddled with *artificial* crags, bogs and stumbling-blocks which invite trouble. Critics may think it unrealistic to eliminate obstacles and unnecessary rules because children need preparation for real life in future, but my analogy assumes that a cultivated landscape contains plenty of natural undulations.

Concluding note on communication, care and control

It may be worthwhile to conclude this chapter with a summary, re-stating some of the ideas underlying the study and introducing a few further thoughts arising from recent pages.

The common factor in these 946 children and adolescents is that they are all at least temporarily living away from their own homes. They are dependent for their daily care upon adults who are not their own parents, yet it seems clear that the treatment they receive varies considerably. It cannot be said that the 561 children in 'good-enough' plus 'more positive' units are *appropriately* receiving better care than the 385 children in 'more negative' units, because all 946 children share common human needs, and delinquent, disturbed or otherwise handicapped children are to be found in each of the three patterns of care. In other words, the less negative units are not able to be so simply because they are catering for less difficult children. Little weight is attached to the argument that only a longitudinal study would show the long-term effects on these children of the different kinds of daily experience they are receiving now, because we already have abundant evidence that negative treatment has negative results.[16]

A basic tenet underlying the study is that benign daily experience is the best way in which previous harmful experience can be counteracted over a period of time. Virtually all the children (except to a large extent the prep-school boys) are living away from home because of their family circumstances and/or their particular problems and handicaps; the separation implicit in residential care and their uncertainties about the future cause them further problems. They are more than ordinarily dependent upon their current care-givers not only to maintain their existence but to build up their confidence in human relationships. In practice, helpful relationships are not shown in woolly idealism but are translated into the daily caring situation. Residential workers (and other kinds of daily care-givers) are exceptionally well placed to offer meaningful relationships by virtue of their close proximity to dependent people within the context of ongoing experience.

Verbal communication between adults and children is not always easy even in comparatively ordinary circumstances; it is likely to be more difficult with disturbed children and with those originating from socio-economic groups which are confined to Bernstein's restricted code.[17] Such children have had limited previous opportunity to learn to respond to personal discussion, explanation and reasoning; they tend to be more accustomed to words used as predictable blunt instruments by parent-figures, often with a rich non-verbal communication running alongside restricted verbal expression. Therefore some children in residential care present a problem to their care-givers in that interaction and control by means of verbal communication is not necessarily effective. Also, group ears are sometimes hard of hearing in that individuals naturally want individual attention, so the workers' words spread over a group of disadvantaged children tend to have less impact.

It follows that residential workers must often supplement their words with non-verbal communication: facial expressions, gestures, movements, touch, play, and all the material, practical elements which abound in residential life, day and night, and whose material importance simultaneously carries emotional significance. C. Winnicott (1968, pp. 66-7) writes about the development of words as symbols linking the infant with those outside himself; she describes how the use of language will go on developing only if the primary needs of food and care continue to be met 'by the person who is the embodiment of the words', and she mentions the danger that young children in disrupted circumstances may lose the capacity for speech, or chatter fluently but meaninglessly. In a safe environment, where words, food and physical care reinforce each other positively, it is likely that children will develop their capacity for verbal interaction. If, as Britton asserts (1970, p. 20) the primary task of language is to symbolize reality in order to handle it, then children who tend to act out their problems should gradually gain more control over their actions when they can be helped to learn how to discuss their feelings. But while they learn, non-verbal communications inherent in daily care remain important.

The prevailing attitudes towards discipline are clearly a vital aspect of non-verbal communication. These attitudes demonstrate continually whether care-givers regard their charges basically as enemies or as friends (Woodmansey, 1966). Friendly attitudes are not only far pleasanter to live with but are also far more effective in ensuring a co-operative response. Friendliness is not synonymous with weak permissiveness based on fear of exerting adult authority; it can co-exist with firmness when required. A few experts on residential work advocate the attitude of 'stern love',[18] but this description could be misinterpreted by workers wanting to justify their own punitive approach—presumably many heretics have been burned at the stake by authority-figures who believed themselves motivated by a spirit of stern love. Bowlby's plea (1958) for 'firm yet friendly intervention whenever a child is doing something we wish to stop' is less open to abuse.

These ideas about friendly control are theoretically sound as well as common sense, but their application to the practical handling of children depends on the workers' emotional willingness and ability to respond positively rather than on intellectual reasoning. The forty-four respondents noted inconsistent attitudes towards controlling children in at least half the sample. While consistent friendliness is obviously a desirable goal, in my view the virtue of consistency has been overvalued in the literature (including books on baby care) with unfortunate results in that many parent-figures feel constrained to attempt the impossible. In deciding to be consistent, a care-giver must calculate the lowest level at which he can maintain an even keel of the right mixture of niceness and firmness —then he must keep to that. (He must also react to children's special requests at face-value rather than be open to underlying messages.) It would not do to let himself be moved by warmer feelings suddenly, lest he felt cooler again next day.

Such conscientious calculation can hardly promote natural relationships, since spontaneity, pleasure, warmth, freedom are lost. In fact children adapt easily to natural inconsistency in their care-givers so long as they receive sufficient evidence enabling them to place some small measure of basic trust in the relationship, or can transfer confidence gained in earlier relationships to the present. If a parent-figure is unable to show some positive feeling towards children in his care, then he may need the offer of skilled help, because he cannot generate confidence-giving attitudes merely by his own will-power. (The inconsistencies mentioned in the study arise less within individual workers and more through fundamental differences of opinion between colleagues about effective methods of control; these clashes are likely to drive both sides into extreme versions of their opposing views.)

In addition to misconceptions about consistency, there is muddled thinking surrounding words such as protection, indulgence, attention-seeking and acceptance. It is sometimes thought that care-givers should be wary of protecting their dependants overmuch,[19] yet secure children show a natural drive towards independence and cannot be held back by genuine protection; over-protection is quite a different phenomenon in that it stems from anxiety, disguised hostility or rejection. The main purpose of flexible discipline and control is to protect children against harming themselves or other people. Again, it is often thought that an indulged child risks becoming 'a spoilt child', though observation suggests that spoiled children are usually materially 'over-indulged' in compensation for the emotional needs which parent-figures cannot meet—spoiled children clamour for whatever gratification they can glean from adults who are withholding affection—there is no danger in trying to meet children's natural needs and wishes as far as possible. Similarly, it can be argued not that attention-seeking children should be ignored as is commonly thought, but that they require extra attention, preferably before and in between those times when they seek it desperately, so they can learn that they do not need to behave in an exaggerated way in order to gain attention from interested adults.

The word confrontation has become fashionable jargon, which is sometimes used to justify hostile tactics (retaliation) in social work but whose main purpose in my opinion is merely as a first step in demonstrating that the worker openly recognizes difficulties in the child's behaviour *and* as a second step can accept them. In other words, confrontation has value in being a prerequisite for acceptance. (Of course there is an art in knowing when it is appropriate to speak frankly and when to let things pass; people cannot live together harmoniously in a perpetual stream of confrontation.) Flabby permissiveness or the weak ignoring of behaviour problems is not acceptance, but implies the worker's indifference, rejection or fear of misbehaviour. Acceptance involves meeting squarely the painful feelings underlying 'unacceptable behaviour' and thus relieving them gradually without the need for fight or flight. Similarly, ventilation of feeling and insight-giving are not of great value in themselves alone; their relevance depends on how the feeling is received (and on how insight is given) by the worker —if the worker's most frequent response is acceptance (entailing freedom from hostility and fear) then the child's discomfort is eased over a period of time and he is on more comfortable terms both with himself and with other people.[20]

The beginning and end of this circular process depends on whether workers are able to show acceptance without experiencing undue strain. Some of these ideas will be developed in the next chapter, whose purpose is to consider the pressures inherent in residential life from the care-givers' viewpoint and to consider how these pressures can be eased, both for their own comfort and for the well-being of the children in their care.

4

Daily life for the care-givers

I didn't see then, as I saw later, that Miss Buss was faced
by a herculean task.... She was a pioneer, and almost single-
handed, in getting some kind of systematic education for
girls.... Now by nature she was generous and kind-hearted,
and did most sincerely long for the co-operation of her pupils in
making the school a success. To this end she delivered every
week a moral lecture, and would frequently enlist our cheerful
compliance with the innumerable rules. 'Multiply the results'
was her great slogan for deciding whether a rule was necessary
or not. She would point out that one girl running downstairs
might not be dangerous, but what if five hundred did? One
shoe-bag untidily hung doesn't matter, but five hundred look
bad. One girl talking makes no disturbance, but five hundred do.
The fallacy of this argument never struck her. Or did it? and
that's why she repeated it so often? I think that her sleep
must often have been broken by the nightmare of five hundred
girls all running amok at once.

Mary Vivian Hughes: *A London Girl of the Eighties*

Out of this nettle, danger, we pluck this flower, safety.

Shakespeare: *King Henry IV, Part I*

The first part of this chapter considers the kinds of difficulty
care-givers commonly experience in residential life. The second
part discusses ways in which care-givers might be helped to
overcome some of the problems inherent in their work, thus
acquiring more self-confidence and a greater sense of personal
safety in their daily life with children.

If the previous chapter aroused passionate concern for children
in residential care because of the evidence that a sizeable proportion of them receive less than good-enough care, then a cor-

responding amount of adverse criticism is likely to have been aroused towards those residential workers who are clearly providing a poor service and whose negative attitudes are actually exacerbating the children's problems. The balance should be redressed in this chapter, but the scales will not be left wavering, with readers wondering whether children or care-givers are more worthy of pity or blame—because ultimately there will be no scales, no judgment as to whose is the harsher predicament. Instead it will be argued that care-givers (in common with members of all the 'helping professions') cannot be expected to give good-enough care unless they receive special consideration themselves.

But it is essential that such consideration be offered directly and exclusively to the care-givers instead of treating them merely as a means to an end, as employees paid to provide an environment in which children receive first priority. That is why the residential workers are considered here in a separate chapter of their own; it is hardly possible to show really effective empathy and concern for both parties of children and their parent-figures simultaneously when they are seriously at odds with each other or when their needs conflict.

DIFFICULTIES COMMONLY EXPERIENCED BY RESIDENTIAL WORKERS

The difficulties enumerated below will form a long but not exhaustive list, compiled from three sources: first, from the literature on residential child care; second, from my own experience both as a residential worker and through listening to many similar workers describing the pressures of their job; third, from evidence in the questionnaires. Although the respondents were expected primarily to observe and describe patterns of care available to children and were less involved in conveying the feelings of the care-givers, there is still much information about the latter, implicit as well as explicit. For instance, every single mention of a child having problems, or showing unco-operative behaviour of any kind, implies that at least one care-giver is affected by the self-same problem through having to deal with it. In other words, chapter 3 could be rewritten, from the care-givers' viewpoint on the other side of the same coin. Rather than engage in such a detailed exercise (though it would be realistic to do so, in order to visualize exactly what is involved for the staff) their problems will be summarized here in compressed form.

Difficulties in relation to children in group care

An obvious starting-point is the difficulty of dealing with children in groups, whether of a widely scattered age-range or with similar growing-pains such as adolescents. (In one unit, the workers quite appreciated having a boy whose leg was temporarily in a plaster-cast, since this marginally reduced the number of legs actively running into mischief.) Moreover, the group is not a coherent, stable family group where each member has been brought up by the same natural parents, taking their ways for granted from the beginning. Outsiders still tend to assume that if a single-minded mother can rear a family of ten children, then it should be possible for a homely, domesticated woman to take on ten assorted, un-related children without undue difficulty. In practice, the pressure of numbers seems (as described earlier in the section about control and discipline) to cause fears of mass unrest and to provoke heightened irritation with individual non-conformists who may prove infectious. These fears and irritations are of course highly uncomfortable for the grown-ups as well as for the children.

In relation to the problem of controlling numbers, there is the difficulty of trying to give individual attention and affection to children in groups—especially as the latter have strong views about fairness. Whilst secure adults may be partially resigned to the fact that life is simply not fair, children still hope to find that it is, all the more so if they have reason for doubt. Their pleas for fairness usually take the form of wanting more rather than less, levelling up rather than down. Parent-figures who themselves feel victimized by unfair experience (as many residential workers may well feel in their present situation, let alone the past) are naturally sometimes over-vulnerable to children's pressurizing demands for fairness, and may therefore make unrealistic efforts to divide their human and material resources into dead equal rations. In practice, these efforts tend to provoke resentment in all parties, with grown-ups feeling that the children are insatiable and children perceiving adults as deliberately withholding gratification.

There is a parallel here with parent-figures' attempts to be completely consistent, in that a striving for strict fairness or for in-human standards of consistency tends in effect to depreciate spontaneous giving and affection. The net result is chronic dis-satisfaction amongst the inmates and debilitating strain in the care-givers. Some residential workers have tried to educate their charges into positive acceptance of the haphazard nature of ordin-ary life—notably Lyward (Burn, 1956, pp. 70-8) who occasionally gave his intelligent, disturbed adolescent boys 'deliberate unfair-nesses' almost as a mark of favour, in preparation for the future:

The real secret of living with children lies in knowing how

to be creative in taking away and in being 'unfair' and haphazard, so that the gift shall never deny the children increasing awareness of the giver.... A gift by itself means nothing.

Through sometimes having their wishes met in surprising ways (with massive plusses or slight minuses) Lyward's boys became less clamorous, grasping, calculating; he described it as a great joy when he discovered how quickly they each sensed the dignity 'unfairness' gave them. (Certainly a useful service is performed by unlinking events from one's deserts if it prevents people from believing natural setbacks are punishments sent by providence.)

However, this seems too idealistic an approach for most children in care, many of whom have already experienced chronic uncertainty and deprivation; also, 'deliberate unfairness' would be a dangerous notion for any worker tempted to derive a sense of power from playing cat and mouse. Probably a more effective approach is to recognize that groups of children are less likely to make exhausting demands for fairness when they receive ongoing experience of their care-givers' willingness to try to meet their individual needs (to try, irrespective of the actual outcome). Children may complain on seeing one of their peers receiving preferential treatment, but surely they do also gain vicarious satisfaction through the realization that this apparent favouritism implies the possibility of any single one of them having his special individual needs met appropriately. A nine-year-old boy at the Mulberry Bush School is quoted (Dockar-Drysdale, 1968b, p. 57; or C. Winnicott, 1964/70, pp. 31-2) as saying, 'Fair play wouldn't be any use to people like us, because it would only mean that we'd all get the same thing and each of us needs something different.' That remarkable statement could only be made in a setting where children are confident not just that their ordinary, basic physical and emotional needs are being met, but that in addition their particular, individual needs and whims will be responded to in a spirit of positive discrimination. (Dockar-Drysdale, 1968b, p. 56, distinguishes between adapting to demands and to expectations, suggesting that children resort to 'demands' when these become chronically 'failed expectations'.)

Often it is impracticable for children's wishes to be granted in full measure at face value, but there can always be an authentic meeting of individual needs in token form. C. Winnicott (1964/70, p. 30) explains the value of a token gesture in demonstrating the care-giver's recognition of the underlying need and a willingness to try to meet it, thus gratifying the child even though his original request may have been far beyond the worker's power or resources.

A child who makes an impossible request can either be snubbed for daring to ask it or he can be comforted in his disappointment by the very person who is unable to grant it. Children's demands seem to depend partly on their perception (coloured by the past) of their adults' generosity and reliability. In any case, friendly parent-figures suffer less emotional arm-twisting; similarly, they are less likely to withdraw or to react harshly through their own discomfort in failing to meet pressing demands. Oliver Twist's request is memorable because he not only remained hungry but also his asking (as group representative) for more food was in itself an outrageous, punishable offence; the incident is an exaggerated version of what still often happens today when children's requests provoke defensive reactions in their grown-ups.

The above four paragraphs are not a digression but a discussion of a central problem. if one believes that 'the essential skill in residential treatment lies in the worker's ability to create a way of living for a group of individuals' (C. Winnicott, 1964/70, p. 31; developed by Beedell, 1970, p. 84). Again, children's misbehaviour, like their importunacy, impinges directly on the staff. In fact much of the literature (for example, Burton, 1968, 1973; Balbernie, 1973) and evidence in the questionnaires suggests strongly that misbehaviour itself is often a disguised request for help, especially if there is a lack of open communication between staff and children. But it seems that adults, when faced by awkward non-conformity, often direct their energy into deciding upon 'a suitable punishment for the crime' instead of trying to meet the underlying distress, or protecting dependants by exerting firm, friendly control when the latter risk harming themselves or others. Workers are likely to feel impotent in exercising gentle authority when their words fall on stony ground; if many of these children are unaccustomed to the person-oriented explanations of Bernstein's 'elaborated code'[1] and apparently already hardened to sharp words and heavy blows, then current care-givers are tempted to rely increasingly on any deterrents at their disposal. One respondent wrote, 'I could not say that any member of staff *always* had to shout or that he *never* had to shout, respect seems to depend on the situation and the mood of both the boy and the staff member.' Another common response is weak permissiveness based on fear.

Care-givers require considerable strength, sensitivity, self-awareness and self-acceptance if they are to deal constructively with the negative feelings aroused in them by insults and threats to their dignity. The outcome depends partly on whether their self-confidence (or dignity) is precarious. Convincing evidence[2] exists to show that experiencing a relentless battle with hostile parent-figures is extremely destructive for children, but it is not always appreciated that the adult combatant is also in a painful position, partly through perceiving the weaker party through a magnifying glass. There seems to be a common misconception that it is a luxury to lose one's temper or to maintain spiteful vendettas, but in fact the overspill of negative feelings can be unpleasant for the punisher as well as for the victim. And the adult would not need to be so intent on 'winning the battle' were he not desperately afraid of defeat. Many parent-figures tilt at windmills quite unnecessarily, but residential workers' careers are sometimes at stake (especially in the introductory stages of a new appointment—for example, Polsky, 1962, ch. 8); even though they are unlikely to be sacked if they lose the upper hand, they may be forced to resign if the group tests their authority to an extent which makes their present post untenable.

It is largely true that parent-figures' natural attitudes are shaped by the kind of treatment they received in childhood; certainly recent studies (for example, Helfer and Kempe, 1968, 1971) suggest that hostility passes from generation to generation. Even if some care-givers recognize the harm they suffered (instead of claiming defensively that it was beneficial to be 'brought up the hard way') and resolve to be different in their turn, they are still under abnormal pressure in the current situation simply through trying to work against their own grain. Possibly fewer people today have the courage of their own convictions in rearing children; they lack the flair of old Mrs May, a character in a children's book,[3] who was 'not strict exactly but she had that inner certainty which does instead'. In earlier times, parent-figures tended to be surer of their moral ground, their own self-righteousness when inflicting punishment; nowadays (though most people continue to hold strong opinions) there is considerable doubt about the concept of punishment, causing three-fold discomforts of inner conflict, uneasiness with difficult children and dissension between colleagues.

To some adults it is unthinkable to forgo their 'right' to punish as they visualize total anarchy resulting; at the other end of the continuum a few gain vicarious satisfaction by inciting children to act out in ways forbidden to themselves in childhood (and who may then punish them afterwards in any case). Confusion is rife, as pointed out in the following excerpts (Redl and Wineman, 1952/65, pp. 230-1):

The confusion in public opinion between punishment as an educational tool and as a simple outlet of adult temper, cruelty, wrath and revenge is indeed a spectacle to behold.... So little thinking has been done about this issue that even professional educators, mental hygienists, and psychiatrists frequently will produce as naïve punishment-beliefs and habits of their own conviction as any nonprofessional person might muster in a hot debate.

And Bowlby (1958, p. 46) goes a step further:

It is a curious thing how many intelligent adults think that the only alternative to letting a child run wild is to inflict punishment. A policy of firm yet friendly intervention whenever a child is doing something we wish to stop not only creates far less bitterness than punishment but in the long run is far more effective.

However, the problem is not so much an academic one, of deciding whether punishment can ever be beneficial or even expedient, as the difficulty actually experienced by grown-ups in managing their own punitive feelings in threatening situations. Hostile behaviour in children starts a vicious circle of hostility in parent-figures, and vice versa. In fact (as argued by Woodmansey, 1971a) the problem is not that 'little thinking has been done' but that adults who are fearful, anxious or angry in the face of delinquency often find their thoughts are distorted or submerged by their feelings. Grown-ups who are tempted to be punitive show great dexterity in producing rationalizations in support of their arguments. In any group discussion about controlling children, someone typically recounts an incident in which he (or she) patiently tried to deal with an awkward child over a period of time and was not successful until he was provoked into a temper outburst which marked the beginning of a much improved relationship between them. These stories sound plausible in attempting to prove that provocative children respond best to spontaneous, natural anger, but possibly the care-giver's original self-discipline contained so much ambivalence that open communication was impossible; warmth was withheld while an over-controlled consistency was maintained. Obviously the child, though not enjoying his care-giver's brief loss of temper, appreciates the aftermath of compensatory positive feelings, and responds accordingly.

Wills (1970, pp. 57-8) describes how he once, under severe provocation, struck a boy in his care; he was shocked at himself but clear in retrospect that one cannot pretend such an incident never happened or that it was a desirable thing to happen—the mistake must be acknowledged in a therapeutic setting, and discussed with those concerned in order to try to prevent its reoccurrence. (I once slapped an adolescent girl on the arm, less than a year after reading the Home Office Rules and deciding I need hardly remember the official warning that a member of staff hitting an inmate risked instant dismissal because I could not at first visualize being driven to that point. In the event, my relationship with the girl seemed little affected either way as my action was overshadowed by the fact that most of the population was beyond control at the time, showing violence day after day; also this particular girl was four stones heavier and immediately hit me back quite gently, so that I was not crippled by remorse and neither of us was hurt except by brief mutual exasperation. Surprisingly however, a few months later during an unavoidable tussle she remarked, 'I'm nearly as strong as you are', so she (or I) evidently misperceived our relative sizes in any case.) Often children are expected to apologize for their contribution to a showdown before they are forgiven, but it is not a sign of weakness for us more appropriately to apologize to them when we temporarily fail them, because again the adult's acknowledgment implies a reassuring underlying wish to behave as reliably as possible.

To outline additional problems in living with uprooted children: there are frustrations, uncertainties and a lack of shared memories in taking on children whose past experience is hazy in detailed information whilst known vaguely to have been traumatic. Even when a comprehensive case-history is available, this is not necessarily the picture as seen by the child and his own family (Beedell, 1970, pp. 61-2). Then there can be natural resentment in residential workers who are given virtually no choice in selecting children likely to blend with the existing population; they frequently feel exploited as 'a dumping ground' and of course any newcomer presents a threat of disruption to the established pattern (Berry, 1972b). It is hard to see how workers in assessment centres and community homes can be given much autonomy over admissions when vacancies are scarce, but at least some willingness from external administrators to discuss selection criteria might lessen the sense of outrage felt by care-givers when expected without question to accept a collection of children whom other people have previously found intolerable. Next comes the uncertainty about how long children will stay once care-givers have grown fond of them (Monsky, 1963). Equally there is the uncertainty of not knowing how to endure living long-term with highly disturbed individuals when no definite end is in sight.

Often workers are worried by not knowing what will happen to a child afterwards: will subsequent parent-figures enhance or undermine all the earlier care invested in him? In its simplest terms, once a care-giver has been responsible for meeting a child's daily needs over a period of time, and has seen him off in clean underclothes, it is distressing to think that the very shirt on his back may be neglected in future. Comparatively trivial details such as a regular supply of darned vests are symbols conveying affectionate concern, but interwoven with the incessant trivia of residential work is the emotional burden of sharing the unusual amount of suffering experienced by these children in their past, present and future lives. To work effectively, C. Winnicott (1964/ 70, p. 43) believes grown-ups must be aware of the strength of their own feelings about the suffering of children. Otherwise workers may deny or minimize the reality of the children's feelings, particularly as suffering is not ennobling except when considered in the abstract. It can be less painful to blame the child for his misbehaviour or to take refuge in domestic busyness than to be open to his pain. Three examples from the questionnaires illustrate outward expressions of suffering and suggest how variously these may impinge on care-givers:

One young child 'said she wanted to join her mother, who was dead'; second, an adolescent coloured girl 'tested out the staff by accusing them of colour prejudice in various ways, hurling abuse of the white scum variety'. Third, most of the physically handicapped children in the nursery unit 'play at hospitals or doctors and nurses. This may be more from familiarity than fear but it seemed they would never be the patient ... but use dolls or adults and themselves are usually doctors. The dolls usually died (sometimes several times) but were generally resurrected by the doctors.'

According to Tod (1968a, p. 103) many adults enter residential work because they feel they have a special contribution to make: they may have 'their own treasured experience of family life which they wish to share'; equally they may hope to compensate deprived children for gaps or distortions in their own childhood experience. Either way, they can be sadly disappointed through discovering that children who have previously been failed are suspicious, testing, and slow to value what is offered. Apparently then, many residential workers are motivated by their own personal needs or problems, and it can be argued that only a strong drive of this kind would be sufficient to bring and keep them in work which is unrewarding in some other ways (Kay, 1971, discusses this factor in relation to foster-parent selection). Probably many find the reality-situation much more difficult than they anticipated, though two-thirds of the current staff in Monsky's sample (1963) said they would have taken the job anyway.

Anthony (1968a) lists some of the discoveries care-givers make, including the fact that there are 'no deep taboos or incest barriers to protect other people's children from our sexuality'. Even an apparently realistic desire to behave protectively towards damaged children is questioned by some experts (for example, A. Rosen, 1971) yet Burton's studies (1968, 1973) imply that numerous children in care bear the personality characteristics of injury-proneness, so again a conflict arises in considering at what point healthy protection becomes 'over-protection'.

It seems as though residential workers risk being first lured and then trapped within the service by their own personal needs (which may never be met in practice); also that administrators unthinkingly exploit the continued existence of these needs. Certainly long-term care-givers commonly describe two states in themselves which seem to be related; one is a sense of being steadily drained of positive feeling, as though they started with a set amount which slowly erodes into a vacuum; the second state (since Nature abhors a vacuum, physicists say) is a sense of being filled to bursting-point with ill-feeling which accumulates as time passes. The finding in chapter 2—that workers in 'more negative' units have a tendency to stay proportionately longer than their opposite numbers in 'better' units—is understandable if one imagines that care-givers affected by these two related states may well find residential life less emotionally demanding if they drift with the tide of negative feeling. This is not to say they are content; such drifting may merely become the lesser of two evils, the line of least resistance.

Difficulties in relation to immediate colleagues

Moving on to relationships between adults in residential child care, an immediate pressure stems from a misconception that childhood, adolescence and adulthood are three quite separate stages; self-aware care-givers are often forcibly reminded that most adults contain aspects of their less mature selves which are liable to emerge under stress. For this reason, Dockar-Drysdale (1973, p. 27) uses the term 'grown-up' rather than 'adult' to emphasize the fact that adults themselves are simply grown-up children. Although many workers are attracted originally to child care because they 'like children', the childishness of fellow-adults is less endearing. Also there is less scope for (and perhaps more friction caused by) projecting one's own childish feelings onto articulate colleagues than onto young children and animals. To illustrate how colleagues may fail to act as reliable, co-operative parent-figures, here follows an incident, suitably disguised, from my experience of working in a unit for adolescent girls (under new management of a strict unit head since the previous example):

Some girls had been sent to the place because it had a small farm and they had earlier expressed 'a love for animals'—disillusionment with human beings had apparently caused some to turn to animals. So there was an excellent chance for me, using the medium of our daily work with farm animals, to begin to form better human relationships. Fay was an extreme example of a wary girl; her record included mention of her breakdown in a long-term foster-home where as a small child she was said to have been tied to a table-leg. One late evening when the girls were in bed and the unit head off duty, I found a hedgehog and gained permission from the deputy (to cover my stepping slightly out of routine, knowing she was on close terms with the head) to keep the hedgehog overnight, and then to show it to Fay next day. Fay had never seen a hedgehog and was wanting to do so. Early next morning I told Fay that when she had milked her cow she could go and find a surprise. Unfortunately I didn't think to ask her beforehand to set the surprise free when she had savoured it; she was slightly indiscreet in sharing her delight with me and my group on our way indoors to breakfast. The unit head happened to observe our well-behaved pleasure from her bedroom window. She reacted angrily, feeling we were interfering with *her* hedgehog (though it was news to me that she had one; she could not have distinguished it from the unusually large population of hedgehogs in the grounds that summer, and it is debatable in any case whether a person can claim possession of an independent creature). Drawing a partial veil over the repercussions of this tiny incident, my efforts to pacify the head proved futile; Fay immediately reverted to her white-faced withdrawnness and was punished quite severely for something which was originally planned to please her—an already damaged adolescent had been treated unkindly and capriciously *once more*.

Perhaps only rarely are all colleagues single-mindedly positive in their attitudes towards the children in their joint care. If it is true that questions of discipline arouse strong feeling, especially when beliefs are being translated into daily practice, then it follows that care-givers are vulnerable in relation to each other as well as with the whole inmate group.[4] Bitter resentment mounts if some workers are felt to be threatening the established order or are weak links in the chain of command. Even though some workers are able to be kinder and more relaxed than others, possibly they rely more than they realize on the firm foundation structured by their colleagues. Unless a staff can communicate effectively as a team, confident in sharing similar positive values as well as different natural abilities, it is easy for them to trade on each other's weaknesses—thus B can afford to seek popularity because A is strict, while C watches D getting into difficulties which E has inflamed, F is punitive in trying to counteract G's softness and H stays in bed with a headache, hoping that B will volunteer for dinner-duty.

These grown-ups (apart from married couples) usually have not chosen each other in the first place as kindred spirits conducive to group-living, even though they exercise greater self-determination than the inmates. Ingram (1961b) speaks from experience in asserting that 'Everything we try to do will depend finally on the quality of the personal relationships of the adults' who are 'seeing each other early in the morning and late in the evening, pleasant or unpleasant, shaved or unshaved, the right side of bed that morning or the wrong side'. Often they are unwittingly repeating the patterns of disharmony which children previously experienced in the relationships between their own parents; perhaps for this very reason children in care are quick to perceive rifts between their care-givers, testing little cracks in the staff façade in a way which may cause splinter-groups. One respondent (amongst others) observed that 'the behaviour of children varies considerably according to the member of staff on duty. Senior staff command more conformity (not necessarily respect though) than junior members. The children adopt certain roles for each member—e.g. they tend to vent their aggression on the more junior members as they are unable to do this with the senior staff because of the far greater risk of punishment. However, the junior staff could not accept this sort of role and this often resulted in conflict. Staff meetings or discussions might have helped to relieve the situation.'

In other cases, older workers seemed more relaxed than their juniors; several respondents mentioned that relief staff had far more difficulty in securing co-operation (as the deputy may also when the head is away on leave). In all, the situation—where a number of workers vary so much in their individual aims, values, experience and skills and are working under pressure—almost invites conflict, which may involve considerable personal misery, rivalry, humiliation, back-biting and discontent. The majority of units appear to have regular staff-meetings but with great variation in effectiveness: some are clearly fruitful, for example in one reception centre where it was agreed, at the special request of several very young, inexperienced members that part of their weekly meeting should be held for them on their own; in addition a few respondents gave instances of staff-meetings bringing about small changes of policy. Several other respondents record that staff-meetings are either non-existent or unprofitable: 'Staff mostly talk about staff; very little case-discussion.' Or 'Those [staff-meetings] I attended seemed to be grumbling about particular individuals who were off duty. There appears to be very little opportunity to discuss pressures.... There is much isolation of staff who are unhappy, tense and feel they are not appreciated or accepted and yet dare not express their feelings. Staff feel their views and opinions are not listened to, the régime is hierarchical and rigid and the only solution is to leave.... The establishment is self-sufficient and contact with "outside" is restricted to senior staff. The lack of opportunity to express discontent together with the inconsistency of an un-structured yet prohibitive régime for the children has presumably been partly the reason why [several members] are leaving.'

Typically, the unit head is vulnerable by virtue of his position as the ultimate authority-figure on the premises; it is small wonder therefore if he sometimes overacts or underplays his role. He is at the end of the internal line (that is, of the staff, and perhaps also of the telephone); he may try to be constantly available to the residents but without receiving much external support himself—one superintendent knows of nobody to whom he can turn except the Director of Social Services *in extremis*. He may be treated not only by the children but by his staff as larger than life-size; his humanity is cloaked with great power for good or ill over the daily lives of all the residents, who tend to see him in black-and-white terms as friend or foe, perhaps in quick succession. 'It seems to happen, too often, that the head or deputy needs to be called to put things right—the head says the staff must have confidence in their own personal reaction to a situation ... that relationships must be based on mutual respect, an acceptance of each other and, in the case of the adult, a real knowledge of self....'

That well-qualified head is clearly under pressure through carrying more than his share of the burden, yet of course his staff cannot develop desirable qualities such as self-confidence by mere exhortation any more than he can exert magical powers of group control.

The picture presented so far suggests a fairly frequent occurrence of interpersonal tension, uncertainty and the worst type of lone-liness—isolation within a crowd, where individuals experience lack of privacy alongside lack of mutual support. In recent years more thought is being given to the accommodation needs of residential workers; new buildings are likely to have self-contained flats so that individuals and married couples can withdraw from the hurly-burly when off duty, and cater for themselves on the premises. Although this is excellent in recognizing that care-givers need a home as well as a work-base, further problems may result in practice—for instance, children are naturally intrigued by the workers' private living-quarters and will want to test whether their presence is welcome there—so where does the worker draw a line between permitting and discouraging visits from other residents, including colleagues? Whilst factors such as salary and conditions of service are important, especially in demonstrating whether workers are valued, previous studies[5] indicate that the workers themselves may be chiefly concerned about staff relationships and second about their free time.

Difficulties in relation to the external environment

Turning to relationships between residential workers and the outside world, once more the picture is sometimes bleak. External contacts might help to dilute interpersonal tensions and renew a sense of perspective, but social isolation seems to extend outwards both in a concrete form and in a more subtle way when outsiders fail to comprehend the nature of residential work. First, the questionnaires show that the inmates' parents, relatives and friends are infrequent visitors to many units; in any case they often have their own problems and may not be able to share much responsibility with the staff, even if the latter could adapt to such a partnership. Second, this study shows that 70 per cent of resident (as opposed to non-resident) staff live in units which are at least fairly isolated within the neighbourhood. Moreover, the limited number of community contacts are sometimes with official bodies rather than with ordinary neighbours, and local people may keep apart in ignorant suspicion or visit only to make complaints about the children's misbehaviour outside.

Third, more than half the sample of units seem to derive little external support in terms of psychiatric or casework treatment for individual children, and care-givers may feel excluded even when therapeutic services are available. Fourth, a few respondents mention an increased sense of isolation in residential units since the recent reorganization of the statutory social services—a feeling that previously well known administrators are now preoccupied within the large new departments and no longer have time to take the same personal interest. This is only the tip of the iceberg depicting a serious area of isolation—the widespread lack of opportunities for external support and consultation with senior workers, which will be discussed further on below.

Fifth, there seems to be a fairly general dissatisfaction over the infrequent or erratic nature of fieldworkers' visits to residential units. Even apart from a subjective feeling in care-givers that field-workers could do far more for children than merely keep essential appointments for reviews and case conferences (which implies that the care-givers themselves feel neglected and to be left holding the baby) there is quite objectively often a real lack of visits—to give one extreme example, over a third of children in a highly negative unit are said not to have seen their fieldworkers for ten months. Ideally, fieldworkers' visits should reassure children that they are not forgotten in the outside world, and be of direct help to care-givers (at all levels) in making children more settled through dis-cussion of plans. But equally the visits are potentially an overtly unsettling reminder of past troubles and present uncertainties, so may sometimes be perceived as unhelpful. Evidence in the question-naires shows marked ambivalence: 'Houseparents feel social workers don't visit the boys often enough ... staff feel boys suffer —they (staff) are not worried.' 'Staff feel fieldworkers' visits are inadequate—however, they do very little to encourage them to visit more often.' 'Staff wish [fieldworkers] came more often, though seem anxious when they do come and may not always be very welcoming.' One respondent in a school for maladjusted girls records a remarkable increase in fieldworkers' visits since the new headmistress has made the school a much happier, more relaxed place, so perhaps they now find it easier and more rewarding to visit. In other cases it is less clear whether regular visiting is a cause or effect of better unit morale.

Traditionally there has been tension and some mutual distrust in the relationship between field and residential workers. The surface reasons for this are usually stated in terms of discrepancies (favour-ing fieldworkers) in their respective salaries and status. In the near future[6] these factors will probably be more evenly balanced, especially when all social workers receive appropriate joint training opportunities and have professional qualifications in common, thus enabling greater flexibility of movement between both types of service. C. Winnicott (1964/70, pp. 33-9) considers some of the deeper underlying sources of potential conflict (while arguing that tensions can be growth-points even if uncomfortable): for one thing, the fieldworker acts partially as the parents' representative both to the child and his current care-givers, and therefore ambi-valence naturally arises. Then, as with foster-parents, care-givers may fear the child is being encouraged in private conversation to express criticism of the care he is receiving, even though children's expression of discontent may provide a safety-valve (P. Barker, 1970). Also the fieldworker may represent impingement and unpredictability from outside in that he brings new admissions, arranges departures, and may be the bearer of bad news. Winnicott sees a fundamental source of tension stemming from the different, though complementary, kind of relationship each of them has with the children for whom they are jointly responsible, which gives scope for possessiveness or resentment if one party appears insufficiently helpful in the total situation (see also Beedell, 1970, pp. 136-8).

In my experience there are three more possible sources of tension : first, rivalry as to which of the two workers has the more demanding job; in fact, potentially both jobs are equally difficult, but the typical pressures of each are quite different. Second, envy sometimes in residential workers that the fieldworker apparently has more freedom, is not confined to barracks doing routine domestic chores but driving around meeting an interesting range of people for short conversations—this is akin to a housewife's feeling that her husband is freer than she to work and play away from childminding and the kitchen sink. Third, and perhaps most important, there may be a vague sense of inferiority in residential workers through observing that fieldworkers seem able to be more consistently friendly towards their clients—a wistfulness that fieldworkers may be nicer people than they are themselves. Characteristically, fieldworkers arrive with disarming apologies for not having visited sooner; will seem cheerful, competent and sympathetic, perhaps able to discuss the child's needs far more dispassionately than the current care-giver who has recently suffered countless vexations in dealing with that child day and night. The child himself may respond more co-operatively with the caseworker simply because he has a different kind of emotional involvement in this relationship.[7] In spite of the fieldworkers' more widely ranging daily pressures, it is obviously easier for them to maintain friendly attitudes when they are not living *en masse* with their clients.

A further point is that fieldworkers nowadays debate whether social work can be designated a profession, and whether professionalism is even a desirable goal, since some suspect it creates role-distance instead of emphasizing their common humanity with people in difficulties. This uncertainty is likely to be magnified in residential staff, partly because a very much smaller proportion are professionally trained for their work. Theoretical knowledge gained during training (in aspects of law, social administration, principles and methods of social work, sociology, psychology, social medicine, human growth and development) may prove useful in practice but is less essential in some people's opinion for living with children, since most parent-figures use their common sense. The plans and decisions made by residential workers are typically on a more insular scale than those of fieldworkers. Perhaps a major impediment to professional aspirations is the aura of domestic service traditionally surrounding residential work. Ordinary mothers can work unpaid seven days a week without losing status in public opinion, but residential staff risk degradation (or may feel they do) through acting as paid domestic servants to other people's children.

At the same time, writers and lecturers often seem to reach a peak of complexity in their arguments where they can only plead for 'more professional attitudes' amongst care-givers (whereas a central argument in this study is that senior administrators themselves should develop 'more professional attitudes' by providing appropriate care for the care-givers). It is almost as though some exponents think, 'We have set such an impossible task for foster-parents and residential workers that we must pay them more money to control their feelings—we must offer a financial incentive or distract them from their immediate preoccupation with the child so that they are obliged to show the right attitudes.' Training and salary are relevant to professionalism but interwoven are two more important elements (in my view): first, a willingness to attend primarily to someone else's needs during working hours. But this is extra difficult for residential staff since their own personal needs (for food and sleep, etc.) have to be met within the work-situation; they experience most of the 'normal' stresses of parenthood[8] plus many more problems—not least role-confusion, as described in chapter 1. But a prerequisite for good-enough parenting is that care-givers should have some confidence in their own identity; they see themselves partly as reflected in the eyes of external colleagues.

The second, most crucial element in professionalism (a corollary of the first) consists of a willingness to accept help with one's difficult relationships—that is, help with the barriers to one's empathy for those one in turn is trying to help. For any parent or care-giver, it is the self-doubts, fears, guilt, resentment, envy, hostility which undermine good-enough relationships with their children. And these painful feelings cannot be overcome just by individual effort, nor by the false professional front deplored by Dockar-Drysdale (1973, p. 5).

Apparently the quality of care is not determined purely by means of parental will-power. E. Newson (1972, pp. 34-5) expressed some pessimism about the nature of parental roles, believing that parents within different socio-economic groups *choose on principle* in child-rearing whether to use democratic, highly verbal means of control (likely to produce self-confident, well-equipped personalities) or whether to use 'a highly authoritarian, mainly non-verbal means of control, in which words are used more to threaten and bamboozle the child into obedience than to make him understand the rationale behind social behaviour' thus producing children who 'expect nothing and are not equipped to do anything about it'. The pessimism arises because she does 'not see how we can easily change principles which are firmly and honestly held'. However, it is argued here that parent-figures (including residential workers) are not so much guided by their *principles* as compelled—or at least influenced—by their own emotional and social *experience* from childhood onwards, especially by their experience in the current work-situation.

Once residential staff have been selected, they bring their internalized experience with them, but surely they are influenced for better or worse by their current experience according to whether they receive helpful support in exceptionally difficult work. Temporarily leaving aside the question whether they are willing to accept such help, it is necessary first to ask what amount and type of support is actually available. The clear answer in this study is that very little external help is offered in the seventeen units graded as 'more negative' while the position in 'better' units is markedly more supportive. Table 2.11 shows that care-givers in the great majority of 'better' units receive at least fairly good (often very good) opportunities for external consultation and support, whereas no fewer than fourteen of the seventeen 'more negative' units have poor opportunities. It might have been expected that negative units would contain a lower proportion of workers with a relevant professional qualification in child care, but in fact there is little difference between 'better' and 'worse' units in this respect—the major factor according to evidence in the questionnaires is whether or not care-givers receive appropriate care themselves.

Therefore the final problem in this list of typical difficulties is a lack of practical concern from people in external positions of authority. 'The workers feel to be out on a limb and have felt this way for a long time.' Or again: 'Management expresses a desire for constructive criticism. However, there is dissension and dissatisfaction amongst the staff over several issues which is wearing thin the little rapport which exists. Management appears oblivious to this and as such is doing nothing to repair the damage.' Several respondents in both more and less negative places record that the unit head is constantly available to all residents, but this is not quite so accommodating in practice as it sounds on paper—it implies a stream of callers with no definite times assigned to individuals. Callers for help may be frustrated by finding that a constantly available head is by definition quite likely to be engaged with someone else in their particular moment of need. Also 'the informal basis for consultation puts the onus on the staff member concerned to initiate it, and this may be difficult for the younger and less experienced.' The general picture shows greater availability of support within units than from outside.

One respondent in a 'good-enough' unit describes a high level of external support which in effect hardly begins to meet the care-givers' real needs: 'The educational psychologist attended daily ... he was felt to be very helpful if occasionally over-academic, but quite skilled at interpreting behavioural symptoms rather than handling of children. Social Services fieldworkers visited more often than child guidance social workers although they rarely saw the "caring" staff ... therefore it was felt they were not vitally important. The area is divided under three psychiatrists ... [one of them] is present at each weekly case conference and their attendance is highly appreciated.... Some staff complained about the different views and lack of overall guidelines.... Because of the strong influence of the psychiatrists [tending to teach in terms of children's pathology] most of the staff did not seem to see their own importance ... as therapists in daily contact with the children. Although uncertain about their role, they did not feel secure enough to question it, because of their "lowly" position in the hierarchical system. The impression was of a ship without a captain, and the crew uncertain of the direction they were travelling in on a daily basis. Despite the apparent avenues for consultation, the mainly young, previously inexperienced student nurses did not seem fully able to use these channels.' This example suggests that theoretical knowledge is not of great practical value unless linked to daily events and backed by attempts to develop and replenish the care-givers' emotional resources.

In this study, care-givers are not expressing their views directly but through student-respondents, so it may be appropriate to include three excerpts from a former unpublished study by Clement Brown (1958, pp. 81-99) who interviewed a sample of professionally trained workers and the seniors responsible for their work:

Among this group [of those more highly regarded in employment than in training] there is, for example, one young woman ... who is recognised still as having considerable personal difficulties, but with opportunities for frequent sympathetic discussion is able to run a home for unstable children with great success where predecessors have failed. There are also several who have done unusually good work but who are described as sometimes 'nervy' or 'despondent', 'a bit temperamental', 'excitable', or 'easily flustered'. All these women, however, seem to have certain all-round qualities of personality which provide them with the necessary resilience to survive their own crises and to discover their own source of strength so that their anxiety can be contained, and does not impinge with damage on children or other adults. It may well be that this is at undue cost to themselves....

One young woman, who had left the work, said

She was disillusioned about the progress she had been led to expect in her training. 'The staff are at war with the children, but it's a cold war now.' She summed up her own feelings, 'I couldn't stay ... my soul was not my own. I had to do something which would give me back my own personality.'

Another, older woman who had stayed in the work

said she was quite satisfied with the life.... She never appears to have felt unduly discouraged in spite of staff difficulties, though she said 'I had to do a bit of talking to myself' about facing up to the work and the life. She could even see the value of the children knowing that it was she who washed their soiled clothes and linen, 'they got the feeling that it wasn't too dirty and horrible for you to care to get it clean for them'.

Apparently that woman refrains from washing her own dirty linen in public; how sad that she was forced to 'talk to herself' while trying to adapt to residential life. Her remark epitomizes the loneliness.

This long list (possibly still incomplete) of care-givers' typical difficulties is largely in the realm of relationships. The list makes the regrettable aspects of the children's daily lives, as described in chapter 3, more understandable. The fact that nearly 60 per cent of children in the sample are said to be receiving at least 'good-enough' care (including nearly 17 per cent in 'more positive' units) demonstrates that the difficulties can be surmounted, but at what personal cost to the care-givers, let alone to the alarming proportion of 40 per cent of children in 'more negative' units? In any case, it is doubtful whether the term 'good-enough' can be taken literally as applied to children whose former experience was poor and who therefore require extra good residential care.

Beedell (1970, pp. 100-2) is realistic in suggesting that a personal resource required by residential workers is the capacity to withstand threatening circumstances; he thinks this quality is perhaps related to acceptance: 'Certainly acceptance becomes more difficult the more one is threatened.' It is argued here that, conversely, the security of having just one available ally increases self-confidence. If there is a limit to the extent to which people in threatening circumstances can contain their own negative feelings, or generate their own positive feelings by spontaneous combustion, then it must follow that care-givers are more able to show genuine acceptance towards their dependants when they themselves receive the same kind of acceptance in the background.

APPROPRIATE CARE FOR THE CARE-GIVERS

Although the climax is reached in this section, it does not pretend to present a startling dénouement as in a detective story. It should come as no surprise now that, if the essence of residential life is living together, communicating through the medium of daily events, and if the daily relationships themselves are simultaneously *the chief means of treatment and the greatest problem* for all concerned, the remedy must also be found within a special relationship.

The proposition now is that care-givers require the experience of a relationship with a skilled person who is in a position to respond appropriately to their particular expressed needs in threatening circumstances. If one believes that in order to give freely, people need similarly to receive, then the relationship must provide a pattern of what it is hoped care-givers will be able to pass on to those with whom they live. It will be necessary to examine the proposition carefully, because it carries overtones of casework help—an idea which may be distasteful to some residential workers and administrators.[9] However, Wills says bluntly (1970, preface), 'Unless he is so insensitive that he ought really to be doing a different job, the most experienced residential worker needs to feel that he has someone to lean on.' Also, the proof of the pudding is in the eating: care-givers are likely to welcome support if their actual experience of receiving it does prove helpful.

The suggestion is that every residential unit requires a special senior supporter who devotes himself to the staff without being directly responsible for the children. This person could be called a consultant, counsellor, supervisor or therapist (but not an inspector); he could by training and experience be a psychiatrist, psychotherapist, a qualified senior residential worker or senior caseworker. It may be an advantage if he is not part of the external or internal hierarchy responsible for that particular unit, so that the staff feel free to use him without fearing that their careers may be influenced by his secret evaluation of them.[10] A more important factor (developed further on) is that he should be unfettered from statutory and departmental duties to the children, so that he is free to attend sympathetically to the care-givers without being hindered by private misgivings about the quality of care received by inmates. For this reason, a basic-grade fieldworker is not an appropriate support-figure except in so far as she offers a reciprocal relationship in her partnership with care-givers. The latter may be far more experienced than many of the numerous fieldworkers visiting a large establishment, so their status would not be enhanced by relying solely on a young caseworker. Also fieldworkers are concerned primarily with individual children and therefore will inevitably focus their discussions on children's needs, rather than on the needs of the staff. Residential workers are realistic in wanting 'better liaison rather than support' from fieldworkers.

The consultant visits at regular intervals by appointment, meeting staff members singly or in groups, and is ready to respond to whatever they wish to discuss at the time—that is, care-givers take the initiative in talking about whatever pressures are uppermost in themselves at the time. In this way, they are not only protected from unwarranted interference into personal problems, but they are actively engaged in the topic they have chosen and are therefore more likely to learn through discussion. (The sessions visualized here are definitely not T-groups, encounter groups or so-called sensitivity groups of the type which encourage uninhibited interaction, with an occasional interpretation from the leader.[11] In my view such groups are a mixed blessing for anybody, and certainly unsuitable for resident colleagues who have more scope for collecting ammunition and more anatomical knowledge of chinks in each others' armour, but who must save face in continuing to live together afterwards.) Often an individual worker would use the session to discuss her own current problem, typically in relation to one of the children's behaviour, so she would be conversing mainly with the consultant while the rest of the group contributed, either openly or in silent participation, perhaps inwardly applying the specific conversation to other similar problems.

An advantage of the method lies in economy of time, effort and money. The therapist would have to spend infinitely more time if he were to attempt to treat individual children; as it is he has a token relationship with the care-givers which may involve him in as little as one hour per fortnight but which spreads like ripples on a pond into the daily caring situation. The consultant may be employed full-time in a range of activities; alternatively a part-time married woman, a retired man, or even a social work tutor could conveniently be attached to one or two local units. Walker (1967) illustrates the help given by a psychiatric social worker visiting schools for severely disturbed children.

Perhaps the consultant's main skill is to listen and respond directly to the care-givers' expressed viewpoint, instead of reasoning with them from the child's viewpoint which is a common but unhelpful approach. Typically a care-giver (who may be a residential worker, foster-parent, natural parent or teacher) begins by complaining about some difficulty she is experiencing with a child, but it is a mistake for the helper to reply by pleading for special consideration to the child, perhaps attempting to give insightful reasons for the child's difficult behaviour, and encouraging the care-giver to show more tolerance in future. That approach not only ignores the care-giver's own needs and discomforts but implies criticism and adds a further burden in the form of exhortations to persevere in bearing a somewhat intolerable situation. The care-giver's problem is not usually that she is basically ignorant of child care principles but that her pressure of negative feeling colours her perception of that particular child and prevents her from putting her principles into practice.

Caseworkers frequently fear that to show any open sympathy with the parent-figure's predicament will only make matters worse by reinforcing the feeling that such a bad child requires stricter handling. In fact the reverse happens: through experiencing the helper's empathy and acceptance of these negative feelings being painful as well as natural, the care-giver is eased and becomes more able to offer a similar experience of unconditional acceptance to the child (Berry, 1972a, ch. 5). There is no need for the consultant to express any opinion about the reality of the child's behaviour (which may or may not be extremely difficult in objective terms); his immediate point of contact lies in acknowledging that the care-giver is finding difficulty, and of course any explicit sympathy with the plaintiff's hostility carries an implicit assumption that such feelings are not desirable from anyone's viewpoint. Usually the care-giver is not devoid of positive feeling but this is submerged or choked by thorny negative feelings; therefore it is essential that the consultant should communicate friendly concern without himself becoming hostile, critical, disapproving or fearful in return.

This draining off or neutralizing of negative feelings sets the reverse process in motion: through being less choked with thorns, the care-giver's very real positive feelings now have room to breathe spontaneously. The process may have to be repeated again and again, depending partly on the amount of prolonged stress present in daily life experience, but meanwhile the care-giver has a sense of background support. Typically the consultant will receive considerable hostility (overt or oblique) directly from the staff: perhaps because his support does not resolve their problems magically for all time, or because his work seems less taxing than theirs or because they resent the implication that they cannot manage without expert help or, as Dockar-Drysdale describes (1973, p. 113) because they envy his apparently superior knowledge and skill. These and other possible grievances are not peculiar to the group's relationship with the consultant but, as seen earlier, pervade most relationships within a residential setting. Far from being a barrier, the care-givers' complaints and negativism directed immediately at the consultant gives him an excellent opportunity to meet it constructively, reducing its sting within himself and drawing it away from their colleagues and children.

Then again at times, the group members' stricter, self-righteous selves (as opposed to their more vulnerable, childlike selves) may feel threatened by the consultant's lenient, relaxed attitudes which seem to be colluding with or indulging their weaknesses, and thus they proceed to attack him or become anxious because of his very lack of reproach towards them. In other words, their punitive sense of what is right and wrong may be provoked or apprehensive because he is not damping them down in the same way as they wish to control or criticize the children. But again, his friendly, unflustered recognition and response to their reproaches eases their discomfort and enables more inward harmony between their inner constraints and their natural urges (between the aspects of themselves which Berne (1964) calls Parent and Child, thus strengthening the Adult self). Since these warring internal elements are exactly the same as those which are in conflict with colleagues and inmates, the experience of the consultant continuing willing to try to help in spite of the obstacles does simultaneously begin to ease relationships all round in the daily caring situation.

These ideas (expanded in Woodmansey's papers) are congruent with ordinary family casework methods and can appropriately be applied to residential workers because of their exceptionally difficult task, and because the method does not involve an intrusive intervention in terms of diagnosis and treatment but a directly helpful response to expressed difficulties. It can be argued (Berry, 1972a, pp. 65-71 and ch. 5) that foster-parents and residential workers require the offer of this kind of help with their relationships in much the same way as any other troubled parent-figure. Several other similar models are available (for example, from Balint, Bettelheim, Caplan, Dockar-Drysdale) which will be examined further below. A common factor in all these methods of consultation is that discussion is confidential between group members and the leader;

clearly members need not only to discover that it is safe to talk in the group but their communication from the outset must be protected against external interference.

Also the situation varies within each residential unit: for instance, the unit head may in fairly exceptional circumstances be able to provide group-consultation (as well as individual support) himself, especially if he is receiving external support. Often he would be too involved with the staff, and they would be too vulnerable in daily relation to him, for him or them to be confident enough to concentrate on their expressed difficulties, but the questionnaires show that the possibility exists. Normally the group should consist of people who see themselves as having similar problems on a par with each other, so they are not inhibited by having to adapt to the needs of more senior or of junior members within the group. So the group could consist of all care-givers in one unit where the head receives separate support, or there could be several groups of staff at similar levels of authority drawn from a number of local units. Obviously much depends on what the people concerned actually want and visualize as appropriate to their particular needs, as well as on what type of help is available locally.

Virtually all the models described in this section assume that support-groups function more comfortably (and therefore more productively) when the individual members can fairly readily identify with each others' needs and problems. To take an analogy from the animal world, a group composed of twelve dogs (not necessarily of similar breed and sex) would probably derive more supportive companionship than a group consisting of four dogs, four cats and four mice. But there is a parallel tendency nowadays to experiment with human groups whose members are naturally vulnerable in relation to each other, in the hope that they will learn to be less mutually defensive if they can stand the strain. For example, Anthony (1968b, pp. 112-19) describes one type of group containing equal numbers of residential staff and children 'expressing their opinions frankly'. He recounts how one little girl asked the staff members what they did with their aggression, and how they denied having any negative feelings at all, claiming that they were there for the good of the children.

> [The little girl] seemed to be saying, 'If I were you, I would feel cross, so where has the crossness gone?' And that's the question, Where *had* the crossness gone? I agreed with the children that it must have gone *somewhere*; had the staff become more tense, more anxious, more persecuted, more negativistic, more

pompous; had they kicked the institution's cat, or developed migraine, abdominal pain or pains in the neck?

However, perhaps a more practical question is whether it is humanly possible for care-givers to expose their sore clay feet, let alone accept chiropody, in the actual presence of the children. Presumably the little girl was not wanting intellectual information about adult aggression but assurance that children in group care need not fear that either they or their adults will be damaged by cumulative ill-feeling. In fact she can best find this out from first hand experience of daily care; she is unlikely to hear anything to her advantage in a mixed discussion group unless the staff are self-confident enough to attend to her needs rather than to their own self-protection, in which case the group would be catering primarily for the children.

Although a few people (for example, D. Winnicott, 1958, ch. 15; Dockar-Drysdale, 1973, p. 14) believe that it can be an advanced step forward for a therapist to verbalize his hatred to a patient, surely this exceptional degree of candour could only be tolerated by a patient who was already confident of strong affection in the relationship; in practice it would seem far simpler, safer and more sensible for the therapist to admit any ambivalence privately to someone else (i.e. to his own support-figure) thereby becoming freer to relate warmly to the patient. Similarly, a group composed of staff and children may sound adventurous in opening up communication but in practice is so over-ambitious as to defeat the object of any exercise designed to support care-givers. Such groups are akin to conjoint family therapy and have the same disadvantage in that the leader cannot hope to show empathy simultaneously to members whose needs and problems are diametrically opposed—it would be unfruitful for the consultant to align himself with a browbeaten child in the presence of that child's punitive adult or vice versa (Berry, 1972a, 152-8). Both parties can meet more positively if the care-giver's opposite viewpoint has been accepted separately.

In other words, it is naïve to suppose that children and their parent-figures should be taught how to communicate positively together; usually they will do so quite spontaneously if the grown-ups have a safe alternative outlet for the negative side of their ambivalence. But the argument here is not against the very real value of mixed groups in the form of 'community meetings' or 'house meetings' (as described for instance by Wills, 1970; H. Jones, 1960; Miller, 1964) which feature in at least three units in my study for the purpose of democratic decision-making in running the unit on lines of shared responsibility. The point is that community meetings are conducted primarily for the benefit of the inmates, not directly for their care-givers, who require their own separate background support if the meetings are to function creatively.

In addition to the Woodmansey model, there are four other models which might be adapted or combined selectively in offering a consultation service. First, Dockar-Drysdale's use of 'context profiles' (1968a, ch. 10; 1973) occurs in a staff-meeting where members pool their individual experience (rather than their cool observations) of what has happened between themselves and a particular child during the past week. These workers have other opportunities for personal support so the focus in this meeting is on building up a multi-dimensional picture of the child in order to discuss his special needs within the daily caring situation, but the process includes the communication of care-givers' feelings in their shared experience with children. Dockar-Drysdale explains the comparatively non-threatening nature of communicating shared experience within the staff-group (1973, p. 15) and she emphasizes (pp. 42-3) that 'the sheer *fact* of communication makes the stress tolerable ... brings the stress within the particular threshold of the individual' so that it can be contained. Because she conceives of panic as a state of unthinkable stress, it follows that communicated stress has become thinkable, containable through the act of communication. At the same time (1973, p. 11),

> I hope that what I have said concerning the need for everyone to be able to communicate stress does not suggest that I am recommending masochistic orgies.... Many people—grown-ups and children—can contain considerable stress within themselves without difficulty. One has no right, I think, to invade the privacy of such people, who will be conscious of stress but able to deal with the problem themselves. What I *am* saying is that, if stress is above this safe level, there needs to be direct communication and sympathetic response.

Balbernie (1973, pp. 23-6) confirms that a breakdown of communication within the staff team inevitably leads to a massive increase of negative acting-out amongst all residents—staff and children.

Second, a business-like model is provided by the Caplans (G. Caplan, 1961, ch. 7; 1970, and R. Caplan, 1972). Professor G. Caplan's special interest in mental health consultation was stimulated as early as 1949 in Israel where part of his small team's responsibilities included supervision of the mental health of about 16,000 new-immigrant children in the Youth Aliyah organization scattered in over a hundred residential institutions. The team quickly discovered the impossibility of providing a therapeutic service directly for the children and began instead to offer their help to the residential staff—particularly since many of the children referred to the team did not appear to be mentally ill—'the problem seemed rather that they were getting on the adults' nerves' (1970, pp. 8-12). Subsequently Caplan has developed and refined a generic approach to offering mental health consultation to a range of key-figures or care-taking agents in the community, individually or in groups: for example, to family doctors, medical specialists, public health nurses, teachers, clergymen, lawyers, welfare workers, and policemen.

He defines consultation (1970, ch. 2) as a process of interaction between a specialist helper and the consultee who seeks help with a current work problem which is causing her some difficulty; the consultant has no administrative authority over the consultee who is free to apply the discussion to her subsequent practice in what-ever way she chooses. In addition, according to the principles underlying crisis-theory (Caplan, 1961; Parad, 1965), timely support with the current problem should enable the worker to deal more confidently with similar problems in future. Caplan differentiates his method of consultation from other specialized methods such as counselling, psychotherapy, supervision and education although it contains elements of these. He may be acutely aware of personal problems within the consultee, which guides his listening and response, but he does not attempt to treat these difficulties directly; the consultee is regarded as a competent colleague who is able to cope effectively with her work on receiving a little clarification and support at her moment of need. In this way, Caplan believes the worker does not become dependent, but retains her autonomy both in the work-situation and in the consultation itself, while she may indirectly be relieved and strengthened in relation to her own small area of private personal difficulties.

Caplan's methods are first outlined simply in his book published in 1961 and with much more comprehensive detail in 1970; then Ruth Caplan (1972) applies the same ideas to experience of groups for clergymen in the USA. She explains (p. 58) that

> this form of intervention can succeed only if it is conducted in a friendly, supportive atmosphere. It will fail utterly if a consultant or members of a consultant group attempt to joke or shame a minister out of his fears, or if they root around in his private life to show him why he is reacting irrationally.... It is the role of the consultant, particularly in group sessions, to create and maintain a companionable atmosphere where only tact and civility are allowed, and where the sensibilities of all the members of the group are respected.

Attempts to evaluate the Caplan method (1970, ch. 12; 1972, ch. 8) indicate that further research should be undertaken in a spirit of optimism.

The third and fourth alternative models are basically similar to those above. Balint (1957) describes a research project in which a group of fourteen general practitioners met regularly with a psychiatrist to discuss their work. Full records of their case-discussions illustrate how the doctors developed more sensitive understanding of their patients as whole persons rather than as symptoms, and became better able to pursue their professional relationships in a mutually satisfying way. Bettelheim (1962) provides the fourth model in his dialogues with groups of mothers of 'normal' young children. His sessions ignored simple rule-giving; he knew from experience that the most carefully explained theory is of little use in handling specific events because overall theories are too broad whilst specific advice never quite fits the real situation. With his residential staff he had already learnt 'to start out with the valid assumption that in asking for help they were interested, not in any theory or advice, but in a way of living more at ease with the children in their care—and hence more at ease with themselves' (p. 5). Effective teaching consisted of efforts to help them discuss 'a particular situation in their own words, on the basis of their own anxieties, notions and hopes.... These were no prearranged situations, but simply those that arose out of everyday living' (p. 6).

In Bettelheim's groups of ordinary mothers, he found that he needed to concentrate at any one moment on reaching the particular mother who was then presenting a problem: 'After all, the way in which I handled my relation to them at any one moment, and theirs to me, presented to all of them an image of how any personal relations may be handled' (p. 12). The way in which the dialogues were conducted introduced these mothers to a long-term method of solving their own problems in future; their natural abilities were enhanced rather than hedged about with theoretical rules. The models presented above are close to the methods developed by fieldwork teachers supervising social work students during their placements, when discussion usually centres on the interaction between a student and his clients rather than on any personal problems he may have.[12] Considerable expertise is already established in social work agencies and on professional training courses about the supervision of fieldworkers, much of which is being applied to residential workers and could be extended further in their direction; this might be called a basic model which is sufficiently familiar not to require elaboration here.

The five models recommended in this section—those practised by Woodmansey, Dockar-Drysdale, the Caplans, Balint and Bettelheim —are not the only ones available but are selected to demonstrate the scope for flexibility in methods of consultation. The five models share more similarities than differences. All five exponents happen to be psychiatrists or psychotherapists but none has a narrow clinical perspective and all have a realistic appreciation of the nature of social work. Their methods are highly adaptable to a wide range of people, either individually or in groups. All share the same basic principle of respect for the care-givers' competence together with the recognition that even thoroughly capable people cannot always be self-sufficient when their work is highly demanding. All five offer a token relationship which aims to enhance rather than to diminish the care-givers' freedom of action in the daily work-situation. All try to provide an emotionally supportive experience rather than intellectual insight-giving, though workers may develop insight and theoretical understanding as a secondary gain. The fact that all focus on real everyday happenings in the workers' current experience gives the participants a parallel experience behind the scenes, with opportunities to integrate thoughts and feelings, theory and practice. And all these groups are optional and confidential.

Perhaps the main difference in the five models is that some consultants, notably Caplan, concentrate deliberately on the work-problem rather than upon the care-givers' feelings about the problem. Further study might determine which approach is more helpful in practice but, in so far as Caplan's method is an attempt to avoid dependency on the consultant, it can be argued that Bowlby's recent formulation (1973, described here in chapter 1) of self-reliance stemming from a 'secure base' shows dependency in a much more favourable light. That is, dependency need no longer be feared as infantile vulnerability to paternalism but as a natural, strengthening, temporary condition for anybody whose daily work revolves round other dependent people—*reculer pour mieux sauter*. The common denominator in all five models is that care-givers are able to communicate their own viewpoint; they are listened to in their own right and this special attention offsets the loneliness without undermining their autonomy. C. Winnicott believes (1964/70, p. 37):

Everyone doing creative work needs a sympathetic audience
if the work is to remain vital, because creative work involves
a giving of oneself, and the audience by accepting at the same
time replenishes the giver.... The mere act of putting feelings

143

into words consolidates the experience, makes it part of the individual, and not something that happens to him or her from outside.

Recent confirmation of the ideas in this section is provided by Krause (1974) who studied staff attitudes towards methods of controlling behaviour in nineteen highly varied child-caring institutions around Chicago. He shows with some precision that attitudes tend to reflect the workers' socialization experiences within the institutions (including supervision and communication between staff members) rather than their personal backgrounds and measured characteristics such as dogmatism, coerciveness and authoritarianism. In other words, the personal qualities of care-givers apparently matter less than the availability of supportive experience within the work-situation—a hopeful finding since it is obviously easier to provide the latter than to attempt to change the former.

CONCLUSION AND RECOMMENDATIONS

The ideas above are not newly conceived in my study; several voices have cried in the wilderness over the past quarter-century.[13] They reappear here as a chorus speaking loud and clear, because if earlier voices had been taken seriously my sample would probably contain a lower proportion than 40 per cent of children living in 'more negative' units and a higher proportion than 17 per cent living in 'more positive' residential units. Therefore my main recommendation is that all residential workers, trained and un-trained, should be offered opportunities for ongoing support and consultation. Further research might indicate the most appropriate forms of support, but meanwhile enough knowledge is available which is adaptable to particular circumstances.

Apparently the Curtis Report was over-optimistic in suggesting that disciplinary methods had become markedly less harsh; public opinion on punishment may have softened, but for individual human beings under stress the temptation remains and it cannot be reduced merely by 'a code of rules' underpinned with 'regular inspection and constant watchfulness that the right atmosphere of kindness and sympathy is maintained' (para. 417). Inspectors of children's institutions have no doubt often come to be regarded as influential friends rather than as watch-dogs but the fact remains that a typical human reaction to inspection is to try to conceal one's deficiencies and to present a polished front, in the hope that the former will pass unnoticed and the latter will be praised. Even if a visiting inspector is perceptive enough to spot trouble, it is still easier to diagnose defects than to remedy them. Care-givers may deny what seems like an accusation, and in any case have limited ability to obey instructions to work less negatively. It is a much greater safeguard if they are given a situation where they can raise their own problems voluntarily and receive effective help in over-coming them. There is less point in sacking a worker who hits a child, because any replacement is also a potential hitter under stress. King, Raynes and Tizard found more child-oriented care in units less subject to inspection (1971, p. 178; also Tizard *et al.*, 1972).

An important recommendation of the Curtis Committee was that residential workers should receive appropriate training. Tremen-dous efforts have been made to set up and develop training courses; renewed efforts are being made now. A large expansion and modi-fication of existing provision is necessary to meet future require-ments;[14] in addition the rate of staff turnover suggests continued wastage and it is unlikely that a position will ever be reached where nearly all residential workers are suitably qualified. The finding in this study that there are similar proportions of professionally trained staff in the 'more negative' and in the 'better' units does not devalue training itself—especially as the proportions, though almost identical, are low—about 20 per cent. The finding does imply that training, however good and however widespread, may not have lasting results. Even everlasting flowers and mummies look desiccated, sapless.

The knowledge, values and skills gained during training are not self-perpetuating, unlike the skill of riding a bicycle which once learnt is never forgotten. Refresher courses give fairly short-lived stimulation. The nature of residential work means that care-givers require an inbuilt support system; no course could prepare them for all future vicissitudes. For example: a new, inexperienced housemother (not in this study) proved able to cope with a wide range of behaviour problems in her group of nine children but she was thrown off balance on discovering their temporary game of urinating into their toothmugs—the selection committee could not have dreamt of asking her beforehand whether this particular phenomenon would upset her and she might not have known the answer in advance in any case. At best, training gives only an excellent foundation for future development. M. Barker (1970, p. 23) quotes an earlier educationalist (Whitehead, 1929):

Whatever be the detail with which you cram your students, the chance of him meeting in after life exactly that detail is almost infinitesimal and if he does he will probably have forgotten what you taught him about it. The really useful training yields a comprehension of a few general principles with a thorough grounding in the way they apply to a variety of concrete details.

Ongoing support within the job has the added attraction that help in the here-and-now situation caters for both untrained and trained staff, including the recently and the long-since-trained; consultation is hand-tailored to meet their particular current needs.

The implications of this study for selection and training of residential workers are three-fold: first, that one factor in selection is assessment of whether an applicant seems likely to respond positively to supportive relationships; this can readily be gauged in the actual interview situation according to whether the candidate shows at least a small measure of trust in the interviewer and a willingness to communicate. Second, during training itself, students should be offered good (more than good-enough) experience of professional relationships individually and in groups with fieldwork supervisors and tutors; if they learn through first-hand experience during training how to accept such a relationship for their own well-being and in order to improve their professional practice, they are more likely to want similar help in future and to use it profitably. Third, while the lion's share of resources will obviously be devoted to basic training provision, some thought should be given to the question of short courses for advanced training in consultancy; in fact this might prove a most economical, quick and effective way of raising standards of residential care—some senior residential workers could well become consultants themselves, thus improving their career prospects.

Finally, the major recommendation of ongoing support and consultation has implications for other areas of difficulty experienced by care-givers. First, it is apparent that residential workers at all levels should be more closely involved in decision-making and planning for those in their care; since empathy combines emotional involvement with an element of objective detachment (Katz, 1963) it is possible that care-givers who themselves receive empathy are in a better position to think clearly about plans. Second, similarly, this study does not consider in detail the administrative organization of residential units, but the overall physical arrangements of rooms, routines and general use of life-space affect relationships within the place; equally, the care-givers' prevailing attitudes to inmates greatly affect the way in which routines are organized.[15] So again, it can be argued that if care-givers are supported they are more likely to make suitable practical arrangements, since it appears that emotional resistance in workers tends to result in restrictive, impersonal or regimented *ménages*. In other words, if care-givers feel free to live comfortably with inmates, they are perfectly capable of applying their common sense to the details of unit organization. External administrators are sometimes criticized for being too preoccupied with material trivialities as an escape from human involvement—not surprisingly, many prefer to pay for the painting of shabby bee-hives rather than to uncover the buzzing relationships within—but the department as a whole cannot afford to ignore the emotional significance of practical matters.

Third, if the very ordinary caring routines are seen as a pervasive means of communication between staff and children, then the care-givers' roles are elevated far above those of domestic servants. They become milieu therapists. This is not merely a grandiose change of name, as from rat-catcher to rodent operative, but gives a complete change of function and purpose. Perhaps more consideration could be given during training to the emotional and social significance of physical care : for example, food as related to affection, security, freedom to choose without coercion; clothing to a sense of identity; pocket money to self-worth; sleep to personal safety and so on.[16] Professional training might narrow the gap between theory and practice if academic disciplines (such as human growth and development, psychology, biology, nutrition) were linked with discussion of residential life as experienced in student placements. Also, if it is desirable that students should develop self-awareness and self-knowledge, there is practical value in residential workers identifying the foibles of their own metabolism; everyone's interests are served through individual workers having some idea of how they personally function at different times of day and night—whether for instance they tend to have more patience at breakfast or at supper-time; whether they are affected more adversely by a delayed mealtime than by broken sleep or vice versa.

It was not the purpose of this study to consider residential treatment in its entirety but to concentrate on its essence as distinct from other methods of social work, so virtually no differentiation is made between the various kinds of children and units in terms of diagnosis and additional treatment facilities (as for example in Balbernie's painstaking study, 1966/73). The one inescapable feature peculiar to residential work (including foster-care) is that those on the receiving end have stomachs to fill, bowels to empty, bodies to be clothed and rested ... but the way in which these needs are met evidently varies enormously even within residential child care. So the argument here is that all people (whatever their individual differences) should have their common human needs met positively not only through respect for their dignity but because positive daily care is milieu therapy—an expedient form of treatment immediately relevant to the reality-situation.

The ideas in these four chapters have now come full circle if the study provides sufficient evidence that the satisfactory care of children (or of dependent people of any age) is interwoven with appropriate care for their care-givers.

5

Summary and conclusions

Nothing ever becomes real till it is experienced—even a
proverb is no proverb to you until your life has
illustrated it.

Letters of John Keats

The most important of all skills, that of living well with
oneself and with others, can be acquired only in a stable
and satisfying environment.... [Parent-figures] cannot
convey to their children what they have never learned
themselves.

Bruno Bettelheim: *Love is not Enough* (p. 334)

The theme of this study is an attempt to dwell on the distinctive
feature of residential work by considering daily patterns of
experience shared by children and their care-givers within the
setting of their life together. When a person of any age is received
into residential care (and whenever one person becomes physically
dependent upon another living under the same roof, irrespective of
the size of the roof) there is an implicit assumption that this entails
catering for his daily needs. The contract is not exactly a promise
to keep body and soul together except in the sense of common
usage that his life will be maintained for the time being. Inevitably
therefore, the residential task revolves round mundane practicalities
such as food, clothes, beds—things which will not be required
spasmodically but in a constant, frequent rhythm as relentlessly as
sunrise and sunset.

The question is whether these inevitable routines can conveniently
be incorporated into a wider, more comprehensive treatment plan in
order to enable greater well-being within the given situation. In
this view of treatment, two meanings of the word 'treat' are
brought together: not only to 'deal with or apply a process' but
actually to try to help the person to feel better (plus a third mean-

ing of 'treat' sometimes, in the sense of giving a rare pleasure). Residential workers are constrained to cater on a daily basis, so it is expedient if they can simultaneously harness their essential activities to some further purpose. Even high physical standards are hollow when divorced from therapeutic attitudes—a holiday in a luxury hotel would be uncomfortable if the manager took offence whenever his guests failed to eat every mouthful of delicious food provided. The quality of care received may be experienced not only as less than life-enhancing but as actively harmful to the inmates directly affected as well as to those for whom present inmates may become responsible in future.

Having introduced these ideas with the implication that they might offer a means of decreasing the arid gap between social work theory and practice, chapter 1 reviewed some previous relevant studies. A few paragraphs quoted from a summary in the Curtis Report (1946) suggest that it is not quite past history yet, even though it caused sweeping changes. Its picture of drab, dreary, impersonal and regimented care seems to have been brightened subsequently by patches of warmer colour rather than completely painted over. Whilst admitting they were unlikely to discover harsh treatment on one short visit to an institution, the Committee members were perhaps sanguine in believing disciplinary methods had already improved then. Today we are more aware that punitive attitudes can continue even though actual methods of punishment seem less extreme (for example, the headmaster in my study who is said to have stopped using the cane because Labour councillors are in control locally, is not necessarily any less punitive, being motivated less by concern for the boys' skin than for his own). With hindsight, it seems that the Curtis Committee was unduly hopeful in thinking that special training for staff, or regular inspection, would of themselves provide adequate safeguards for children in care.

Three further studies were mentioned: first, King, Raynes and Tizard's research (1971) is relevant in giving precise information about patterns of residential child care, showing that remarkable differences exist between institution-oriented hospital wards and the more child-oriented care found in community homes and hostels. Second, Bettelheim (1950/71) describes milieu therapy practised within daily caring routines, and how 'love for children' implies willingness to go to some trouble in meeting children's spoken and unspoken needs. Third, the Newsons' studies (1963, 1968) highlight the fact that socialization of young children happens largely through communication, verbal and non-verbal, with their parents in ordinary everyday life, and moreover, emphasize the fact that mothers often experience great pressures in the situation. From this realization arose a discussion on the changing, increasingly complex expectations of the role of care-givers other than 'birth parents', with the suggestion that a prolonged theoretical debate may militate against open acknowledgment of the extreme difficulties inherent in these ambiguous roles, and act as a defence in postponing the offer of appropriate help to care-givers in order that they may care more self-confidently for those with whom they live. Chapter 1 ends with a case-illustration of one brief, detailed experience in residential life.

As chapter 2 gives a complete outline of the present study, with most of the tables and numerical details, it may be useful to repeat some central points here in simplified form. The study is based on questionnaires completed by forty-four students, mainly on professional social work training courses, during their residential placements in a range of institutions for children and adolescents: fourteen observation and assessment centres, twenty-one community homes including ten ex-approved school units, six special schools for maladjusted and otherwise handicapped children, and three miscellaneous places—a boys' prep-school, a family rehabilitation hostel and a ward in a psychiatric hospital. This is not a random sample, though it represents most types of provision (except wards in subnormality and general hospitals) mainly of the kind which King, Raynes and Tizard (1971) would expect to be 'better' in offering child-oriented rather than institution-oriented care.

These forty-four units contain 946 children and adolescents: 690 boys and 256 girls, of whom approximately 70 per cent are in care or subject to care orders. They range in age from four months to eighteen years old, although 90 per cent of the sample are eight to sixteen years old, and the biggest single group consists of fourteen to fifteen-year-old boys. Over 150 children are placed with at least one sibling. Some are resident during a short crisis-period, but 69 per cent of the total have lived in their present unit for over three months, 39 per cent for over one year and nearly 13 per cent for over three years—sizeable spans of childhood, with twelve years being the longest stretch in any one place. Future plans are many and various, though more than half the sample could expect to remain where they were for the time being, including 122 children for whom there were no definite plans. Almost one-fifth of the children are said to be unsettled or very unsettled, which gives some indication of the repercussions on care-givers.

A tentative attempt was made to grade patterns of care in each unit on the basis of twelve aspects of daily life from dawn until beyond dusk, including methods of discipline and staff reactions to children who are unco-operative in their daily routines. Accordingly, twenty-one units containing approximately 43 per cent of the children appear to offer a mid-point standard of good-enough care, with 17 per cent living in six more positive units, and 40 per cent living in seventeen more negative units. Some allowance was made for the fact that various types of unit differ in their specific functions but since the study is concerned primarily with basic human needs (in terms of care, communication and control) rather than with additional treatment facilities, it is argued that the whole range of units can legitimately be compared in this way, especially as difficult, disturbed children are spread thickly throughout the sample (except in the boys' prep-school, although one boy there is in care).

The three patterns emerge without rigid boundaries. (For instance, if five grades had been used instead of three, there might have been two very positive units, seven fairly positive, eighteen good-enough, eleven rather negative and six very negative.) So the exact proportions of children in each of the three patterns is less important than the obvious finding of remarkable differences in the quality of care provided. Decisions in grading patterns (checked by two other social workers independently) were based on overall impressions of daily care, communication and control. Methods of control show some flexibility in units other than those where discipline is consistently strict; even so, almost half the respondents record seriously conflicting attitudes within units about methods of handling children in group care. Rewards as well as punishments seem almost irrelevant in the more positive units, whereas there is great reliance on both in the more negative units where children not only have to earn 'privileges' such as pocket money and home leave but are subjected to far more scolding, threats, restrictions, official and unofficial corporal punishment than in the good-enough units.

Once delineated, the three patterns of care can be related to various factors such as unit type, relationships between residents and within the neighbourhood, staff qualifications, length and conditions of service. Patterns within units stand out all the more sharply because in many cases there is limited communication with the outside world. Thirty-one units (nearly three-quarters of the sample, including nearly 90 per cent of negative units) are said to be somewhat isolated within the neighbourhood; the fairly few existing community contacts are not always friendly; only four units are said to be well integrated into the neighbourhood. Visits from parents and relatives are uneven in frequency, partly because a fair proportion of children are going home regularly for weekends and holidays. But at a rough estimate 25 per cent of inmates (excluding the boys' prep-school) rarely if ever see their parents.

Therefore relationships with current care-givers are magnified in importance; though in any case these grown-ups immediately responsible for dispensing daily bread are bound to be significant figures. Staff-child relationships are not easily evaluated, but respondents indicate that over the whole sample, 46 per cent of children are on good terms with their care-givers, 38 per cent are on fairly good terms and 13 per cent on poor terms. More seems to depend on individual children being likeable and amenable than on their common need for acceptance. In the positive units, 90 per cent are said to be on good terms with care-givers as opposed to 35 per cent in more negative units. Relationships between children seem to mirror the above proportions on a lower parallel plane; overall 33 per cent are said to be on good terms with each other, 46 per cent on fairly good terms and nearly 18 per cent on poor terms; 57 per cent of children in more positive units seem to enjoy good relationships together, in contrast with only 26 per cent in more negative units. In many cases a child on poor terms with care-givers is also on poor terms with his fellows and generally unsettled.

Typically then, residential workers not only have the problem of handling groups but they also have to try to share their affection amongst clamorous youngsters who are ambivalent towards parent-figures and each other, in a place which may be isolated from the outside world. Working hours are long, and even when a shift system enables greater predictability of hours, this affords less opportunity for the whole staff to meet for discussion. Domestic help seems adequate or even plentiful in almost three-quarters of the sample, though care-givers in over a third of units sound pre-occupied with household chores; also, in nearly a third of units (typically in remand homes and to a lesser extent in ex-approved schools), adolescents themselves undertake most chores with varying degrees of willingness. The sample provides details about 416 workers: 43 per cent men, 57 per cent women—slightly more married than single women; 70 per cent of the total are resident, 30 per cent non-resident. The workers span a wide age-range, from late teens up to retiring age, with the largest proportion in the mid-thirties to mid-fifties group.

With regard to length of stay, approximately 33 per cent of workers have stayed in their present unit for less than one year; 40 per cent from one up to four years, 18 per cent from four up to nine years, and 6 per cent for over nine years. When length of service over two years, and over four years in one place, was linked to the three patterns of care, it was found that workers not only do stay in the more negative units but they tend to stay proportionately longer than those in the 'better' units. Perhaps generalized concern about staff turnover and wastage has obscured a different problem of authoritarian durability. Numerous speculations were explored—one being the possibility that workers in 'better' units may exhaust themselves more quickly by trying to give positive care against heavy odds. Speculations revolved particularly around the aspects of training and subsequent support within the work-situation.

The general picture for training throughout the sample is that approximately 20 per cent of workers have a relevant qualification in child care (higher than the present national average, which is explicable in terms of these units having been selected for student placements); 14 per cent are primarily trained as teachers, 7 per cent as nurses; 7.5 per cent have none of the above qualifications but have had further or higher education of some kind; nearly 15 per cent have in-service training and nearly 30 per cent have had no training at all. These figures, related to the three patterns of care, show that there are almost identical proportions of 'child care trained' workers in negative units as in 'better' units (though negative units contain a higher proportion of workers without any kind of training); in fact senior workers in charge of negative units appear to be even slightly better qualified than their counterparts elsewhere. This depressing finding need not imply that professional training for residential work has little value; however, it does highlight a gulf between theory and practice, and the fact that initial training cannot be expected to prepare workers for all the subsequent pressures and hazards they will meet on the job.

Respondents were asked about the general pattern of visits from parents, relatives, friends and fieldworkers; about the number and type of staff-meetings, the number of visits from fieldworkers and external senior workers; about opportunities for consultation, and whether any children were receiving casework help or psychiatric treatment. Apparently more than half the sample of workers (particularly in negative units) feel that they derive little benefit from services offered directly to children. The question about fieldworkers' visits aroused strong feelings of isolation, frustration, resentment (particularly in negative units) about a lack of effective co-operation from fieldworkers and poor participation in planning. The majority of units have formal staff-meetings at widely ranging intervals, but meetings in some units seem merely a dead formality, and staff relations in a few negative units militate against open discussion.

The question about external support and consultation for care-givers seems to be of outstanding significance, even though responses are impressionistic (and even ambiguous in a few cases). On the whole, opportunities for consultation and staff development seem to emanate from within units, with many more opportunities in 'better' units. But although there is in general rather less external than internal support, it is clear that the majority of 'better' units have at least fairly good (often very good) opportunities for external support, whereas the vast majority of negative units have poor opportunities. Therefore the factor of ongoing support for care-givers within the current work-situation appears to be of greater influence in determining the quality of care than the factor of training.

If chapter 2 represents the skeleton of the body of my book, then chapter 1 is the head and heart containing thoughts and feelings underlying the study; this final chapter 5 is the skin (a comparatively superficial finishing touch) and chapters 3 and 4 represent the flesh and blood. That is, chapter 3 considers in some detail the daily patterns of residential life as experienced by children and adolescents, while chapter 4 is devoted to their care-givers' viewpoint. Because the latter concentrates on the constellation of extreme difficulties commonly experienced by residential workers (largely in terms of their relationships with inmates, and with internal and external colleagues) it seems possible now to state bluntly that the respondents reveal a miserable existence for some children in residential care—indeed, there is no room for complacency in so-called 'good-enough' units.

To repeat just a few memorable phrases from the questionnaires in order to illustrate contrasting experience and the compelling nature of daily routines:

'On being called, the children are expected to put their feet on the floor right away and then make their beds.' 'They are allowed to waken at their own pace.' 'They commence [mealtimes] by standing behind their chairs until silence prevails and prayers.' 'I did not always enjoy the mealtimes—always a great deal of tension present amongst the boys.' '[Mealtimes are] a very relaxed and happy time.' 'There is of course a set routine of wearing best shirts for dinner.' 'A high standard [of housework] is not expected but they are all made to feel that they each have a part to play in the running of the unit.' 'The staff leave [the dormitories] when every girl has settled down for the night.'

Similarly, in descriptions about the experience of care-givers, a few respondents convey examples of effective teamwork, whereas a typical contrasting note is sounded elsewhere: 'The staff feel to be out on a limb and have felt this way for a long time.' Overall, the main impression is that the daily care itself is a continuous communication, for better or worse, of adults' attitudes, particularly in relation to unco-operative children. Responses to children's needs, naturally enough, seem to be determined less by theoretical principles than by the care-givers' own pressures of frustration, fear, uncertainty, irritation in the heat of the moment. And all too often, children receive either mediocre or blatantly poor experience, whilst care-givers remain stranded in threatening circumstances. Tension arises particularly in the aspect of discipline and control, causing destructive conflict between children and workers in at least seventeen units, and serious divisions between colleagues within units in almost half the sample. There seems to be a debilitating equation in the minds of many care-givers that the dependent person will prosper only at their own expense—the recipient waxes while the giver wanes in direct proportion. Thus a tired mother may feel her toddler grows all the more obstreperous as she becomes drained, or a nurse with backache may feel her patient is lazing in bed, gaining weight, becoming harder to lift.

No doubt the ordinary world abounds with reciprocal relationships but these are less characteristic of situations requiring social work help; in any case, once the waning process sets in, the care-giver is less motivated to encourage sturdy independence in someone who may later take advantage of her weakness. Fear of waning may indeed cause some workers to take on the outward appearance of frighteningly powerful people (Stevenson, 1972). Apparently the best way of making the equation viable is for care-givers themselves to be given something by a third party; an emotional subsidy appears to be effective even though it does not represent the full equivalent of the care-givers' expenditure—even a small token of attending to the care-givers' viewpoint can be sufficient. Although residential work is exceptionally taxing, the necessary consultation service is similar to that which is required by workers in all 'helping professions' if they are to make a positive contribution.

Summing up then, the findings represent a fairly widespread incidence of personal isolation, tension, distress, lack of self-confidence amongst grown-ups as well as children—much of which could be prevented. It is relatively unimportant to establish a fact that 40 per cent of children are living in negative units—because in any case this number does not include other individuals elsewhere who may be receiving less than good care even though they live in 'better' units where the majority are treated with some measure of friendship. Similarly, the finding that workers in twenty-seven units are managing somehow to provide 'better' care is clouded by the suggestion that this is often at undue personal cost to themselves. The central, indisputable fact is that a sizeable proportion of children have a comparatively poor experience of daily care in residential life, and that this appears to be linked with their care-givers receiving similarly poor experience of ongoing support.

The findings in this study could perhaps be discounted on the grounds of their being insufficiently amenable to statistical analysis, too impressionistic. However, it would be unrealistic to dismiss subjective evidence wholesale if any of it rings true, especially since real personal experience of residential life in the flesh is undoubtedly impressionistic rather than statistical. Care-givers and inmates do not usually count the exact number of times they are spoken to during one day, nor can they measure in degrees Fahrenheit the temperature of each interaction, but they do none the less have a very real ongoing impression. Therefore, it seems fitting that at least some research in this area should concern itself with sub-jective experience rather than attempt precise fact-finding in matters of close human relationships which defy scientific analysis at any meaningful depth.

A further argument is that inmates and care-givers not infre-quently gain the impression that outsiders 'do not want to know', perhaps because such knowledge might cause discomfort, especially if there seems to be no solution to the problems; so it would be unfortunate if the impressions recorded here were similarly ignored or dismissed (for example, Harrison, 1974; K. Jones, 1974). Even supposing the findings are exaggerated, which is fairly unlikely in view of the efforts made to prevent distortion, there is room for concern if only a fraction of the evidence is objectively accurate. Also, several previous studies (for example, Goffman, 1961; and others mentioned by K. Jones, 1967) expose shameful skeletons in the residential cupboard but stop short on a critical note likely to undermine the workers' confidence still further, whereas this study not only combines a positive and negative exposure but takes the next step of suggesting an attainable remedy. The second half of chapter 4 outlines five similar models of consultation for current care-givers, designed to meet their immediate problems in the work-situation as expressed by them to a reliable external support-figure both for their own job-satisfaction and for the sake of their fellow-residents.

Attempts were made to demonstrate that the offering and acceptance of ongoing support denotes professional attitudes in both parties and is the prerequisite for giving positive daily care without undue personal strain. Both the service to inmates and the parallel service to their care-givers are seen in terms of daily experience, since consultation tends to focus on daily happenings from the care-givers' viewpoint, thus enabling them to practise a form of milieu therapy with a supportive oasis (or 'secure base from which to operate' in Bowlby's terms, 1973) in the background. The experiential focus in consultation promotes integration of thought and feeling, theory and practice; the method is equally applicable to trained and untrained staff, to beginners and veterans. So the major recommendation arising from the study is that the widespread availability of consultancy services should prove both to be the biggest single influence in raising standards of residential care and the most economical method.

Corollaries arising from the major recommendation (expanded towards the end of chapter 4) relate both to training and practice. First, selection for training (and/or employment) should include some assessment of whether applicants are likely to respond positively to supportive relationships (with tutor, fieldwork teachers, fellow-students) during training, on the assumption that appropriately trained residential workers will appreciate the value of such experience and wish it to continue during subsequent employment. (One proviso is that these skilled helpers should not impose themselves in a paternalistic way; realistic support does not include intrusive insight-giving but is available on terms acceptable to the workers and their expressed needs; the offer of help is justified by the fact that these care-givers are engaged in exceptionally demanding work.) Second, ongoing support in the background implies that care-givers should be better equipped to participate in the organizational and planning aspects of their work; they may also become more aware of the emotional symbolism inherent in daily events as these affect inmates and themselves—in short, they gain stature as well as personal satisfaction.

These ideas can be applied, with variations on the basic generic theme, not only to residential child care but to all types of residential work and day care (including ordinary schools), to foster-care, to the care of children at risk in their own homes, and to virtually any situation in which one person, young or old, depends upon another in a manner likely to cause prolonged stress. The concept of care is visualized at two levels, each feeding the other since both are interwoven. Appropriate care for care-givers under pressure appears to provide an experience which can be passed on in a positive way.

Appendix A Questionnaire

(Compressed here; actual questionnaire spread over nine foolscap sheets.)

Department of Sociological Studies
University of Sheffield

See notes on last page (sheet 9).

AMENDED

Questionnaire on aspects of daily life in residential treatment

Purpose It is hoped that about 50 students may complete these questionnaires during their placements in a variety of settings. This could prove to be a useful focus during the placement itself, but the main purpose is to gather some information on aspects of daily life as experienced by the staff and by the children for whom these places exist. Individual places will remain anonymous throughout any subsequent study of them: it is certainly not intended to criticize them in an unconstructive way—indeed, we recognize from the outset that the staff and administrators of residential units are faced with an exceptionally difficult task. There seems to be some general doubt about what is involved in residential 'treatment'; the idea underlying this study is that it is *not* dependent on the immediate availability of highly qualified therapists practising inside or outside residential units, but that the real treatment consists largely in the staff's day-to-day handling of ordinary, routine events. We also wish to consider what kinds of support the staff require to enable them to cope with the daily stresses involved in meeting children's needs as helpfully as possible. Therefore many aspects are covered in this questionnaire; the students are asked to complete it as far as possible *from their own observations* rather than by direct questioning. The students are also asked to inform the person in charge of the residential unit that he/she wishes to complete a questionnaire. We shall be very grateful to have permission for this to be done (and the students will do it unobtrusively); we shall also be grateful if the *completed questionnaire could be regarded as confidential between the student and the social work tutor concerned*—but the unit head shall choose whether he/she wishes to see the completed questionnaire.

Please state here whether SEEN or UNSEEN by unit head after completion
. . . .

1 (a) *Type of residential unit* (e.g. small home for children in local
authority care)
(b) *Number of children/young persons*
(c) *Number of staff:*
How many resident?   How many non-resident?
(d) *Design of unit* (e.g. purpose-built, blending with housing estate
on city outskirts)

Sheet 2

2 STAFF (refer to each by title (Mr/Mrs/Miss) and one alphabetical
letter, listing them in order of responsibility)

Name	Position	Approx. age	How long resident	Training
E.g. Mrs A	Housemother in charge	early middle age	2½ years	In-service

Sheet 3

3 CHILDREN/YOUNG PERSONS (refer to each by Christian name only.
Indicate siblings in same family)

Name	Approx. age	How long resident	Any future dept plans	Degree of settlement (say whether *settled* or *fairly settled* or *unsettled* or *very unsettled*)	Relationships with staff/children (say whether on *good terms* or on *fairly good* or on *poor* terms with staff, and with children) With whom is he closest?
E.g. Tim	12	18 months	to stay here until school-leaving age	speaks of this as 'home'	Tolerated by most children. Staff regard him as likeable though cheeky. He depends mainly on Mrs A

Sheets 4 and 5

4 DESCRIBE THE TYPICAL PATTERN OF THE FOLLOWING ASPECTS OF DAILY
ROUTINE AND THE ROLE PLAYED BY STAFF IN EACH :
  (a) Getting up in the morning
  (b) Washing/dressing/bathing/toilet
  (c) Meal-times
  (d) Getting off to school/work
  (e) Returning from school/work
  (f) Leisure activities during weekdays/weekends
  (g) Management of clothing/pocket money
  (h) Child's responsibility for household chores
  (i) Bed-time
  (j) Incidents during night
  (k) General pattern of visits from parents/relatives/friends/field-
  workers

Sheet 6

5 STAFF
  (a) Approx. hours worked during a typical day
  (b) Time off each week
  (c) The amount of time spent on routine chores
  (d) Availability of outside domestic help
  (e) Interaction with children during daily routines
  (f) Opportunities for playing/talking with children
  (g) Number and type of staff discussions
  (h) Number of visits from fieldworkers/senior workers outside (say
  whether staff *feel* they get enough outside support)
  (i) Opportunities for consultation (about children/pressures of job/
  own development)

Sheet 7

6 Are any of the children receiving casework help/psychiatric treatment of any kind?
Do the staff consider this effective?

7 What sort of methods are used by the staff to encourage reasonably
co-operative behaviour in the children? (Is discipline *strict* or *quite
firm* or *relaxed*? Are the children in general co-operative, and is it very
important to the staff that they should conform?)

8 Give examples of rewards/punishments used here:

9 Give examples of incidents arising during daily routines. E.g. How
did staff members handle a child who returned tearful from school/
criticized the food/wet the bed/was awkward after a visit from relatives. . . .

Sheet 8

10 Give examples of children talking about or acting out their personal worries/hopes/fears

11 What is your impression of the unit's integration into the immediate neighbourhood? Reply in terms of the number and nature of community contacts. (Say whether the unit is *well* integrated into the neighbourhood or *fairly well* or *isolated* with few contacts)

12 How frequently do parents visit? How many children have no visits from parent(s)?

13 How many days did you stay here?

14 Give brief details of your age; course; previous fieldwork experience; career intention. Male or female.

Sheet 9

Notes for guidance on the completion of the questionnaire on aspects of daily life in residential treatment

It is important that both the person in charge of the residential unit and the appropriate external administrator should know beforehand that you intend to complete this questionnaire. They are welcome to see it beforehand if they wish, but it should be regarded as confidential once completed. Please return it to me as soon as possible.

The material you collect will be of three kinds:

(a) *Factual*—this should be simple enough. Do not refer to the full name of anybody in the unit—i.e. list children by their Christian name only, and indicate which are siblings—e.g. Tim, brother of Bill and Anna. List members of staff by consecutive letters of the alphabet—e.g. Mr A, Miss B, Mrs C; but use the same letter if they are married to each other—e.g. Mr A, Mrs A.

(b) *Descriptive*—you need a free hand here. I shall be glad to have clear details, and hope to gain as vivid and graphic a picture as possible. *Under question 4* (sheets 4 and 5) try to indicate whether these routine patterns are geared flexibly to meet the children's needs or whether the routines themselves have in some cases become more important than the people involved in them.

(c) *Opinion/assessment*—it will be helpful in subsequent collation of the material if there is some standardization of comments

Therefore:

(i) *Under question 3* (sheet 3), the column headed *Degree of settlement*, include mention of whether each child seems settled, *or* fairly settled, *or* unsettled, *or* very unsettled. And in the column headed *Relationships with staff/children*, include mention of whether each child seems to be on good terms with most of the staff, *or* on fairly good terms, *or* on poor terms. Remember to say with whom on the staff each child seems closest.

(ii) *In section (h) of question 5* (sheet 6), the answer will be largely subjective, according to whether the staff in general feel they do or do not receive sufficient support from fieldworkers and external senior staff.

(iii) *Under question 7* (sheet 7), describe the prevailing attitudes about discipline—whether this is strict, *or* quite firm *or* relaxed. And describe the sort of methods used by the staff to control the children —e.g. threats, withdrawal of privileges, verbal coercion, reasoning. Do the children in general behave co-operatively, and is it very important to the staff that they should conform?

(iv) *Under question 11* (sheet 8), indicate whether the unit seems well integrated into the neighbourhood, *or* fairly well, *or* seems isolated with few contacts.

If you need more space for any section, continue overleaf on that same page, marking clearly the number of the question/section.

Thank you *very* much for your help.

Juliet Berry (Miss J. H. Berry)
Department of Sociological Studies
University of Sheffield

Appendix B Stencilled letter

(Sent by course tutors to the administrator responsible for arranging placement(s) in each department concerned.)

Dear

We are glad that   is able to have a residential placement in your department, at   beginning on   , 1972/3.

This is to explain that we have agreed to co-operate in a study being undertaken at present by Miss Juliet Berry, a social work teacher in the Department of Sociological Studies, The University of Sheffield. The study is on patterns of daily care in residential treatment, and it will be based on material collected in questionnaire form by a large number of students during their residential placements. The residential units and the local authorities, staff members and children/adolescents concerned will remain *anonymous* throughout the study.

If you agree, I shall be very grateful if   could complete one of these questionnaires during the above placement in your department. He/she will tell the person directly in charge of the residential unit about this soon after his/her arrival there, and will complete it discreetly on receiving permission to do so. The staff are welcome to see the questionnaire beforehand if they wish, and it would also be possible for the unit head to see the completed questionnaire if he particularly wished, though it would be preferable from the research point of view if it could remain confidential between Miss Berry and the student.

Although it seems unlikely that any difficulties would arise, I thought I should inform you beforehand about this questionnaire so that you have opportunity to tell me if you feel it would be unwise for its completion to be attempted in this particular placement. But if I do not hear from you, I will take it that you are agreeable to the idea.

Yours sincerely,

Appendix C Additional tables

C1 *Age of students*

Age	21–25	26–30	31–35	36–40	41–45	46–49	Totals
Men	9	9	2	1	1	1	23
Women	2	12	1	2	4	–	21
Totals	11	21	3	3	5	1	44

C2 *Frequency distribution of children according to unit type (see Table 1.1)*

Key to Tables C2, 3, 4.

RC = reception centres   BCS = boys' community schools
RH = remand homes   GCS = girls' community schools
SCH = small children's homes   SS = special schools
LCH = larger children's homes   OP = other places

No. children per unit	RC	RH	SCH	LCH	BCS	GCS	SS	OP	Totals
4–10	2	–	4	–	–	1	1	2	10
11–15	2	–	1	1	2	2	–	–	8
16–22	2	1	–	4	1	–	1	–	9
23–29	1	1	–	1	2	1	1	–	7
30–37	2	3	–	–	–	–	2	–	7
38–45	–	–	–	–	–	–	1	–	1
70–72	–	–	–	–	1	–	–	1	2
Totals	9	5	5	6	6	4	6	3	44

C3 *Number of whole/part units related to sex and unit type (Key as for C2)*

		Whole units			Units part of larger centre		Totals
		Boys	Girls	Mixed	Boys	Girls	Mixed	
	RC	–	–	6	2	–	1	9
	RH	4	1	–	–	–	–	5
	SCH	–	–	3	1	–	1	5
	LCH	–	–	5	1	–	–	6
BCS &	GCS	1	1	–	5	3	–	10
	SS	1	1	3	–	–	1	6
	OP	1	–	1	–	–	1	3
	Totals	7	3	18	9	3	4	44

C4 *Unit type and number of children in three patterns of care (Key as for C2)*

		More positive				Good-enough				More negative			
		Boys	Girls	Total	%	Boys	Girls	Total	%	Boys	Girls	Total	%
	RC	0	0	0	–	50	40	90	9·5	53	27	80	8·5
	RH	0	0	0	–	21	0	21	2·2	98	26	124	13·1
SCH & LCH		20	3	23	2·4	47	24	71	7·5	52	20	72	7·6
BCS & GCS		70	0	70	7·4	28	56	84	8·8	64	0	64	6·8
	SS	49	15	64	6·8	19	41	60	6·3	45	0	45	4·8
	OP	0	0	0	–	74	4	78	8·2	0	0	0	–
	Totals	139	18	157	16·6	239	165	404	42·5	312	73	385	40·8

C5 *Length of children's stay in present unit*

Time	<1 wk	1–5 wks	6–11 wks	3–6 mths	7–11 mths	12–17 mths	18–23 mths
Boys	13	116	84	119	71	82	44
Girls	4	52	21	65	30	24	13
Totals	17	168	105	184	101	106	57

Time	24–30 mths	31–35 mths	3<4 yrs	4<5 yrs	5<6 yrs	6<7 yrs	7 yrs & over
Boys	68	3	46	20	8	4	10
Girls	13	2	17	3	3	2	7
Totals	81	5	63	23	11	6	17

N=944 (2 not known)

C6 *Length of service in present unit* (simplified in Figure 2.7)

	Men No.	%	Women No.	%	Total No.	%
Under 3 months	14	7·9	22	9·3	36	8·7
3-6 months	27	15·2	29	12·3	56	13·5
7-11 months	18	10·1	25	10·6	43	10·4
12-17 months	14	7·9	26	11·0	40	9·7
18-23 months	15	8·4	12	5·1	27	6·5
Over 2 years	17	9·5	26	11·0	43	10·4
„ 3 years	22	12·3	30	12·7	52	12·5
„ 4 years	8	4·5	10	4·2	18	4·3
„ 5 years	6	3·4	11	4·7	17	4·1
„ 6 years	9	5·0	5	2·1	14	3·4
„ 7 years	4	2·2	8	3·4	12	2·9
„ 8 years	3	1·7	10	4·2	13	3·1
9-14 years	4	2·2	8	3·4	12	2·9
15-20 years	6	3·4	1	0·4	7	1·7
Over 20 years	4	2·2	1	0·4	5	1·2
„ 30 years	1	0·6	0	—	1	0·2
Not known	6	3·4	12	5·1	18	4·3
Totals	178	100	236	100	414	100

C7 *Length of service over two and over four years in three patterns of care (see Table 2.7 and Figure 2.8)*

Time of staff stay	More positive No.	%	Good-enough No.	%	More positive and good-enough No.	%	More negative No.	%	Total No.	%
All known staff	72	100	170	100	242	100	154	100	396	100
2+ years	35	48·6	73	42·9	108	44·6	86	55·8	194	49·0
4+ years	20	27·8	34	20·0	54	22·3	45	29·2	99	25·0
Total known men	35	100	57	100	92	100	80	100	172	100
2+ years	23	65·7	17	29·8	40	43·5	44	55·0	84	48·8
4+ years	15	42·8	8	14·0	23	25·0	22	27·5	45	26·2
Total known women	37	100	113	100	150	100	74	100	224	100
2+ years	12	32·4	56	49·5	68	45·3	42	56·7	110	49·1
4+ years	5	13·5	26	23·0	31	20·7	23	31·1	54	24·1
Single women	23	100	65	100	88	100	23	100	111	100
2+ years	9	39·1	26	40·0	35	39·8	9	39·1	44	39·6
4+ years	3	13·0	11	16·9	14	15·9	4	17·4	18	16·2
Married women	14	100	48	100	62	100	51	100	113	100
2+ years	3	21·4	30	62·5	33	53·2	33	64·7	66	58·4
4+ years	2	14·3	15	31·2	17	27·4	19	37·2	36	31·8
Married women working with husband	4	100	15	100	19	100	22	100	41	100
2+ years	0	—	9	60·0	9	47·4	14	63·6	23	56·1
4+ years	0	—	4	26·7	4	21·0	7	31·8	11	26·8
Married women working without husband	10	100	33	100	43	100	29	100	72	100
2+ years	3	30·0	21	63·6	24	55·8	19	65·5	43	59·7
4+ years	2	20·0	11	33·3	13	30·2	12	41·4	25	34·7

N=396 (omitting 18 workers whose length of service is unknown. These 18 workers account for 4·3 per cent of the sample and comprise 6 men and 12 women; 11 workers in good-enough units and 9 in more negative units. Because numbers in more positive sub-groups are small, bar-charts in Figure 2·8 show the more positive units combined with good-enough units.)

C8 *Staff training in relation to three patterns of care* (see Figure 2.9)

Qualification	More positive No.	%	Good-enough No.	%	More positive and good-enough No.	%	More negative No.	%	Total No.	%
Child care	13	18·1	40	22·1	53	20·9	31	19·0	84	20·2
Teaching	10	13·9	31	17·1	41	16·2	18	11·0	59	14·2
Nursing	7	9·7	22	12·2	29	11·5	1	0·6	30	7·2
In-service	12	16·7	32	17·7	44	17·4	18	11·0	62	14·9
Other	13	18·1	12	6·6	25	9·9	6	3·7	31	7·5
None	17	23·6	44	24·3	61	24·1	63	38·6	124	29·8
Not known	0	—	0	—	0	—	26	16·0	26	6·3
Totals	72	100	181	100	253	100	163	100	416	100

(Because numbers in more positive units are comparatively small, the central section shows these combined with good-enough units. The above table includes unit heads with the whole sample.)

C9 *Training of unit head in relation to three patterns of care* (see Figure 2.10)

Qualification	More positive No.	%	Good-enough No.	%	More positive and good-enough No.	%	More negative No.	%	Total No.	%
Child care }	1	16·7	10	47·6	11	40·7	8	47·1	19	43·2
Advanced }	1	16·7	1	4·8	2	7·4	1	5·9	3	6·8
Teaching	2	33·3	5	23·8	7	25·9	2	11·8	9	20·5
Nursing	1	16·7	3	14·3	4	14·8	0	—	4	9·1
In-service	0	—	0	—	0	—	3	17·6	3	6·8
Other	1	16·7	1	4·8	2	7·4	0	—	2	4·5
None	0	—	1	4·8	1	3·7	0	—	1	2·3
Not known	0	—	0	—	0	—	3	17·6	3	6·8
Totals	6	100	21	100	27	100	17	100	44	100

(Again, because numbers in more positive units are extremely small, the central section shows these combined with good-enough units.)

Notes

Chapter 1   Ideas underlying the study

1   (a) Beedell (1970, pp. 4-5) estimates approximately 92,000 children and young persons in residential care (in over 3,300 establishments with over 20,000 staff). This includes 15,000 in local authority children's homes; 11,800 in voluntary societies children's homes; 6,000 in specialist units (e.g. nurseries, reception centres, hostels); 8,000 in approved schools; 1,100 in remand homes; 20,500 in special schools; 17,000 mentally subnormal in hospital wards/units; about 9,000 in borstals, detention and remand centres. (In addition about 141,000 in 'ordinary' boarding schools.)

(b) The CCETSW *Discussion Document* (1973) gives figures of 89,838 children in 3,240 residential establishments (residential nurseries, children's homes, reception centres, remand homes, approved/training schools, special schools, hostels for working children) with 20,737 staff.

2   (a) Confirmed in recent correspondence with Miss S. Clement Brown, one of the few surviving members of the Curtis Committee.

(b) Early evidence of increased popularity of foster-care is available in the *Seventh Report on the Work of the Children's Department*, HMSO, November 1955. In England & Wales, at end November 1949, 35 per cent of children in care of local authorities were boarded out; at end November 1954, 44 per cent were boarded out—a remarkable increase considering the substantial rise in the total number of children in care during that period. The impetus to board out came largely from the Children Act, 1948, Section 13(1) which placed a duty on local authorities to board out every child in their care, unless this was 'not practicable or desirable for the time being'. Also the Seventh Report (p. 11) states that between May 1951 and the end of 1954, about 130 large long-stay children's homes were closed; about 200 small 'family group homes' (more akin to foster-care than to institutional care) were opened.

3   The phrase coined by C. H. Kempe *et al.* in July 1962.

4   E.g. *From Birth to Seven*; Davie, Butler and Goldstein (1972) is one of many books emerging from the National Child Development Study (1958 Cohort) combining a medical, social and educational approach.

5   B. Akhurst (1972) quotes several studies showing the high level of mental, physical, emotional and social disorders found in children in care.

Also Beedell (1970, pp. 6-7) describes the likely incidence of disturbance amongst a group of twenty children in residential care.

6 E.g. Dockar-Drysdale (1968a) implies the influence of Bettelheim in daily life at the Mulberry Bush School; Ziegler (1972) describes milieu therapy in Norway.

7 E.g. Bayley (1973, ch. 15) describes the daily grind experienced by parents of mentally handicapped adults living at home.

8 For historical accounts, see Carlebach (1970) or Balbernie (1966/73, ch. 2).

9 E.g. Crellin, Pringle and West's study (1971) of children born illegitimately; Seglow, Pringle and Wedge's study (1972) of adopted children; particularly Kadushin's work (1970) on the adoption of older children.

10 Demonstrated in James and Joyce Robertson's films of Kate, Jane, Thomas, Lucy—young children in foster-care during brief separation experiences.

11 Beedell (1970, pp. 9-15) outlines a 'sample day' in a reception centre.

12 Endorsed for example by Axline (1966); Berry (1972a, chs 1, 2, 3, 4); Wolff (1969) and by many more.

13 C. Winnicott (1964/70, pp. 29-30) also says acceptance involves an active effort by the worker 'to reach behind the delinquent act and the deceitful language to the suffering in the human being which causes the symptoms which we see'.

14 Ibid. (pp. 9-10). Although both residential and fieldworkers are concerned with past, present and future aspects of children's lives, the point here is that a fieldworker often has to take precipitate action in emergency and then tries to help the child through discussion afterwards.

Chapter 2 Outline of the study

1 Dockar-Drysdale (1973, p. 41) suggests that students may use theoretical knowledge as a defence against having real residential experience and that this is more likely to happen if they are being supervised from outside the unit (c.f. Mattinson, 1968; also Rigby, 1972).

2 K. Jones (1967, p. 10) uses this phrase to describe several recent studies (e.g. Goffman's Asylums) criticizing institutional organization to an extent likely to undermine staff.

3 Heraud (1966, pp. 13-16) studied experiences of fifty-five students (men and women, aged 19-46) in two-month residential placements; three-quarters were apprehensive but only 15 per cent continued dissatisfied. Irrespective of age or length of previous experience, 11 per cent had bad experiences during placements; 44 per cent had mixed feelings; 45 per cent had good experiences. Important factors were whether they felt welcome on arrival; whether they appreciated links between theory and practice, and particularly whether they enjoyed good relationships with their supervisor in the unit.

4 (a) Davies, Best and B. Jones (1966, pp. 53-63)—a social worker, housemother and housefather—discuss the advantages and disadvantages of 'family group homes'.

(b) Brill and Thomas (1964, part 2) describe the broad range of types of residential provision for children and adolescents.

(c) Richardson (1969) deals specifically with adolescent girls in approved schools.

5 See note 5 for chapter 1 mentioning the work of Beedell and Akhurst.

6 The Williams Committee Report survey (1967) shows a ratio of staff

to children of 1:4 in children's homes; 3:2 in reception centres; 1:4·8 in hostels.

7 (a) *Ibid*. In this survey, boys in children's homes outnumbered girls by 3:2.

(b) Capes, Gould and Townsend (1971) made a five-year study of the psychiatric treatment, schooling and care of 153 adolescents in Wessex (104 boys, 49 girls); a major finding was the long history of disturbance, usually from before the age of five years.

(c) Seglow, Pringle and Wedge (1972, pp. 144-7) show that although adopted children compare very favourably with others in the National Child Development Study (1958 Cohort), adopted boys showed a higher incidence of maladjustment than either adopted girls, or boys in the whole cohort.

(d) Evidence in a paper by Wolkind and Rutter (1973).

8 E.g. Irvine (1967) believes that 'hard-to-like families' need more than good-enough parenting from the worker; as with the maladjusted child in residential care 'they now need a parental figure who will be more understanding ... more patient than the majority of parents are, once earliest infancy is over'. Other examples: Wolff (1969, p. 226); Beedell (1970, p. 21); Flint (1967, ch. 16).

9 Kraak (1961 or 1967, pp. 156-7) studied methods of punishment in children's homes in Germany—an additional item in his list (c.f. mine), is ridicule. Trained staff more often punished by isolation and less often by sending to bed; staff aged under thirty used less corporal punishment and more often related the punishment to the offence.

10 Children in care under Section 1 of the Children Act, 1948; Fit Person Orders and Approved School Orders are replaced by Care Orders under the Children and Young Persons Act, 1969.

11 The higher success rate of very young children in long-term foster-care is a major finding of Parker (1966) confirmed by George (1970, p. 190).

12 E.g. Ferguson (1966)—a study of young adults earlier in foster-care, compared with Davis and Heimler's study (1967) of a small group of adults earlier in care of Barnardo's Homes.

13 George (1970, pp. 186-8) cannot give a precise indication of the risks involved in foster-placements of siblings together but stresses that such placements require very great care. Rowe and Lambert (1973, pp. 64, 71-2, 96) found the obstacle to placement most frequently mentioned was siblings.

14 Parker (1971) stresses the importance of exploring the complex reasons why comparatively little long-term planning for children in care actually takes place. See also L. Davis (1971).

15 George (1970, ch. 5) found a discrepancy between theory and practice in that workers often failed to include parents and/or children in discussion of plans. See also Keyte (1974), and Thorpe (1974).

16 A major finding of Rowe and Lambert (1973) was that 22 per cent of their sample (of 2,812 children aged under 11 in care for more than six months) were awaiting placement in a substitute family.

17 Evident in J. and J. Robertson's film series of *Young Children in Brief Separation*, 1967-73. Also Robertson (1958/70, 1971).

18 D. Winnicott (1957, p. 114) observes that children in group care are often content to let one of their number represent them in testing out the staff, thus proving to the group that the unit can contain them. See also Redl (1966, part 3).

19 Conway (1957 or 1967, pp. 137-40) studied 220 children in an orphanage;

houseparents were asked whether or not they had a good relationship with each child. Houseparents (mostly unmarried and untrained) gave more favourable assessments than teachers. Amongst older children, lengthy stay and being reconciled to separation from home were associated with good relationships. Houseparents' assessments of relationships reflected their own personality differences as well as those of the children. Heal, Sinclair and Troop (1973) studied the differing perceptions of residents. Triseliotis (1973) deals with relationships in adoptive families.

20 (a) Stanley (1954) observed the main causes of friction amongst children in a small home, rating them in this order: personal needs, lack of privacy, shared playthings, possessions, boy-girl rivalry, interruption of games.

(b) Ingram (1961b) points out that although foster-care may make more intimate emotional demands, group life is stressful for children as well as for staff.

(c) Dockar-Drysdale (1973, pp. 34-40) emphasizes that 'unintegrated children' are highly disruptive to the group, and a few such children are likely to be found in any residential unit other than ordinary boarding-schools.

21 Wills (1971, pp. 15-19, 25-9) describes vicious subcultures characteristically found amongst inmates who parody the staff in punitive institutions. Polsky (1962, 1970) depicts the pervasive influence of the inmate subculture. H. Jones (1960) uses a sociometric approach.

22 (a) The Williams Report survey (1967) found that 80 per cent of all staff in children's homes were women; two-thirds single women but decreasing in availability. Further findings (relevant later in this chapter and in chapter 4): The average home replaced one-third of its staff during the preceding year. Privacy was the least satisfactory aspect of staff accommodation. Seventy per cent of all full-time care staff were without formal qualifications. Some recommendations: Rules and restrictions for staff should be minimal; experiment with use of non-resident staff; training is essential; supervision should be provided.

(b) Henry (1965) and J. Davies (1961) write about the value of male residential workers.

(c) Clement Brown (1957, 1958 or 1967) studied the selection, training, and subsequent career at least two years later of 147 residential child care staff. About half had been in only one post since qualifying. Trained staff spent a slightly longer time in one job; single men changed jobs most frequently and married couples least frequently. Further findings (relevant later in chapters 2 and 4): 37·3 per cent of those qualified, including a high proportion of married couples, were rated Group I (good) for their work; 49 per cent Group II and 13·7 per cent Group III. About 80 per cent proved at least as good as expected at selection. Of single women, a larger proportion of Groups I and III had left the work, mainly because of the narrow life, lack of emotional satisfaction, or physical exhaustion. Staff relationships was the main reason given by single men for leaving jobs later. Views of past students on training: 48 per cent thought highly of it (including more Group I subjects); 33 per cent quite favourable; 19 per cent very critical. The commonest criticism was that classroom teaching was not related closely enough to the actual work. In placements while training, staff relationships was the most important factor; 42 per cent of single women mentioned staff being helpful; 38 per cent said staff were hostile or unsympathetic to children. Of homes used for placements, 8 per cent were later criticized as shocking by students whose judgment was considered reliable. Some of thirty-five specific recommendations: married couples appear to be the best investment but need special help in rearing their own children. The early years of employment are crucial: sympathetic discussions, meetings, etc. help junior staff to feel valued. Staff relationships appear to be all important: two sources of dissatisfaction are low status of assistants, and hostility between trained and untrained staff. The latter might be eased by having someone from headquarters available for consultation.

23   The Williams Report (1967) makes recommendations on working conditions. Also Potts (1965) studied eighty-eight trainees currently in training with an average of four years previous experience; fifty considered salaries adequate—their comments mostly stressed the need for more free time for staff. Hulley (1973) discusses staff accommodation. See also Hazel (1968).

24   Monsky (1963 or 1967) studied attitudes of present residential staff (528 women) and ex-staff (309 women) plus 125 children's officers to find reasons for heavy staff wastage. Children's officers said continuity was the most valuable attribute in staff; that most suggestions for improvement, except better staff communications, would increase costs; that during one year 37 per cent of residential posts fell vacant (half being losses to the service rather than transfers). Most current staff found the work worse than expected but 64 per cent would have taken the job anyway. Trained staff appeared very slightly more permissive than untrained staff. Assistants described housemothers as much less permissive than the latter believed themselves to be; assistants were less likely to leave democratic housemothers. Relative importance of problems: first, long hours and lack of privacy (more important than salary), then difficult children, and losing children to foster-homes; 25 per cent were dissatisfied with relationships with the Children's Department. Stayers compared to leavers: leavers were younger, more likely to be married with children; a majority were rated satisfactory by children's officers. Stayers tended to be more authoritarian, and to find adults harder to get on with than children. Ex-staff reported less permissiveness than current staff; assistants were far more likely to have left an authoritarian home; ex-housemothers were more permissive than current. Nearly half of all leavers had left during their first year; about half felt something could have been done to help them stay. Of all staff, 85 per cent thought changes could reduce wastage; their main recommendations all concerned staff relations. One of Monsky's recommendations is that staff communications should be improved by appointing someone in the Department solely to help staff and to arrange group discussions.

25   The Discussion Document, *Training for Residential Work* (CCETSW, February 1973) recommends a single pattern of training for residential staff and fieldworkers, with training provision at two levels; all staff should have the right to training advice. (This is confirmed in the subsequent Report, CCETSW Paper no. 3, November 1973.)

26   *Ibid.*, pp. 8-9. Over the past twenty-five years, a total of 6,184 staff received the CRCCYP, the Senior CRCCYP and recently the CRSW; the total still working may be only about 2,000. Current qualification figures are available for approximately 8,500 residential staff (in homes for people of all ages); of these about 15 per cent are trained child care staff. Of the 8,500, 23 per cent have some relevant training (i.e. in residential social work, in-

service study, teaching, nursing etc.); at least 62 per cent of staff are without any form of qualification or training.

27 *Ibid.*, appendix IV gives a history of rapid developments in training for residential work, starting in 1946 with the Interim Report of the Curtis Committee on Training in Child Care.

28 The Central Training Council in Child Care issued a Report (1972) on Criteria for Selection for Qualifying Residential Child Care Courses; p. 20 emphasizes the need for careful selection; p. 23 the complex motivation of applicants.

29 (a) As early as 1957 in the Report of the European Seminar on Training of Personnel for Children's Institutions (Director, Miss Clement Brown), it was recognized that training requires to be followed by personal supervision during the early years of employment.

(b) Mehringer (1959) explains that, just as ordinary parents need to discuss together the problems of bringing up their children, residential workers need to discuss difficulties as they arise.

(c) Also C. Winnicott (1964/70, pp. 37-9); Dockar-Drysdale (1973); Hodder (1968); RCCA Study Group (1969, pp. 28-9); Towle (1945/73, part 3).

30 (a) Timms and Itzin (1962) questioned small samples of child care officers, foster-parents and residential staff about the role of child care officers; replies revealed some confusion, and a very wide range of expectations.

(b) R. Parker (1967) believes residential staff need more support internally and externally; field staff are overloaded, so visits to homes receive low priority.

Chapter 3 Daily life for the children

1 Towle (1945/73, part 2); RCCA Study Group (1969); also Berry (1972a, pp. 2-3) quotes Etzioni (1968) in arguing for the usefulness of the concept of basic human needs whilst recognizing that this concept is controversial, being considered unproductive by many sociologists.

2 Although consensus of opinion through experience may suggest that there is more nutritional value in food eaten in a pleasant emotional climate, it is not easy to discover definite evidence. Numerous colleagues have been consulted (in the University of Sheffield Departments of Sociology, Psychology, Psychiatry, Human Biology and Anatomy) but it seems the academic question must be approached somewhat indirectly, often in terms of extreme conditions such as obesity or dwarfism. Relevant references appear to be Bruch (1973), Schachter (1973); a treatise on the stomach offers some clues (Wolf, 1965); also four references all mentioned by Rutter (1972, pp. 92-9) are Patton and Gardner (1963), Provence and Lipton (1962), Silver and Finkelstein (1967) and Widdowson (1951). The latter is most pertinent in describing two orphanages in Germany, concluding that psychological stresses due to harsh and unsympathetic handling may seriously curtail growth rates—the attitudes of children's supervisors seemed more significant than their dietary supplements. Miller (1964, pp. 178-81) says it was possible in his therapeutic hostel catering for young, institutionalized delinquents 'to pinpoint tension by the milk consumption taken on a daily basis'. Two further papers are first Lowenberg (1968) writing in practical terms as a consultant in nutrition to children's services in the USA; she emphasizes the emotional significance of food and how adults may set the stage for successful eating by associating children's food with pleasure. Second, Wood-

mansey (1967) inquires into the causes and prevention of functional disorders of defecation; successful treatment depended on helping parents with emotional problems in relation to their children—it seems reasonable to suppose therefore that both ends of the alimentary canal may be sensitive to the prevailing emotional climate. Undoubtedly the boy later in this chapter who was sick after being forced to eat swedes derived little nutriment from that particular meal.

3 Evocative descriptions of parent-figures' reactions to criticism of their food are provided by the Newsons (1963, pp. 32-67; 1968, ch. 8) and by Stevenson (1965, pp. 52-3; 1972, p. 11). Slater (1969) describes a similar phenomenon amongst elderly residents, and Berry (1972b, p. 431) amongst newcomers of all ages to residential care.

4 The Newsons (1968, ch. 10; E. Newson, 1972) are impressed by the extent to which many parents, in the privacy of their own homes, are prepared to meet their children more than half-way by responding to requests for rituals, some of which might appear slightly ridiculous to an outsider.

5 E. Newson (1972, pp. 30-3) observes how parents, in striking such a bargain, uphold a dual role as advocates of society's demands and as defenders of the child against those same demands within the privacy of his family.

6 References (e.g. Kahn and Nursten, 1968, pp. 46-7) hint that children living away from home tend to find less difficulty in attending day school; this is not to say that long-term removal from home is an appropriate solution to the problem.

7 S. Parker (1971) illustrates the premium placed on leisure nowadays. References slanted specifically to leisure activities in residential child care include Brill and Thomas (1964, ch. 7), RCCA Review (1967), Vincent (1968, pp. 83-8), Ingram (1961a), Redl (1972), Redl and Wineman (1952/65, ch. 2), Styrt and Styrt (1972), Green and Clark (1972), Flint (1967, ch. 7). Oswin (1971) studies the empty hours of mentally handicapped children in institutions.

8 Burn (1956, pp. 29, 38, 60-1) illustrates an extraordinary range of activities chosen by Mr Lyward's boys. The therapeutic value of animals is discussed by Berry (1960), Levinson (1972), Vincent (1968, p. 88).

9 Beedell (1970-1) describes a more positive experiment offering super-vised, spontaneous activities in the cellar of a reception centre.

10 Additional references on the theme of daily life and routines in resi-dential child care include Burmeister (1949, 1960), Brill and Thomas (1964, chs 5, 6), Vincent (1968), Flint (1967, ch. 6), Lennhoff and Lampen (1968), Redl (1966), Redl and Wineman (1952/65), Trieschman, Whittaker and Brendtro (1969), Whittaker and Trieschman (1972), Wills (1970), ACCC (1970). Similarly, Bayley (1973, ch. 15) describes daily care at home of mentally handicapped adults; Hanson (1972) observes routines in an old people's home round the clock. Douglas (1971) edits papers on understanding everyday life on a broader sociological basis. Finally, the recent work of Tizard *et al.* is relevant (1971, 1972, 1974).

11 Although children in classifying and remand centres may be in resi-dential care for only brief periods, theories about the susceptibility to influence of people in crisis-situations suggest that short-term residential care could carry lasting significance in these circumstances—Parad (1965), G. Caplan (1961), RCCA Study Group (1969, para. 20).

12 Capes, Gould and Townsend (1971) discuss the incidence, care and treat-ment of children who 'act out' their problems; also Dockar-Drysdale (1968a,

1973), Miller (1964), Redl and Wineman (1952/65).

13   Wills (1971) discusses effective treatment of bullying; more specifically Mercurio (1972) studied caning as an educational rite and tradition from the viewpoints of schoolmasters, pupils and parents. Johnston, Savitz and Wolfgang (1970) edited papers on the sociology of punishment and correction.

14   The Newsons (1968, pp. 476-82) discuss varying parental responses to temper-tantrums in four-year-old children; Kemp (1971) describes how parents visiting their children (in a residential centre) for substantial periods weekly can learn alongside staff how to handle temper-outbursts more constructively. Pringle (1972-3) discusses the roots of violence and vandalism.

15   References to behaviour modification include Jehu (1967, 1968, 1972), Beech (1969), Cohen and Filipczak (1971), Eron, Walder and Lefkowitz (1971), Krasner and Atthowe (1971), Ullmann and Krasner (1965), Pizzat (1973).

16   This is a bold statement : evidence is available in Woodmansey's papers (especially 1971a) and in his references to former studies; also Wills (1971), Newson (1968 and studies not yet published), Redl and Wineman (1952/65), Helfer and Kempe (1968, 1971), Rochlin (1973), Burton (1968, 1973). Equally convincing evidence from a behavioural approach is provided by Eron, Walder and Lefkowitz (1971), who studied the learning of aggression in over 800 children during a five-year period.

17   Bernstein (1971, 1973) has developed theories about 'elaborated' and 'restricted' codes of language which he sees as crucial in the context of children's socialization. His work is discussed by the Newsons (1968, ch. 14), Day (1972, ch. 4), Berry (1972a, pp. 44-6) amongst others, and adversely criticized by H. Rosen (1972).

18   The concept of 'stern love' is mentioned for instance by Burn (1956, p. 59), Wills (1970, p. 18) though in these contexts it is similar to Bowlby's phrase of 'firm yet friendly intervention'.

19   A. Rosen (1971) found unanimous agreement amongst thirty-three houseparents that children in residential care are 'over-protected' in some important ways. Burton (1968, 1973) describes characteristics of injury-prone children.

20   The ideas outlined towards the end of this chapter are developed in Woodmansey's papers (particularly 1966).

Chapter 4   Daily life for the care-givers

1   Bernstein (1971, 1973), Berry (1972a, pp. 44-6), Day (1972, ch. 4), etc., again questioned by H. Rosen (1972). See also Cicourel, and Speier, in papers edited by Douglas (1971).

2   In Woodmansey's papers (particularly 1966, 1969, 1971a) and others quoted by him; Helfer and Kempe (1968, 1971), Burton (1968), Wills (1971), Eron, Walder and Lefkowitz (1971), Pringle (1972-3).

3   *The Borrowers,* by Mary Norton, p. 1.

4   At the European Seminar (1957, pp. 57-8) Miss Clement Brown said that the greatest single influence upon whether residential staff settle down is not whether they can tolerate children but whether they can get on with one another. She quoted Aichhorn (1925) : 'The attitude of the worker towards the leader determines itself the relationship between the worker and the child', and went on to speculate whether training courses could include aspects designed to help reduce staff tensions on the job.

Wills (1971) describes graphically the inter-personal vulnerabilities of residential workers.

5 For example, Heraud (1966), Clement Brown (1958), Monsky (1963), Potts (1965). Also S. Parker (1971), a sociologist writing in general terms about work and leisure, refers specifically to residential social workers (pp. 85-90).

6 The development of a single pattern of training for field and residential social workers was both a central issue in the Discussion Document (CCETSW, February 1973) and a major recommendation in the Report (CCETSW, November 1973). See also Bartlett (1970).

7 This different kind of emotional investment can be compared with E. Newson's comment (1972, p. 31) about the confusion arising from the different kind of relationships a child has with parents and teacher. The child's teacher may appear to parents to have magical powers in calming temper-tantrums but a simpler explanation is that children are less likely to have tantrums in less intimate company.

8 Perlman (1968) says that parenthood requires a basic, consistent, continuous willingness to give or lend oneself to the nurture and protection of another.

9 Sawdy (1974, pp. 731-2) records a national meeting of social work students, whose 'biggest complaint was the common experience of being "caseworked" in the name of training'. Students felt that tutors are reluctant to consider the political nature of social work and have an unfortunate tendency to resort to 'casework techniques' (in the form of unwelcome 'insight-giving'?) when faced by negative responses of any sort. Yelloly (1972, ch. 5) reviews the concept of insight.

10 Leader (1966, p. 77): 'Some workers openly expressed their anxiety about using the agency's executive staff as consultants for fear of being "evaluated" ... more workers than we had anticipated have shied away from consultation.' Ranjan (1970) describes an experiment in Ontario where social workers and residential workers discussed the latter's day-to-day problems with residents. Questionnaires showed that 86 per cent of respondents (residential workers) found social workers easily accessible and co-operative; 83 per cent found it helpful to discuss problems with them; 80 per cent felt social workers and themselves met on an equal footing. Residential workers were feeling less fatalistic about the value of consultation but had not yet overcome their initial suspicions.

11 ACCC (1971, Discussion Paper 5) deals with the implications of participation in these and other types of groups during professional training, from the viewpoints of tutors and students. Paper 3 in the same collection discusses residential placements. Other references include Kydd (1970-1), Ottaway (1970-1). Gibbs (1968, ch. 6) mentions difficulties arising when the children's therapist is also a senior administrator within the residential unit; presumably similar factors would affect a staff support-group whose leader was also a senior colleague within the unit. Also Kahn and Thompson (1970).

12 References on the fieldwork supervision of students include Kent (1969), Pettes (1967), Towle (1945/73, ch. 7), Young (1967).

13 In addition to the chorus in the text, others include the European Seminar Report (1957), Irvine (1959, 1964), Mehringer (1959), R. Parker (1967), Beedell (1970), Hodder (1968), Ranjan (1970), Riley (1958/68) writing through direct experience of group consultation enhancing her daily work, and Ainsworth (1971) describing the plight of prison staff.

14 Numbers involved in future expansion are estimated in CCETSW docu-

ments (February and November 1973). At present less than 4 per cent of existing 65,000 residential staff (working with children and older people) have had a relevant social work training. If, by 1980, only 25 per cent of the likely staff establishment is to be trained (possibly at two levels) there will need to be at least 8,000 students in training at any one time. 'We estimate that at least 700 tutors will be required and many more teacher/ practitioners' (November 1973, paras 223, 228).

15 Organization in terms of 'life-space' is discussed in detail by Beedell (1970), Redl and Wineman (1952/65), Whittaker and Trieschman (1972), ACCC (1970).

16 Para. 41 of the CCETSW Paper (November 1973) suggests that residential workers, because of their special experience of non-verbal methods of communication, would (when trained jointly with other kinds of social workers) be able to contribute to fieldworkers' understanding of the daily pressures experienced by relatives caring for handicapped children/adults in their own homes.

Bibliography

ADVISORY COUNCIL ON CHILD CARE (1970) *Care and Treatment in a Planned Environment: a Report on the Community Homes Project*.

ADVISORY COUNCIL ON CHILD CARE (1971) *Fieldwork Training for Social Work* (Paper 3: *The Residential Placement*. Paper 5: *Working with Groups*).

AICHHORN, A. (1925) *Wayward Youth*, London, Imago.

AINSWORTH, F. (1971) 'Attitudes and resources within the penal institution', *Social Work Today*, 1, 10, January.

AKHURST, B. (1972) 'The effects of long stay care', *Concern*, no. 9, National Children's Bureau.

ANTHONY, J. (1968a) 'Other people's children', in *Children in Care*, ed R. J. N. Tod.

—— (1968b) 'Group therapeutic techniques for residential units', in *Disturbed Children*, ed R. J. N. Tod.

AXLINE, V. (1966) *Dibs: in Search of Self*, Harmondsworth, Penguin.

BALBERNIE, R. (1966/73) *Residential Work with Children*, Oxford, Pergamon.

—— (1973) 'The management of an evolving care system', in *Residential Establishments* (Conference Report), University of Dundee.

BALINT, M. (1957) *The Doctor, his Patient and the Illness*, London, Pitman.

BARKER, M. (1970) 'Education for social work: a teacher's viewpoint', *Social Work Today*, 1, 9, December.

BARKER, P. (1970) 'Conversations with a child', *Child Care News*, no. 98, May.

BARTLETT, H. (1970) *The Common Base of Social Work Practice*, New York, National Association of Social Workers.

BAYLEY, M. (1973) *Mental Handicap and Community Care*, London, Routledge & Kegan Paul.

BEECH, H. (1969) *Changing Man's Behaviour*, Harmondsworth, Penguin.

BEEDELL, C. (1968) 'The residential setting and the worker's task within it', *Annual Review Residential Child Care Association, 16*, pp. 65-73.
—— (1970) *Residential Life with Children*, London, Routledge & Kegan Paul.
—— (1970-1) 'Provision for play groups in a reception centre', in *Groups*, RCCA Review, *18*, pp. 107-33.
BERNE, E. (1964) *Games People Play*, Harmondsworth, Penguin.
BERNSTEIN, B. (1971) *Class, Codes and Control*, vol. 1, London, Routledge & Kegan Paul.
—— (1973) *Class, Codes and Control*, vol. 2, London, Routledge & Kegan Paul.
BERRY, J. (1960) 'Therapeutic farming?', *Case Conference, 6*, 9, March.
—— (1969) 'The use of humour in social work', *Case Conference, 16*, 6, October.
—— (1972a) *Social Work with Children*, London, Routledge & Kegan Paul.
—— (1972b) 'The experience of reception into residential care', *British Journal of Social Work, 2*, 4.
—— (1973) 'The authenticity of parenthood by adoption', *Child Adoption, 73*, 3.
BETTELHEIM, B. (1950/71) *Love is not Enough*, London, Collier-Macmillan/Avon.
—— (1962) *Dialogues with Mothers*, London, Collier-Macmillan.
BOSS, P. (1971) *Exploration into Child Care*, London, Routledge & Kegan Paul.
BOWLBY, J. (1958) 'Psychoanalysis and child care', in *Psychoanalysis and Contemporary Thought*, ed J. Sutherland, London, Hogarth.
—— (1973) *Separation, Anger and Anxiety*, London, Hogarth.
BRILL, K. and THOMAS, R. (1964) *Children in Homes*, London, Gollancz.
BRITTON, J. (1970) *Language and Learning*, Harmondsworth, Penguin.
BRUCH, H. (1973) *Eating Disorders*, London, Routledge & Kegan Paul.
BURMEISTER, E. (1949) *Forty-five in the Family*, New York, Columbia University Press.
—— (1960) *The Professional Houseparent*, New York, Columbia University Press.
BURN, M. (1956) *Mr Lyward's Answer*, London, Hamish Hamilton.
BURTON, L. (1968) *Vulnerable Children*, London, Routledge & Kegan Paul.
—— (1973) 'Injury-prone children', in *Stresses in Children*, ed V. Varma.
CAPES, M., GOULD, E. and TOWNSEND, M. (1971) *Stress in Youth*, for Nuffield Provincial Hospitals Trust, London, Oxford University Press.
CAPLAN, G. (1961) *An Approach to Community Mental Health*, London, Tavistock Publications.
—— (1970) *The Theory and Practice of Mental Health Consultation*, London, Tavistock Publications.

BIBLIOGRAPHY

CAPLAN, R. (1972) *Helping the Helpers to Help: Mental Health Consultation to Aid Clergymen in Pastoral Work*, New York, Seabury Press.

CARLEBACH, J. (1970) *Caring for Children in Trouble*, London, Routledge & Kegan Paul.

CENTRAL COUNCIL FOR EDUCATION AND TRAINING IN SOCIAL WORK (1973) *Discussion Document on Training for Residential Work*, February 1973.

—— (1973) *Social Work: Residential Work is a Part of Social Work* (report of working party on education for residential social work), CCETSW Paper 3, November 1973.

CENTRAL TRAINING COUNCIL IN CHILD CARE (1972) *Report: Criteria for Selection for Qualifying Residential Child Care Courses.*

CICOUREL, A. (1971) 'The acquisition of social structure: toward a developmental sociology of language and meaning', in *Understanding Everyday Life*, ed J. Douglas.

CLEMENT BROWN, S. (1957) 'Training for residential work', *Child Care, 11*, 1, pp. 14-18.

—— (1958) 'The training of houseparents for work in children's homes', unpublished thesis, Nuffield College, Oxford (abstract in Dinnage and Pringle, 1967, pp. 191-5).

COHEN, H. and FILIPCZAK, J. (1971) 'Programming educational behaviour for institutionalized adolescents', in *Behavioural Intervention in Human Problems*, ed H. Rickard.

CONWAY, E. (1957) 'The institutional care of children—a case history', Ph.D. thesis, University of London (abstract in Dinnage and Pringle, 1967, pp. 137-40).

CRELLIN, E., PRINGLE, M. L. K. and WEST, P. (1971) *Born Illegitimate*, London, National Foundation for Educational Research.

CTCCC/CCETSW (1972) *Developing Residential Student Supervision*, July.

CURTIS REPORT (1946) Report of the Care of Children Committee, Cmd 6922, HMSO.

DAVIE, R., BUTLER, N. and GOLDSTEIN, H. (1972) *From Birth to Seven*, London, Longman and National Children's Bureau.

DAVIES, J. (1961) 'Father and the deprived child', *Child Care, 15*, 4.

——, BEST, K. and JONES, B. (1966) 'Family group homes—a trilogy', *Child Care, 20*, 2.

DAVIS, L. (1971) 'Recommendation, placement and provision: reception centre survey', *Social Work Today, 1*, 10, January.

DAVIS, N. and HEIMLER, E. (1967) 'An experiment in the assessment of social function', *The Medical Officer, 3052, 117*, 3, pp. 31-2.

DAY, P. (1972) *Communication in Social Work*, Oxford, Pergamon.

DINNAGE, R. and PRINGLE, M. L. K. (1967) *Residential Child Care—Facts and Fallacies*, London, Longman.

DOCKAR-DRYSDALE, B. (1968a) *Therapy in Child Care*, London, Longman.

—— (1968b) 'The problem of making adaptation to the needs of the individual child in a group', in *Disturbed Children*, ed R. J. N. Tod.

—— (1973) *Consultation in Child Care*, London, Longman.

DOUGLAS, J. (ed) (1971) *Understanding Everyday Life*, London, Routledge & Kegan Paul.

ERON, L., WALDER, L. and LEFKOWITZ, M. (1971) *Learning of Aggression in Children*, Boston, Little & Brown.

ETZIONI, A. (1968) 'Basic human needs, alienation and inauthenticity', *American Sociological Review*, *33*, 6, December, pp. 870-85.

EUROPEAN SEMINAR REPORT (1957), *Training of Personnel for Children's Institutions* (Director: Miss S. Clement Brown), United Nations, Geneva.

FERGUSON, T. (1966) *Children in Care—and After*, London, Oxford University Press.

FLINT, B. (1967) *The Child and the Institution*, London University Press.

GEORGE, V. (1970) *Foster Care: Theory and Practice*, London, Routledge & Kegan Paul.

GIBBS, J. (1968) *Patterns of Residential Care for Children*, National Children's Home Convocation Lecture.

GOFFMAN, E. (1961) *Asylums*, Harmondsworth, Penguin.

GOLDSTEIN, J., FREUD, A. and SOLNIT, A. (1973) *Beyond the Best Interests of the Child*, New York, Free Press.

GREEN, R. and CLARK, W. (1972) 'Therapeutic recreation for aggressive children in residential treatment', in *Children Away from Home*, ed J. Whittaker and A. Trieschman.

HALL, H. (1965) 'Building and design of children's homes', *Annual Review of the Residential Child Care Association*, *13*.

HANSON, J. (1972) *Residential Care Observed*, London, Age Concern/ National Old People's Welfare Council.

HARRISON, P. (1974) 'The old under control—a case study', *New Society*, *27*, 591, pp. 249-52.

HAZEL, N. (1968) 'Institutional care—for whose benefit?', *Case Conference*, *15*, 3, July.

HEAL, K., SINCLAIR, I. and TROOP, J. (1973) 'Development of a social climate questionnaire for use in approved schools and community homes', *British Journal of Sociology*, *24*, 2, June.

HELFER, R. and KEMPE, C. H. (eds) (1968) *The Battered Child*, Chicago University Press.

—— (1971) *Helping the Battered Child and his Family*, Chicago University Press.

HENRY, R. (1965) 'The man in residential child care', *Annual Review of the Residential Child Care Association*, *13*, pp. 52-7.

HERAUD, B. (1966) 'Students in institutions: a survey', *The Child in Care*, September, pp. 13-16 (or *Case Conference*, *13*, 7).

HEYWOOD, J. (1959) *Children in Care*, London, Routledge & Kegan Paul.

—— (1969) 'Childhood and Society 100 Years Ago', National Children's Home Convocation Lecture.

HITCHMAN, J. (1960) *The King of the Barbareens*, Harmondsworth, Penguin.

HODDER, J. (1968) 'The residential task—the role of the residential services adviser in the support of houseparents', *Child in Care*, February.

HOME OFFICE (1955) *Seventh Report on the Work of the Children's Department*, HMSO.

HOME OFFICE (1971) *Absconding from Approved Schools*, Home Office Research Unit Report.

HULLEY, T. (1973) 'No home from home', *New Society*, 25, 571, 13 September.

INGRAM, E. (1961a) 'Play and leisure time in the children's home', *Case Conference*, 7, 7, January (also in *Children in Care*, ed R. J. N. Tod).

—— (1961b) 'Living together in the children's home', *Case Conference*, 7, 8, February.

IRVINE, E. (1959) 'The use of small group discussions in the teaching of human relations', *British Journal of Psychiatric Social Work*, 5, 1.

—— (1964) 'Mental health education in the community', *British Journal of Psychiatric Social Work*, 7, 3.

—— (1967) 'The hard-to-like family', *Case Conference*, 14, 3, July.

JEHU, D. (1967) *Learning Theory and Social Work*, London, Routledge & Kegan Paul.

—— (1968) 'Childhood phobias—treatment in residential settings', *Child Care Quarterly Review*, 22, 3, July.

—— et al. (1972) *Behaviour Modification in Social Work*, London, Wiley-Interscience.

JOHNSTON, N., SAVITZ, L. and WOLFGANG, M. (eds) (1970) *The Sociology of Punishment and Correction*, New York, Wiley.

JONES, H. (1960) *Reluctant Rebels*, London, Tavistock Publications.

JONES, K. (1967) 'The development of institutional care', in *New Thinking about Institutional Care*, Association of Social Workers.

—— (1972) 'Better services for the mentally handicapped', in *The Year Book of Social Policy in 1971*, London, Routledge & Kegan Paul.

—— (1974) 'Violence and the mentally handicapped', *New Society*, 27, 591, pp. 247-9.

KADUSHIN, A. (1970) *Adopting Older Children*, New York, Columbia University Press.

KAHN, J. and NURSTEN, J. (1968) *Unwillingly to School*, Oxford, Pergamon.

—— and THOMPSON, S. (1970) *The Group Process as a Helping Technique*, Oxford, Pergamon.

KATZ, R. (1963) *Empathy: its Nature and Uses*, New York, Free Press.

KAY, N. (1971) 'Foster parents as resources', in *Social Work in Foster Care*, ed R. J. N. Tod.

KEMP, C. (1971) 'Family treatment within the milieu of a residential treatment center', *Journal of the Child Welfare League of America*, 50, 4, April.

KEMPE, C. H. et al. (1962) 'The battered child syndrome', *Journal of the American Medical Association*, 181, 1, pp. 17-24.

KENT, B. (1969) *Social Work Supervision in Practice*, Oxford, Pergamon.

KEYTE, M. (1974) 'Caring', *Social Work Today*, 5, 1, April.

KING, R., RAYNES, N. and TIZARD, J. (1971) *Patterns of Residential Care*, London, Routledge & Kegan Paul.

KONOPKA, G. (1968) 'Effective communication with adolescents in institutions', in *Children in Care*, ed R. J. N. Tod.

KRAAK, B. (1961) 'Die Praxis des Strafens im Heim' (abstract in Dinnage and Pringle, 1967, pp. 156-7).

KRASNER, L. and ATTHOWE, J. (1971) 'The token economy as a rehabilitative procedure in a mental hospital setting', in *Behavioural Intervention in Human Problems*, ed H. Rickard.

KRAUSE, K. (1974) 'Authoritarianism, dogmatism and coercion in child caring institutions: a study of staff attitudes', *Journal of the Child Welfare League of America*, 53, 1, January, pp. 23-30.

KYDD, R. (1970-1) 'The residential child care course as an educational community', in *Groups*, Annual Review of the Residential Child Care Association, 18, pp. 143-8.

LAMBERT, D. (1968) 'Residential staff and their children', *Annual Review of the Residential Child Care Association*, 16, pp. 46-57.

LEADER, A. (1966) 'A new program of case consultation', in *Supervision and Staff Development*, New York, Family Service Association of America.

LENNHOFF, F. and LAMPEN, J. (1968) *Learning to Live*, Shotton Hall Publications.

LEVINSON, B. (1972) 'Pets: a special technique in child psychotherapy', in *Children Away from Home*, ed Whittaker and Trieschman.

LOWENBERG, M. (1968) 'Food means more than nutriture', in *Children in Care*, ed R. J. N. Tod.

MATTINSON, J. (1968) 'Supervising a residential student', *Case Conference*, 14, 12, April.

MEHRINGER, A. (1959) 'The training of educators in institutions' (translated title), *Unsere Jugend*, 11, 11 and 12.

MERCURIO, J. (1972) *Caning: Educational Rite and Tradition*, New York, Syracuse University Press.

MILLER, D. (1964) *Growth to Freedom: the Psycho-social Treatment of Delinquent Youth*, London, Tavistock Publications.

MONSKY, S. (1963) 'Staffing of local authority residential homes for children', *The Social Survey* (abstract in Dinnage and Pringle, 1967, pp. 200-5).

NEILL, A. S. (1962) *Summerhill: a Radical Approach to Education*, London, Gollancz.

NEWSON, E. (1972) 'Towards an understanding of the parental role', in *The Parental Role* (Conference Papers), National Children's Bureau.

NEWSON, J. and E. (1963) *Patterns of Care in an Urban Community*, Harmondsworth, Penguin.

—— (1968) *Four Years Old in an Urban Community*, Harmondsworth, Penguin.

BIBLIOGRAPHY

—— (1975) *Seven Years Old in the Home Environment*, London, Allen & Unwin.

OPIE, I. and P. (1969) *Children's Games in Street and Playground*, Oxford, Clarendon Press.

OSWIN, M. (1971) *The Empty Hours: a Study of the Weekend Life of Handicapped Children in Institutions*, London, Allen Lane, Penguin Press.

OTTAWAY, K. (1970-1) 'Non-directive groups in professional training', in *Groups*, Annual Review of the Residential Child Care Association, *18*, pp. 134-42.

PARAD, H. (ed) (1965) *Crisis Intervention: Selected Readings*, New York, Family Service Association of America.

PARKER, R. (1966) *Decision in Child Care*, London, Allen & Unwin.

—— (1967) 'The residential care of children', *Case Conference*, *13*, 9, January.

—— (1971) *Planning for Deprived Children*, National Children's Home Convocation Lecture.

PARKER, S. (1971) *The Future of Work and Leisure* (Sociology Series, *5*), London, MacGibbon & Kee.

PATTON, R. and GARDNER, L. (1963) *Growth Failure in Maternal Deprivation*, Springfield, Illinois, C. C. Thomas.

PERLMAN, H. (1968) *Persona: Social Role and Personality*, Chicago University Press.

PETTES, D. (1967) *Supervision in Social Work*, London, Allen & Unwin.

PIZZAT, F. (1973) *Behaviour Modification in Residential Treatment for Children*, New York, Behavioural Publications.

POLSKY, H. (1962) *Cottage Six*, New York, Wiley Science Editions.

—— (1970) 'Social structure in a juvenile institution', in *The Sociology of Punishment and Correction*, ed N. Johnston *et al.*

POTTS, D. (1965) 'An enquiry into the staff of children's homes who are on Home Office training courses in May 1965', available at National Children's Bureau.

PRINGLE, M. L. K. (1972) 'Are parents necessary?', in *The Parental Role* (Conference Papers), National Children's Bureau.

—— (1972-3) 'The roots of violence and vandalism', *Concern*, National Children's Bureau, *11*, Winter.

PROVENCE, S. and LIPTON, R. (1962) *Children in Institutions*, New York, International Universities Press.

PUGH, E. (1968) *Social Work in Child Care*, London, Routledge & Kegan Paul.

RANJAN, G. (1970) 'Role of professionals in an institutional setting— a case study', *Social Work Today*, *1*, 9, December.

RCCA REVIEW (1967) *Play in Child Care*, *15*, Residential Child Care Association.

—— (1968) *Residential Staff in Child Care*, *16*, Residential Child Care Association.

—— (1970-1) *Groups, 18*, Residential Child Care Association.

RCCA STUDY GROUP (1969) *The Residential Task in Child Care*, Residential Child Care Association.

REDL, F. (1966) *When We Deal with Children*, London, Collier-Macmillan.

—— (1972) 'The impact of game ingredients on children's play behaviour', in *Children Away from Home*, ed Whittaker and Trieschman.

—— and WINEMAN, D. (1952/65) *Controls from Within*, New York, Free Press.

RICHARDSON, H. (1969) *Adolescent Girls in Approved Schools*, London, Routledge & Kegan Paul.

RICKARD, H. (ed) (1971) *Behavioural Intervention in Human Problems*, New York, Pergamon.

RIGBY, A. (1972) 'Residential placements', *Social Work Today*, 3, 11, September.

RIGHTON, P. (1972) 'Parental roles in residential care', in *The Parental Role* (Conference Papers), National Children's Bureau.

RILEY, M. (1958) 'Psychiatric consultation in residential treatment: the child care worker's view', *American Journal of Orthopsychiatry*, 28, 2 (and in *Disturbed Children*, ed R. J. N. Tod).

ROBERTSON, J. (1958/70) *Young Children in Hospital*, London, Tavistock Publications.

—— and J. (1967-73) *Young Children in Brief Separation* (film series), Tavistock Institute of Human Relations.

—— and J. (1971) 'Young children in brief separation—a fresh look', *Psychoanalytical Study of the Child*, 26, reprinted Chicago, Quadrangle Books.

ROCHLIN, G. (1973) *Man's Aggression: the Defence of the Self*, London, Constable.

ROGERS, C. (1951) *Client-centered Therapy*, London, Constable.

—— (1961) *On Becoming a Person*, London, Constable.

ROSEN, A. (1971) 'Are children in children's homes overprotected?', *Child in Care*, 2, 2.

ROSEN, H. (1972) *Language and Class—a Critical Look at the Theories of Basil Bernstein*, Bristol, Falling Wall Press.

ROWE, J. (1971) 'The reality of the adoptive family', in *Social Work in Adoption*, ed R. J. N. Tod.

—— and LAMBERT, L. (1973) *Children who Wait*, London, Association of British Adoption Agencies.

RUTTER, M. (1972) *Maternal Deprivation Reassessed*, Harmondsworth, Penguin.

SAWDY, M. (1974) 'A social work students' association?', *Social Work Today*, 4, 23, February.

SCHACHTER, S. (1973) 'Obesity and eating', in *Psychology in the Service of Man*, ed M. Karlins, London, Wiley.

SEGLOW, J., PRINGLE, M. L. K. and WEDGE, P. (1972) *Growing Up Adopted*, London, National Foundation for Educational Research.

SILVER, H. and FINKELSTEIN, M. (1967) 'Deprivation dwarfism', *Journal of Paediatrics*, 70, p. 317.

SLATER, R. (1969) 'Criticism amongst residents of old people's homes', *Social Work*, 26, 3.

SPEIER, M. (1971) 'The everyday world of the child', in *Understanding Everyday Life*, ed J. Douglas.

STANLEY, W. (1954) 'Frictions in a children's institution', M S W thesis, University of Toronto (abstract in Dinnage and Pringle, 1967, p. 226).

STEVENSON, O. (1965) *Someone Else's Child*, London, Routledge & Kegan Paul.

—— (1972) 'Strength and weakness in residential care', Quetta Rabley Memorial Lecture, London, Bookstall Services.

STYRT, J. and STYRT, M. (1972) 'Spontaneous play in resolution of problems—a brief example', in *Children Away from Home*, ed Whittaker and Trieschman.

THORPE, R. (1974) 'Mum and Mrs So-and-So', *Social Work Today*, 4, 22, February.

TIMMS, N. (1973) *The Receiving End*, London, Routledge & Kegan Paul.

—— and ITZIN, F. (1962) 'The role of the child care officer', *Child Care News*, March; and *British Journal of Psychiatric Social Work*, 6, 2, pp. 74-83.

TIZARD, B., COOPERMAN, O., JOSEPH, A. and TIZARD, J. (1972) 'Environmental effects on language development: a study of young children in long-stay residential nurseries', *Child Development*, 43, pp. 337-58.

—— and REES, J. (1974) 'A comparison of the effects of adoption, restoration to the natural mother, and continued institutionalization on the cognitive development of four-year-old children', *Child Development*, 45, pp. 92-9.

TIZARD, J. and TIZARD, B. (1971) 'The social development of two-year-old children in residential nurseries', in *The Origins of Human Relations*, ed H. Schaffer, New York, Academic Press.

TOD, R. J. N. (ed) (1968a) *Children in Care (Papers on Residential Work*, vol. 1) London, Longman.

—— (1968b) *Disturbed Children (Papers on Residential Work*, vol. 2) London, Longman.

—— (1971a) *Social Work in Adoption*, London, Longman.

—— (1971b) *Social Work in Foster Care*, London, Longman.

TOWLE, C. (1945/73) *Common Human Needs*, London, Allen & Unwin.

TRASLER, G. (1957) 'The effect of institutional care upon emotional development', *Case Conference*, 4, 2, pp. 35-40.

TRIESCHMAN, A., WHITTAKER, J. and BRENDTRO, L. (1969) *The Other 23 Hours: Child Care Work in a Therapeutic Milieu*, Chicago, Aldine.

TRISELIOTIS, J. (1970) *Evaluation of Adoption Policy and Practice*, Edinburgh University Press.

—— (1973) *In Search of Origins*, London, Routledge & Kegan Paul.

ULLMANN, L. and KRASNER, L. (eds) (1965) *Case Studies in Behaviour Modification*, New York, Holt, Rinehart & Winston.

VARMA, V. (ed) (1973) *Stresses in Children*, London University Press.
VINCENT, B. (1968) *Begone Dull Care*, London, HMSO.
WALKER, A. (1967) 'Some aspects of social casework in residential schools for severely disturbed children and adolescents', *Case Conference*, *13*, 12, April.
WHITEHEAD, A. N. (1929) *The Aims of Education*, London, Macmillan.
WHITTAKER, J. and TRIESCHMAN, A. (eds) (1972) *Children Away from Home: a Sourcebook of Residential Treatment*, Chicago, Aldine.
WIDDOWSON, E. (1951) 'Mental contentment and physical growth', *Lancet*, 6668, p. 1316.
WILLIAMS COMMITTEE REPORT (1967) *Caring for People: Staffing Residential Homes*, London, Allen & Unwin.
WILLS, D. (1970) *A Place Like Home*, London, Allen & Unwin.
—— (1971) *Spare the Child*, Harmondsworth, Penguin.
WINNICOTT, C. (1964/70) *Child Care and Social Work* (collected papers), London, Bookstall Publications.
—— (1968) 'Communicating with children', in *Disturbed Children*, ed R. J. N. Tod.
—— (1972) 'Comment', *Social Work Today*, *3*, 11 and 12, September.
WINNICOTT, D. (1957) *The Child and the Outside World*, London, Tavistock Publications.
—— (1957/64) *The Child, the Family and the Outside World*, Harmondsworth, Penguin.
—— (1958) *Collected Papers*, London, Tavistock Publications.
WOLF, S. (1965) *The Stomach*, New York, Oxford University Press.
WOLFF, S. (1969) *Children under Stress*, Harmondsworth, Penguin.
WOLKIND, S. and RUTTER, M. (1973) 'Children who have been "in care"— an epidemiological study', *Journal of Child Psychology and Psychiatry*, *14*, pp. 97-105.
WOODMANSEY, A. C. (1962) 'The psychiatrist as adjuvant in medical social work', *Case Conference*, *8*, 9, March.
—— (1966) 'The transmission of problems from parents to children', in *Mental Illness in the Family: its Effect on the Child* (22nd Child Guidance Inter-clinic Conference Papers), NAMH.
—— (1967) 'Emotion and the motions: an enquiry into the causes and prevention of functional disorders of defecation', *British Journal of Medical Psychology*, *40*, pp. 207-23.
—— (1969) 'The common factor in problems of adolescence', *British Journal of Medical Psychology*, *42*, pp. 353-70.
—— (1970) 'First principles in psychiatric education', *Lancet*, 7647, p. 610.
—— (1971a) 'Understanding delinquency', *British Journal of Criminology*, *11*, 2, April.
—— (1971b) 'Psychotherapy in the student health service', *Lancet*, 7709, p. 1122.
—— (1972) 'The unity of casework', *Social Work Today*, *2*, 19, January.

YELLOLY, M. (1972) 'Insight', in *Behaviour Modification in Social Work*, D. Jehu *et al.*

YOUNG, P. (1967) *The Student and Supervision in Social Work Education*, London, Routledge & Kegan Paul.

ZIEGLER, S. (1972) 'Residential treatment of disturbed children in Norway', *Journal of the Child Welfare League of America*, *51*, *5*, May.